THE REFERENCE SHELF   VOLUME 44 NUMBER 2

STABILIZING AMERICA'S ECONOMY

EDITED BY

GEORGE A. NIKOLAIEFF

THE H. W. WILSON COMPANY
NEW YORK   1972

THE REFERENCE SHELF

The books in this series contain reprints of articles, excerpts from books, and addresses on current issues and social trends in the United States and other countries. There are six separately bound numbers in each volume, all of which are generally published in the same calendar year. One number is a collection of recent speeches; each of the others is devoted to a single subject and gives background information and discussion from various points of view, concluding with a comprehensive bibliography. Books in the series may be purchased individually or on subscription.

Library of Congress Cataloging in Publication Data

Nikolaieff, George A   comp.
   Stabilizing America's economy.

   (The Reference shelf, v. 44, no. 2)
   Bibliography: p.
   1. Wage-price policy--United States. 2. Dollar,
American--Devaluation. 3. United States--Economic
policy--1971-   I. Title. II. Series.
HC110.W24N55   330.9'73'0924   72-3361
ISBN 0-8242-0465-4

PREFACE

In the inventory of things which constitute the American way of life few carry as much weight as the "free enterprise system." Indeed, those given to using such imagery claim that free enterprise is more than just a pillar of our society. It is, they say, the very cornerstone of our social order, the one that the other American institutions and beliefs rest on.

There have, of course, been occasional skeptics who felt an economy based on free enterprise left much to be desired. They have been scoffed at or ignored. American opinion in general—especially the more conservative segment represented by the Republican party—has successfully kept the ideal intact and very nearly sacred.

A casual observer might thus be forgiven if he found himself completely confused in August of 1971. For in the middle of that month, a Republican President who had chastised the previous Democratic Administration for meddling too much in business affairs, suddenly initiated a controlled economy. In a very rapid sequence of events President Richard M. Nixon first declared a ninety-day freeze on wages and prices; then he replaced that with Phase II, a period in which a hastily assembled bureaucracy ruled on how much pay and prices could be increased.

It was a sweeping, unprecedented series of steps. The only time that controls of this scope had been imposed before had been in wartime—most recently in the Korean War in the early 1950s. And though some might hold that the Nixon moves did not make the US economy a controlled one in the sense that the Socialist economies are controlled (with the state owning the means of production), that is only quibbling. The essence of a free enterprise economy is that prices and wages are determined by the unfettered

3

interaction of people and business. Once that interaction is not free, then the economy can no longer be fairly called a free enterprise economy.

Yet, curiously enough, the President's action was met with a wave of popular support. The stock market, a sensitive indicator of public confidence, surged upward. Businessmen, labor leaders, and government officials responded, by and large, to an extraordinary degree. Even though there was almost no mechanism by which the Government could check on prices and wages there was a high degree of co-operation. (It should be noted that organized labor's initial enthusiasm cooled rather quickly. Labor leaders felt the workingman was bearing the hardships in the policy while businessmen were getting the benefits. The discontent escalated and, in the spring of 1972, four of the five labor members of the Pay Board resigned. While that registered the degree of labor's discontent the move had little effect on the general direction of policy.)

There was a reason, of course. The fact is that by the summer of 1971, anyone remotely aware of what was going on in the nation knew that the economy was in deep trouble. It was on a seemingly unending spiral of wage increases following price increases that threatened to erase years of prosperity. First of all, business activity was slow. The economy had just gone through a recession. Technically the recession was over, but as a practical matter there was little to be cheerful about. At the same time the rate of unemployment continued to rise. Over the two previous years it had gradually inched its way toward 6 percent of the labor force, and there was no indication that it was going to reverse itself.

That alone would have been reason for concern. But while all this was going on the nation found itself in the clutches of the worst inflation in decades; constantly rising prices were eating away at the purchasing power of money. As if that weren't enough, the Administration faced still another dilemma. Because of inflation the dollar had been weakened in relation to the currency of other nations. American-made goods were costing more and more, and becoming less and less competitive abroad. As a result, the balance of trade, which had run in favor of the United States since 1893, was about to disappear.

What to do? The classical solutions seemed stymied. One could get the economy moving again with a variety of stimuli —such as a tax cut, easier money, or deficit spending. But if one did that it would only fuel the inflationary fires. On the other hand, if one were to do something about inflation, then one ran the risk of hurting the economy even more. That step would be hard to take, especially since the Nixon Administration faced elections in 1972.

So the President came up with a very inventive set of steps. To keep wages and prices from rising he first imposed the ninety-day freeze and then followed it up with wage and price review boards. Then he devalued the dollar—returning it to a more viable level in international trade. And finally, he moved to stimulate the economy with massive Federal spending.

All these events came in rapid-fire order and this book is published just as the first effects of these steps are making themselves felt on the economy.

The first section of the book focuses on each of the major steps the President has taken to revitalize the economy while halting inflation. The second section steps back in time to 1965, when our current set of difficulties began. The third section deals with the first half of 1971, a period in which each of the major problems plaguing the economy became clear and the economy itself was on the very edge of a full-blown crisis. Section IV contains articles that examine what the Nixon Administration did—or failed to do —to head off the crisis. Section V examines the popular reaction to each of the President's major moves and takes a look at the early effects they have had on the economy itself.

The sixth and last section takes a look at the long-term implications of the President's New Economic Policy.

The editor would like to thank the authors and publishers who have graciously consented to have their material included in this compilation. As always, special thanks is due to Rosalind Nikolaieff for her help and encouragement during the project.

GEORGE A. NIKOLAIEFF

April 1972

CONTENTS

III. THE CRISIS

IV. WHAT WENT WRONG?

I. THE GUNS OF AUGUST

EDITOR'S INTRODUCTION

In the spring and early summer of 1971 President Richard Nixon was beginning to be sharply criticized by the nation's press. Usually, concern with the economy is left to businessmen, economists, and perhaps a handful of political figures —in short, all those people with an immediate stake and interest in it. The rest of the nation seems content to pay attention to other, perhaps more exciting, events.

But this period was quite different, for the economy was beginning to intrude into the conscious lives of millions of people. Inflation was soaring at such an alarming rate that everyone was starting to feel its painful effects. Unemployment was rising. Business in general was lackluster—and showed little sign of improvement any time soon.

Thus the press was blaming Mr. Nixon for not doing enough to change the situation. As the summer wore on, the warnings and forecasts grew more dire. It was time, editors and columnists said, to do something, anything, to get the economy back on the right track.

And that was when Richard Nixon really surprised everyone. For that is just what he did. He took bold action. He implemented a series of controls whose aim it was to contain inflation while the pace of economic activity picked up. The surprise was all the more keen because Mr. Nixon had repeatedly said that his Administration would never do anything so rash as to impose controls of any kind on the economy.

But, of course, he did. This section of the book deals with the nature of those controls: what they are and what purpose they are meant to serve. The first selection is the text of the

11

President's speech in which he announced Phase I of his
economic program. The second, from *Time* magazine, gives
a report and analysis of Phase II—a time when Government
review boards rule on wages and prices. The third article
deals with devaluation of the dollar. While Phases I and II
were meant to deal primarily with the domestic situation,
the dollar devaluation was meant to cope with the economy's
international difficulties.

The final selection focuses on the stimulus that the Nixon
Administration is giving the economy. No incumbent President seeking a second term can afford high unemployment
in an election year. And so it is not surprising that to round
out his economic program the President is spending heavily
on generating jobs.

PHASE I [1]

Good evening. I've addressed the nation a number of
times over the past two years on the problems of ending the
war. Because of the progress we have made toward achieving
that goal, this Sunday evening is an appropriate time for us
to turn our attention to the challenges of peace.

America today has the best opportunity in this century
to achieve two of its greatest ideals: to bring about a full
generation of peace and to create a new prosperity without
war.

This not only requires bold leadership ready to take bold
action; it calls for the greatness in a great people.

Prosperity without war requires action on three fronts.
We must create more and better jobs; we must stop the rise
in the cost of living; we must protect the dollar from the
attacks of international money speculators.

We are going to take that action—not timidly, not half-
heartedly and not in piecemeal fashion. We are going to

[1] Text of President Richard M. Nixon's television speech to the nation
announcing Phase I of the New Economic Policy, as recorded by the New York
Times. New York *Times*. 120:14. Ag. 16, '71.

move forward to the new prosperity without war as befits a great people, all together and along a broad front.

New Economic Policy

The time has come for a new economic policy for the United States. Its targets are unemployment, inflation and international speculation, and this is how we are going to attack those targets:

First, on the subject of jobs. We all know why we have an unemployment problem. Two million workers have been released from the armed forces and defense plants because of our success in winding down the war in Vietnam. Putting those people back to work is one of the challenges of peace, and we have begun to make progress. Our unemployment rate today is below the average of the four peace-time years of the 1960s, but we can and we must do better than that.

The time has come for American industry, which has produced more jobs at higher real wages than any other industrial system in history, to embark on a bold program of new investment of production for peace. To give that system a powerful new stimulus I shall ask the Congress when it reconvenes after its summer recess to consider as its first priority the enactment of the Job Development Act of 1971.

I will propose to provide the strongest short-term incentive in our history to invest in new machinery and equipment that will create new jobs for Americans: a 10 percent job development credit for one year effective as of today with a 5 percent credit after August 15, 1972.

This tax credit for investment in new equipment will not only generate new jobs. It will raise productivity; it will make our goods more competitive in the years ahead.

Second, I will propose to repeal the 7 percent excise tax on automobiles effective today. This will mean a reduction in price of about $200 per car.

I shall insist that the American auto industry pass this tax reduction on to the nearly eight million customers who are buying automobiles this year. Lower prices will mean that more people will be able to afford new cars, and every additional 100,000 cars sold means 25,000 new jobs.

Third, I propose to speed up the personal-income-tax exemptions scheduled for January 1, 1973, to January 1, 1972, so that taxpayers can deduct an extra $50 for each exemption one year earlier than planned.

This increase in consumer spending power will provide a strong boost to the economy in general and to employment in particular.

The tax reductions I am recommending, together with this broad upturn of the economy, which has taken place in the first half of this year, will move us strongly forward toward a goal this nation has not reached since 1956, fifteen years ago; prosperity with full employment in peacetime.

Looking to the future, I have directed the Secretary of the Treasury [John B. Connally, Jr.] to recommend to the Congress in January new tax proposals for stimulating research and development of new industries and new techniques to help provide the 20 million new jobs that America needs for the young people who will be coming into the job market in the next decade.

To offset the loss of revenue from these tax cuts, which directly stimulate new jobs, I have ordered today a $4.7 billion cut in Federal spending.

Tax cuts to stimulate employment must be matched by spending cuts to restrain inflation. To check the rise in the cost of Government I have ordered a postponement of pay raises and a 5 percent cut in Government personnel.

I have ordered a 10 percent cut in foreign economic aid. In addition, since the Congress has already delayed action on two of the great initiatives of this Administration, I will ask Congress to amend my proposals to postpone the implementation of revenue sharing for three months and welfare reform for one year.

Priorities Reordered

In this way, I am reordering our budget priorities so as to concentrate more on achieving our goal of full employment.

The second indispensable element of the new prosperity is to stop the rise in the cost of living. One of the cruelest legacies of the artificial prosperity produced by war is inflation. Inflation robs every American, every one of you. The 20 million who are retired and living on fixed incomes—they are particularly hard hit. Homemakers find it harder than ever to balance the family budget. And 80 million American wage earners have been on a treadmill.

For example, in the four war years between 1965 and 1969, your wage increases were completely eaten up by price increases. Your paychecks were higher, but you were no better off. We have made progress against the rise in the cost of living. From the high point of 6 percent a year in 1969, the rise in consumer prices has been cut to 4 percent in the first half of 1971. But just as is the case in our fight against unemployment, we can and we must do better than that. The time has come for decisive action—action that will break the vicious circle of spiraling prices and costs.

I am today ordering a freeze on all prices and wages throughout the United States for a period of ninety days.

In addition I call upon corporations to extend the wage-price freeze to all dividends. I have today appointed a Cost of Living Council within the Government. I have directed this council to work with leaders of labor and business to set up the proper mechanism for achieving continued price and wage stability after the ninety-day freeze is over.

Let me emphasize two characteristics of this action. First, it is temporary. To put the strong vigorous American economy into a permanent straitjacket would lock in unfairness;

it would stifle the expansion of our free-enterprise system, and second, while the wage-price freeze will be backed by Government sanctions, if necessary, it will not be accompanied by the establishment of a huge price-control bureaucracy.

For Voluntary Cooperation

I am relying on the voluntary cooperation of all Americans—each one of you: workers, employers, consumers—to make this freeze work. Working together, we will break the back of inflation, and we will do it without the mandatory wage and price controls that crush economic and personal freedom.

The third indispensable element in building the new prosperity is closely related to creating new jobs and halting inflation. We must protect the position of the American dollar as a pillar of monetary stability around the world.

In the past seven years, there's been an average of one international monetary crisis every year. Now who gains from these crises? Not the working man, not the investor, not the real producers of wealth. The gainers are the international money speculators: because they thrive on crises, they help to create them.

In recent weeks, the speculators have been waging an all-out war on the American dollar. The strength of a nation's currency is based on the strength of that nation's economy, and the American economy is by far the strongest in the world.

Accordingly, I have directed the Secretary of the Treasury to take the action necessary to defend the dollar against the speculators.

I directed Secretary Connally to suspend temporarily the convertibility of the dollar into gold or other reserve assets except in amounts and conditions determined to be in the interest of monetary stability and in the best interests of the United States.

Now what is this action—which is very technical—what does it mean to you? Let me lay to rest the bugaboo of what is called devaluation. If you want to buy a foreign car or take a trip abroad, market conditions may cause your dollar to buy slightly less.

But, if you are among the overwhelming majority of Americans who buy American-made products, in America, your dollar will be worth just as much tomorrow as it is today.

The effect of this action, in other words, will be to stabilize the dollar. Now this action will not win us any friends among the international money traders. But our primary concern is with the American workers, and with their competition around the world.

To our friends abroad, including the many responsible members of the international banking community who are dedicated to stability in the flow of trade, I give this assurance: The United States has always been and will continue to be a forward-looking and trustworthy trading partner.

New Monetary System

In full cooperation with the International Monetary Fund and those who trade with us, we will press for the necessary reforms to set up an urgently needed new international monetary system. Stability and equal treatment is in everybody's best interest. I am determined that the American dollar must never again be a hostage in the hands of international speculators.

I am taking one further step to protect the dollar, to improve our balance of payments and to increase jobs for Americans. As a temporary measure I am today imposing an additional tax of 10 percent on goods imported into the United States.

This is a better solution for international trade than direct controls on the amount of imports. This import tax is a temporary action. It isn't directed against any other country. It's an action to make certain that American products will not be at a disadvantage because of unfair exchange rates.

When the unfair treatment is ended, the import tax will end as well. As a result of these actions the product of American labor will be more competitive and the unfair edge that some of our foreign competition has will be removed.

This is a major reason why our trade balance has eroded over the past fifteen years.

At the end of World War II, the economies of the major industrial nations of Europe and Asia were shattered. To help them get on their feet and to protect their freedom, the United States has provided over the past twenty-five years $143 billion in foreign aid.

That was the right thing for us to do. Today, largely with our help, they have regained their vitality. They have become our strong competitors, and we welcome their success.

But now that other nations are economically strong, the time has come for them to bear their fair share of the burden of defending freedom around the world. The time has come for exchange rates to be set straight, and for the major nations to compete as equals.

There is no longer any need for the United States to compete with one hand tied behind her back.

The range of actions I have taken, and proposed tonight on the job front, on the inflation front, on the monetary front, is the most comprehensive new economic policy to be undertaken in this nation in four decades.

We are fortunate to live in a nation with an economic system capable of producing for its people the highest standard of living in the world, a system flexible enough to change its ways dramatically when circumstances call for change, and, most important, a system resourceful enough to produce prosperity with freedom and opportunity unmatched in the history of nations.

The purposes of the Government actions I have announced tonight are to lay the basis for renewed confidence, to make it possible for us to compete fairly with the rest of the world, to open the door to new prosperity.

But Government with all of its powers does not hold the key to the success of a people. That key, my fellow Americans, is in your hands. A nation, like a person, has to have a certain inner drive in order to succeed. In economic affairs that inner drive is called the competitive spirit.

Every action I have taken tonight is designed to nurture and stimulate that competitive spirit, to help us snap out of the self-doubt, the self-disparagement that saps our energy and erodes our confidence in ourselves.

Whether this nation stays number one in the world's economy or resigns itself to second, third or fourth place, whether we as a people have faith in ourselves or lose that faith, whether we hold fast to the strength that makes peace and freedom possible in this world or lose our grip—all that depends on you.

All that depends on you, on your competitive spirit, your sense of personal destiny, your pride in your country and in yourself.

We can be certain of this: As the threat of war recedes, the challenge of peaceful competition in the world will greatly increase. And we welcome competition, because America is at her greatest when she is called on to compete.

Voices Will Be Heard

As there has always been in our history, there will be voices urging us to shrink from that challenge of competition, to build a protective wall around ourselves, to crawl into a shell as the rest of the world moves ahead.

Two hundred years ago a man wrote in his diary these words: "Many thinking people believe America has seen its best days." That was written in 1775, just before the American Revolution, the dawn of the most exciting era in the history of man.

And today we hear the echoes of those voices preaching a gospel of gloom and defeat, saying the same thing: We have seen our best days. I say, "Let Americans reply, 'Our best days lie ahead.' " As we move into a generation of peace, as we blaze the trail toward the new prosperity, I say to every American: Let us raise our spirits, let us raise our sights, let all of us contribute all we can to this great and good country that has contributed so much to the progress of mankind. Let us invest in our nation's future. And let us revitalize that faith in ourselves that built a great nation in the past and that will shape the world of the future.

PHASE II [2]

President Nixon [in a speech on October 7, 1971] has summoned a "volunteer army" of wage earners, corporate executives, bankers and consumers to march against inflation—under a blurry banner emblazoned so far with only an official emblem, an organization chart and row upon row of question marks.

What the White House aims to create is a national consensus on wage-price policy that will be mostly self-policing. Standards for pay and price rises are to be set by representatives of labor, management and "the public," not directly by Government officials. The stick of Federal compulsion will be available to back up their decisions, but it will fall most heavily on a relative handful of giant corporations and major unions. Drafters of the program have deliberately not provided enough enforcement officers to do anything more than spot-check the wages and prices at small machine shops, corner laundries and car washes. That essentially voluntary

[2] "A Blurry Banner for Phase II." *Time*. 98:12-17. O. 18, '71. Reprinted by permission from *Time*, the weekly newsmagazine; © Time Inc. 1971.

approach is a gamble that will succeed only if Americans display a spirit of economic self-sacrifice that, historically, they have shown only in times of all-out war.

The Hard Questions

Nixon tried to arouse that spirit on television. He left most details of his program for others to announce—probably wisely because it is not easy to stir patriotic fervor by unfurling an organization chart. Instead, he concentrated on exhortation. Said the President: "I call upon all of you tonight to look at this program not as Democrats or Republicans, workers or businessmen, farmers or consumers, but as Americans. We cannot afford a business-as-usual attitude anywhere, because fighting inflation is everybody's business."

Nixon left unanswered all the hard questions about what will happen after the wage-price freeze ends November 13 [1971]. Workers had no clearer an idea than before of how big a raise they can expect, or if they can expect any at all. Company executives were not told what prices they will be able to increase or by how much. Tenants were still wondering when, if and by what amount their landlords will be permitted to raise the rent.

The White House specified only an interim goal: cutting the rate of inflation roughly in half by the end of 1972, so that prices then will be rising an average of only 2 percent to 3 percent a year. In order to achieve that, some Administration aides imply, wages and benefits will have to be held to a 5 percent to 6 percent annual increase. How to get there from here will be decided largely by persons not yet chosen for boards, commissions and other bodies not yet created.

No Cheers for Notre Dame

The organization chart for Phase II of the President's New Economic Policy is imposingly detailed. Nixon set up three committees, two commissions, one council, one administration and one board (with a committee inside it). The key bodies are to act partly as think tanks calculating formulas for allowable wage and price boosts, partly as courts ruling on pleas from businessmen and union chiefs for exceptions from the general standards, partly as prosecuting attorney's offices seeking injunctions and fines against violators of their decisions. White House aides gave some details in a long briefing-paper and background sessions, but these details also raised questions. Major points:

1. A Pay Board and a Price Commission will be created as the heart of the Phase II apparatus.

The Pay Board will have fifteen members—five each from management, labor and the public at large. They will establish yardsticks for permissible increases in wages, salaries, pensions and other fringe benefits, bonuses, salesmen's commissions and the like. A committee within the board will formulate rules for executive pay boosts. Meanwhile, the Price Commission will do the same for prices and rents. The commission will consist of seven "public" members.

What sort of people will Nixon choose for the crucial posts of "public" representatives on the Pay Board and Price Commission? Judges? Lawyers? Professors? Labor arbitrators? Over the weekend, Nixon men gave the first hint. They named to the Pay Board William G. Caples, president of Kenyon College in Ohio and a former vice president of Inland Steel. Otherwise, Administration officials have been silent. They will say only that they are looking for "tough" people. They are much clearer about whom they do *not* want: anyone like the Reverend Theodore Hesburgh, president of Notre Dame, who is regarded in the Nixon White House as a wishy-washy liberal.

2. After devising general rules, the Pay Board and the Price Commission will weigh particular increases case by case.

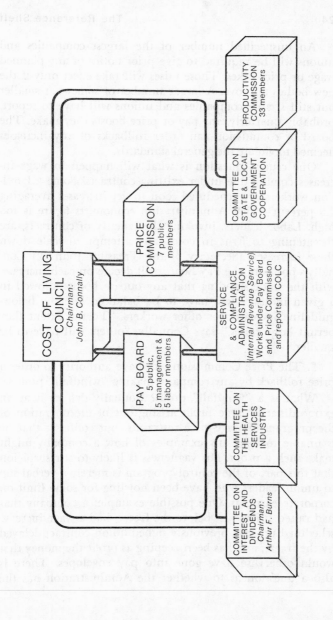

An unspecified number of the largest companies and unions will be required to give prior notice of any planned wage or price hikes. Those raises will take effect only if the new bodies approve. A larger number of somewhat smaller but still sizable companies and unions will have to report, probably quarterly, any pay or price boosts they make. The board or commission can order rollbacks of any increases deemed to violate the general standards.

One crucial question is what will happen to wage increases coming due under existing contracts? Some 2.1 million workers are scheduled soon to get increases averaging 7.6 percent which Administration economists figure is too high. Labor leaders, invoking the sanctity of contracts, are threatening to fight in court any attempt to scale down these increases. [Secretary of the Treasury John B.] Connally's position: the Pay Board will decide on each increase, with the understanding that any outsize boosts allowed in a given industry will have to be balanced later by below-guideline increases for other workers. "To the extent they permit large raises," says Connally, "others will have to be smaller."

3. The Price Commission will have authority to order a price rollback by any company making "windfall" profits.

What is a "windfall" profit? Connally defines it as an extraordinarily large profit arising out of the operation of the program of wage-price restraints, but confesses that he is unable to offer any examples of how a company might make such a profit. His vagueness is likely to stir suspicion that this part of the control program is merely a verbal sop to union leaders who have been howling for some limit on corporate earnings. One possible example: a company that had raised prices just before the freeze, had a wage increase scheduled under a previously signed union contract delayed by the freeze, and has been keeping as profit the money that would otherwise have gone into pay envelopes. There is also a question as to whether the Administration has the legal authority to order price cuts as well as stopping price increases.

4. Several lesser, but still important bodies will be set up.

A Committee on the Health Services Industry will advise the Pay Board and Price Commission on how to adapt wage and price standards to doctors' fees and hospital charges. A Committee on State and Local Government Cooperation will advise on wage standards for public employees. An Interest and Dividends Committee of high Government officials, headed by Federal Reserve Chairman Arthur F. Burns, will try, presumably by jawboning, to persuade bankers to hold down loan rates voluntarily and corporate executives to hold down dividend payouts. Nixon will also ask Congress for standby authority to set legal ceilings on interest.

5. A Service and Compliance Administration will handle enforcement.

This administration will really be the Internal Revenue Service wearing a second hat; it will be staffed by 3,000 IRS agents working out of 360 field offices around the country. They will investigate complaints of pay or price violations by the big companies and unions that report to the Pay Board and Price Commission. The agents will also spot-check the books of small companies in order to make sure that they are complying with the national wage and price guidelines as well as with the tax laws.

The chairmen of the Pay Board and Price Commission will have authority to seek injunctions and fines against violators big or small; such cases will be prosecuted by the Justice department. The fine for each violation will be $5,000. That is not as small as it sounds. A machine-tool maker, for example, could conceivably be fined $5,000 for every tool shipped at a higher price than the Price Commission proposes to allow.

6. Connally's Cost of Living Council will sit atop the whole structure.

The COLC will stay out of day-to-day administration and will not hear any appeals from the decisions of the Pay Board and Price Commission. Connally says, though, that it will "review" the standards set by the various boards, commissions and committees to see that they are "in balance" with each other and show real promise of cutting the inflation rate in half by the end of next year. Just what the word review may mean has been left deliberately vague, apparently in order to give Connally maximum scope in guiding the decisions of the other bodies without explicitly threatening their independence.

This whole structure reflects the often-voiced and bitter reminiscences of Richard Nixon, a veteran of the World War II Office of Price Administration, which deployed a bureaucratic army of price inspectors across the country. In contrast to the OPA, the number of employees of the new mechanism will be fairly small.

The new program, though, has many jurisdictional oddities. Both a self-employed television repairman and a TV repairman who works for a company will have their incomes regulated—but by different bodies. The Price Commission will set standards applying to the fees that the self-employed repairman can charge; the Pay Board will draw up rules governing what wages the employee repairman can collect. Doctors may eventually be visited by those much-feared IRS agents, inquiring into complaints of "excessive" charges for operations or consultations. But lawyers who are partners in a firm will face no such investigations; income from partnerships will be considered profits, which are unregulated.

These quirks result largely from the fact that the Phase II machinery has been set up to give something to everybody. Labor demanded a tripartite board, including union representatives, to determine pay, while business insisted that only public representatives chosen by a Republican White House rule on prices. Each won its point. Labor in addition got some Government gestures toward control of interest rates and profits—but the limits on "windfall" profits are so far not strict enough to anger corporate chiefs.

Economic Home Run

The first public reaction to this program was a mixture of approval and uncertainty. The most volatile economic indicator, the stock market, wobbled nervously. On the day after Nixon's speech, the Dow Jones industrial average fell nearly eight points, and it closed the week at 894. Investors found it difficult to appraise the program, and they were particularly unsure about what actions the new Interest and Dividends Committee might take.

The nation's businessmen and bankers generally supported the President's actions. Said A. W. ("Tom") Clausen, president of the Bank of America: "We believe his program will begin to make possible an orderly transition out of the freeze." With liberal use of metaphor, Dow Chemical Chairman Carl Gerstacker responded in terms that sports fan Nixon understands best: "The President has hit another home run in the fight against inflation." Chrysler Corporation Chairman Lynn Townsend voiced the hope that the Price Commission will allow some increases on 1972 models, which came out during the freeze. Said he: "We price only once a year, and the freeze caught us at the worst possible time."

Professional economists were more cautious, but mostly approving. Robert Nathan and Beryl Sprinkel, two members of *Time*'s Board of Economists, believe that the President was wise in trying to form a consensus on wages and prices before establishing specific guidelines. Sprinkel, although an ideological opponent of economic controls, added that Nixon acted realistically in setting his goal as 2 percent to 3 percent inflation by the end of 1972, rather than specifying some lower number that would be more attractive but un-reachable.

Many economists and businessmen, however, were more inclined to stress the indefinite nature of much of the program. "Until I see the flesh on the skeleton, I can't tell whether the girl is beautiful or not," quipped Arthur Okun, former chairman of the Council of Economic Advisers. Joseph Pechman, director of economic studies at the Brookings Institution, complained that Nixon "is providing machinery, but not yet a policy for restraining wages and prices." In the judgment of George Sheinberg, treasurer of Bulova Watch Company, the impact of the program "is going to depend almost entirely on the people whom Nixon appoints. He needs more men like Connally—people who really take hold and are effective in a short time."

The Buck Blocker

The program indeed seems largely designed both by and for John Connally. The Phase II structure was planned mostly by budget boss George Shultz and economic adviser Herbert Stein, and it reflects their horror of controls imposed directly on the economy by Government officials. A mild joke in the White House is that "the only reason that Phase II may work is that the people who designed the controls do not believe in them." It was Connally, however, who insisted that the Administration commit itself to the simple objective of lowering price increases to a 2 percent or 3 percent rate about a year from now. He did so against the advice of some members of the Cost of Living Council, notably Shultz, who wanted no numerical guideline at all, and against others who wanted specific, low figures for wages and prices to be reached quickly. A program that would move toward a fairly clear goal, but in ways and at a pace to be defined pragmatically as it proceeded, especially suited Connally's talents as a maker of coalitions and manipulator of pressure groups.

Connally put some of those talents on display at his jammed press conference the day after the President's announcement. He airily asserted that the Pay Board and Price Commission have "a world of time" in which to formulate wage and price standards before the freeze ends November 13 [1971]—in full knowledge that his Cost of Living Council has authority to promulgate temporary rules if they fail. He disclaimed any role as economic czar, contending that the COLC would not "veto" any standards formulated by the other bodies—and managed to make his stand sound forceful. "We will not let these groups pass the buck up to us," he said sternly. "If the Price Commission permitted prices that patently were exorbitant," he added, "or if the Pay Board announced their own goal of a 6 percent rate of inflation instead of 2 percent to 3 percent—well, at that point we'd lock horns." His self-assured manner left no doubt who would win.

Unspoken Implication

Connally's main job at the press conference was to allay the suspicions of AFL-CIO President George Meany. Fearing above all that an unfriendly Republican Administration would overrule the wage decisions of a tripartite board, Meany had demanded that the Pay Board be completely independent of the Government. He had initially decided to cooperate with the program, but withdrew his support even as President Nixon was speaking Thursday night. Briefings of newsmen by White House aides had led Meany to believe that Connally's COLC would exercise veto power over the Pay Board.

Connally adroitly put Meany on the spot before the nationwide TV audience. Asked if Meany would be on the Pay Board, Connally happily issued a public invitation: "I expect him to be. I hope he will be. He's been asked. I can't imagine that he couldn't make a great contribution." The obvious, but carefully unspoken implication was that if Meany declines to serve and sets organized labor to fighting the program in the courts or on the picket lines, he will be largely to blame for the failure of the most promising effort yet to check inflation.

Whether Meany will be won over is still highly doubtful. He has reserved his decision, pending a meeting this week of the AFL-CIO's thirty-five-man executive council. Leonard Woodcock of the United Auto Workers and Frank Fitzsimmons of the Teamsters, who head the two largest unions in the country, will also attend, even though their unions are not in the AFL-CIO. Both have been asked to sit on the Pay Board along with Meany, although Woodcock has echoed Meany in declining to do so unless he is assured that the board will be independent. [When the Pay Board was set up, the labor members were Woodcock, Meany, and Fitzsimmons plus I. W. Abel (the president of the United Steelworkers) and F. E. Smith (the president of the International Association of Machinists and Aerospace Workers). On March 22, 1972, Meany, Abel, and Smith resigned, followed on March 23 by Woodcock.]

The labor leaders, however, know that they run an immense risk of outraging public opinion if they do not at least go on the Pay Board and see if it can be made to work. If they do join the Pay Board, there will still be rich potential for conflict. Meany intends to demand that all pay raises held up by the freeze be paid when it ends, a step that the White House has said will not be permitted.

Auspicious Indicators

If Nixon and Connally can win labor's grudging acceptance, the stabilization program stands at least a fair chance of success. Economically, Phase II is being set up at an auspicious time. Wholesale prices in September showed their largest drop, 0.4 percent, in five years. The unemployment rate inched down from 6.1 percent to 6 percent—nothing to arouse wild cheers, but still a move in the right direction.

A major imponderable is the attitude of the President. The machinery for Phase II has been designed to operate at not one, but two removes from the White House. In part, that is not a bad idea. Interference by the head of Government eventually undermined the authority of Britain's Prices and Income Board in the 1960s. The President and his aides shaped the Phase II machinery after listening to British veterans of that board advise that the wage-price mechanism be insulated from political meddling.

At some point, however, the President will have to place the prestige of his office directly behind the machinery. Sooner or later, the Pay Board and the Price Commission will have to issue rulings that will be hotly disputed. Nixon will be asked if he supports them. If he dodges, public support will wither. The owner of a corner grocery may obey a ruling backed by the President, but not one on which the President is noncommittal.

The administrative machinery is cumbersome, and the different bodies could find themselves working at cross purposes. The Pay Board, for example, could approve wage increases that would force price boosts larger than the Price Commission wants to allow. The Health Services Committee could advise allowing rises in medical-care costs that would wipe out any gains achieved by holding industrial prices down. Making sure that all parts of this machinery move in unison is the job of, above all, that enigmatic, smiling, charming, menacing, tough Texan—John B. Connally. It is a task to tax even his vaulting ambitions.

DEVALUATION [3]

When the free world's foreign-exchange markets reopen, a lot more than money values will be very different.

[3] Article "The New Dollar," by Richard F. Janssen, Washington correspondent. *Wall Street Journal.* p 1+. D. 20, '71. Reprinted with permission of the *Wall Street Journal.*

Under the weekend pact among the Group of Ten key industrial nations, the Nixon Administration made a contingent promise to devalue the dollar by raising the official gold price 8.57 percent to $38 an ounce from the historic $35. The Japanese yen and the West German mark are being revalued sharply higher, and many other currencies are being reset one way or another.

But if the hard-won monetary realignment works out as hoped, strategists say, the United States will also have:

—Cleared the way for considerably more domestic job creation by regaining this country's competitive ability to export more than it imports

—Swerved the world away from a swamp of protectionism that might have mired many nations in a severe 1972 recession

—Enhanced chances that Mr. Nixon's coming summitry in Moscow and Peking will help produce a more peaceful future, because his pride-swallowing retreat after earlier rough shoving has brought the Western allies back together

"More Peaceful World"

It is "the most significant monetary agreement in the history of the world," a beaming Mr. Nixon said Saturday evening when he unexpectedly appeared at the Smithsonian Institution to end the suspense. "The whole free world has won," he declared, because the new financial stability will mean that "competition can be more fair" and that there can be "more true prosperity" and in the long run "a more peaceful world."

Any number of predictable setbacks could prevent the benefits from matching Mr. Nixon's billing, of course. In any case, Treasury Secretary John B. Connally cautions that it would be too optimistic to think that the monetary pact itself could cure the chronic US balance-of-payments deficit; such a deficit occurs when foreigners acquire more dollars than they return in all dealings.

And the gains that do result may be slow in coming. Experience of other countries shows that it often takes two years before a currency devaluation produces all the desired export and employment upturns.

Some things should happen swiftly, though.

The Government is allowing foreign-exchange markets in this country to open as usual today, and Paul A. Volcker, Treasury under secretary for monetary affairs, predicts that exchange rates will immediately leap to the agreed new levels. Other major nations generally intend to close their currency markets today. But within a day or so they are also due to be dealing at the new relationship to the dollar— about a 12 percent average change from the old fixed rates (weighted according to these countries' volume of trade with the United States). The 12 percent calculation excludes Canada; the Canadians refuse to halt the "float" of their dollar, but Mr. Connally predicts its value will rise, too.

End to Surcharge Pledged

The Administration intends to remove the 10 percent import surcharge "right away," Mr. Connally says, and this will permit already-scheduled "Kennedy Round" cuts in regular tariff rates to take place January 1 [1972]. Scrapping of a "buy-American" limitation in the newly restored 7 percent tax credit for business equipment purchases is to take place simultaneously with the lapse of the import surcharge. Both these measures were designed to pressure other countries into the upward currency revaluations they now have agreed on—revaluations that will make foreign goods costlier in this country and American wares cheaper abroad.

Also effective immediately, the conferees agreed, currencies will be allowed to fluctuate more widely than before around their new par values, or official rates. In contrast to the old rule limiting market-price movements to 1 percent either way, the Group of Ten communiqué provides for a 2¼ percent margin up or down. The aim is to discourage disruptive international flows of "hot money" motivated by interest-rate advantages or currency-rate speculation; the wide range will increase the risk of loss for speculators. (The 118-country International Monetary Fund, which gave up trying to enforce its old 1 percent band earlier this year, yesterday formally approved the wider band as a "temporary regime.")

Almost immediately may come the foreign action that is a prerequisite for US legislation to devalue the dollar in terms of gold. Mr. Connally reports that talks aimed at wringing short-term trade concessions from Canada, Japan and the European Common Market are in high gear; he says there is ample time for at least token lowering of barriers before Congress reconvenes in mid-January. Only when America's major trading partners thus demonstrate cooperation, the Group of Ten agreed, will the US Administration actually "propose to Congress a suitable means for devaluing the dollar in terms of gold to $38 an ounce."

Minor Concessions First

The imminent trade concessions, though, will come on relatively minor items, such as US orange exports to Europe, officials of European nations say. And they see years of hard bargaining ahead on more major issues such as nontariff barriers against heavier US cars. The mandate given by authorities of the European Common Market to their trade negotiators is only "barely" satisfactory, Secretary Connally complains. Europeans counter testily that the United States still hasn't come across with some concessions promised almost a decade ago.

The United States has further to go to rebuild its foreign-trade position than is generally realized, warns William Eberle, the President's top trade negotiator. He sees a $2 billion trade deficit this year, the first since 1893. That is on the favorable basis the United States uses to keep its books, he notes. If the United States included shipping and in-

surance costs on imports as other countries do, the trade
deficit "would be closer to $7 billion," he estimates. On that
basis, the US foreign-trade position has been in the red
since 1967 and will take "two or three years" to swing into
the black, he says.

The expected employment gains for the United States
will probably be spread over about two years, too, according
to Peter G. Peterson, the White House international economic policy chief. Each $1 billion of payments turnabout
will create 60,000 to 80,000 jobs, he estimates. Thus, attain-
ing the Connally goal of a $9 billion swing for the better
could mean more than 700,000 additional jobs by late 1973;
that in itself would be enough to lower the unemployment
rate to about 5.2 percent from . . . [November 1971's] 6
percent.

The currency realignment didn't come in the way the
United States originally wanted, of course. Messrs. Nixon
and Connally favored only upward revaluations by other
nations and no devaluation by this country. But by bowing
to the foreign demand for a gold-price increase, analysts say,
the United States has gained something useful that the others
had all along: the ability to alter the international exchange
value of its currency as an added tool of economic policy.

In so doing, the United States has also shed its sancti-
monious attitude that the dollar alone is immune from devaluation. This means it can deal more as an equal with
its traditional post—World War II allies, some observers
assert.

While devaluation is rather humbling, they add, the
monetary accord shores up the Western Alliance just in time
for Mr. Nixon to present a much stronger front in his 1972
missions to the Soviet Union and China. A major objective
of Soviet policy, in particular, is to split the United States
and its allies in Western Europe; Moscow's propagandists
love to crow about any sign of "disunity in the capitalist

world." But now the Kremlin will find it harder to drive a wedge through the West.

Moreover, analysts add, the Group of Ten agreement also spares the President from domestic political charges of running roughshod over old Free World friends while courting the Communists.

Major Monetary Questions

Major monetary questions remain to be resolved with the Western allies, however, and some insiders suspect that this will take at least a year or two of delicate dickering.

At present, for instance, the United States is still keeping its $10.1 billion (at the old $35-an-ounce price) of gold locked up and leaving it to other countries to stabilize the dollar in their foreign-exchange markets. Foreign central banks will do this by buying dollars with their own currencies in order to hold the market value of those currencies down within the permissible limits. But other countries are loath to continue adding indefinitely to their hoard of an estimated $45 billion without assurance that the United States will once again offer to accept excess dollars in return for gold or other reserve assets.

Along with this controversial issue of currency convertibility, the authorities also face other tricky monetary reform problems: the future division of responsibilities for stabilizing currencies; the proper roles of reserve assets including gold, dollars and the IMF's [International Monetary Fund's] Special Drawing Rights, or "paper gold"; a permanent version of the temporary "wider band" for currency values; and control over short-term capital movements.

An Easing of Suspense

If things go halfway right, though, the coming discussions probably won't cause the high suspense that marked the past weekend's meeting. The conferees arrived . . . with expressions of hope that they could quickly end the floating of currency values that had been bogging down international trade and investment since mid-August. But none wanted to appear very anxious for fear of weakening his bargaining power.

With the authorities secluded in the turreted red sandstone Smithsonian headquarters (built in 1855 to resemble a twelfth century European monastery), clashing rumors of breakthroughs and collapse constantly whipped through some five hundred newsmen confined to an adjacent building. Just when pessimism was at its peak, Treasury spokesman Calvin E. Brumley alerted reporters to a "nice surprise" soon, and President Nixon popped in shortly before 6 P.M. Saturday, stood under the Wright Brothers' 1903 airplane, and congratulated the assembled finance ministers and central-bank governors for solving the crisis that many of them had accused him of provoking.

Evidently, what brought the final breakthrough was the sense that nothing but trouble could come from further delay. The foreign powers (France, Germany, England, Japan, Canada, Italy, Sweden, Belgium and the Netherlands) feared that congressional protectionists soon would buffet their wobbling economies with restrictive import quotas. And the US delegation doubtless feared that disappointment after the buildup of expectations would send the stock market into a new slump, dashing the confidence considered crucial to a strong 1972 election-year economic recovery.

THE BIG SPENDER [4]

Lower income taxes, less unemployment, and reduced inflation along Main Street, USA, in 1972 and 1973.

If this is a perennial promise of Federal budgets, it also has the usual too-big-to-hide price tag—another crimson deficit.

[4] Article, "Nixon Primes Economy With Deficit Tide," by Courtney R. Sheldon, chief of Washington bureau. *Christian Science Monitor.* p 1+. Ja. 25, '72. Reprinted by permission from *The Christian Science Monitor.* © 1972 The Christian Science Publishing Society. All rights reserved.

The true name of President Nixon's fiscal-year budget game is bring down the unemployment rate—and never mind the old Republican theories about balanced budgets.

The unemployed figure now stands at a towering 6.1 percent. Mr. Nixon would have it slim down into the neighborhood of 5 percent by the end of the year.

The Democrats agree heartily with Mr. Nixon's job-stimulation goal. And deficits don't alarm them particularly. They have piled up some handsome ones in their time.

Only such conservative Republicans as Representative John M. Ashbrook of Ohio can't swallow the verbiage on the need for a whopping deficit.

Ceiling Urged

The political and economic touchiness of the deficits was evident in a Nixon statement issued as an afterthought to his budget message.

He urged Congress "to enact a rigid ceiling that will prevent the Government spending more than the $246 billion" he requested in his budget.

"Those who increase spending beyond that amount will be responsible for causing more inflation," he warned.

The question remains—and it could be the big one of the election year—could Mr. Nixon have foreseen the job squeeze?

Should he have taken action earlier and thus avoided taking the nation so deeply into debt?

For the 1972 fiscal year now ending, Mr. Nixon estimates the country will go $38.8 billion more in the hole. One year ago, he estimated it would be only $11.6 billion.

Dialogue on Deficits

For fiscal 1973, Mr. Nixon figures the deficit at $25.5 billion. This time, the public is assured again, matters won't get so out of hand.

How did these burdensome deficits come about and is anyone to blame?

In this election year, the dialogue seems destined to go something like this:

Mr. Nixon: We have had to absorb into our job force thousands of returning Vietnam war veterans and convert industry to a peacetime economy. It is a tremendous task.

The Democrats: You apparently had no program to ease soldiers into civilian jobs and now you are desperate to do almost anything as the election approaches.

Mr. Nixon: We acted decisively to curb inflation in August [1971] by setting up price and wage controls. We cut taxes and authorized spending to create jobs. We have made American goods more competitive in the foreign market.

The Democrats: We advocated all those things years earlier and you stuck by your laissez-faire economic program until it was almost too late.

Mr. Nixon: The whole mess began when war expenditures rose during the Johnson Administration and the domestic consequences were not reckoned with.

The Democrats: That argument might have been persuasive even with us during your first two years, but you have had enough time to take corrective action.

Progress Possible, but . . .

This kind of acid debate will probably rage on even if the economy continues to improve right up until election day in November.

It is quite possible that there will not be enough visible progress for Mr. Nixon to point to it with great pride.

On the other hand, every improved statistic will make it harder for the Democrats to make their case against Republican neglect.

The focus will be mainly on the unemployment.

The advance indications are that the Nixon Administration will not rely wholly on a lowered rate of unemployment to make its economic case to the public.

Secretary of the Treasury John B. Connally, Jr., told newsmen the Administration has a study under way which will analyze just who the unemployed are.

Mr. Connally then added that roughly 1.25 million jobless would be affected.

Full Employment

Such a study could well confirm Administration suspicions that it is unrealistic to shoot for a full-employment goal of 4 percent.

One reason is that the work force now has in it increasing numbers of working wives and teen-agers.

George P. Shultz, director of the Office of Management and Budget, said one reason for hope for a downward trend in unemployment is that the phasing out of military-related jobs "is fundamentally behind us."

Mr. Connally was asked how many would be removed from unemployment rolls if the rate is sliced to 5 percent.

"I haven't calculated it. I can add, but I can't subtract very well," Mr. Connally quipped.

Mr. Shultz interrupted with a smile: "That is the basic trouble with the budget process."

In the budget briefings by Mr. Connally and Mr. Shultz and in Mr. Nixon's budget messages, much was made of "the full-employment budget concept."

The dictum of this concept is that spending be held only to the level of tax revenue that would be collected if the jobless rate were at the full-employment level of 4 percent.

Mr. Nixon adopted it last year fully. Many economists have favored it for years.

Even this was violated by the Administration in the 1972 fiscal year budget. That full-employment budget is expected to be $8.1 billion in deficit ($38.8 billion by old calculations).

In 1973, Mr. Nixon estimates there will be a $0.7 billion surplus by full-employment budget-accounting procedures.

Budget Balancing

The idea is that good times economically eventually will bring legitimate surpluses which will offset the deficits in emergency years.

Though the $270.9 billion Nixon budget for fiscal 1973 is about $20 billion over last year, it does not appear to have large bulges of new spending.

He does ask some $3 billion more than Congress was willing to spend for defense the last time around. But there is no guarantee Congress will go along, despite the strong plea to strengthen the Navy and new strategic-weapons programs.

Mr. Shultz emphasized that taxes have now been cut back to the point where the Government cannot count on new large sums of tax money being generated annually simply by the growth of the economy.

"Government," said Mr. Shultz, "is very much on the spot."

II. THE DANGERS OF TOO MUCH SUCCESS

EDITOR'S INTRODUCTION

How did the nation get itself into such a predicament that it had to resort to wage-price controls? Since economic policy is deeply involved in the political process, there is no shortage of answers to that question. One thing that most economists agree on, though, is that the difficulties stem at least partially from the success of earlier policies.

In the early 1960s the United States—under President Kennedy—moved to induce prosperity. It was the theory of British economist John Maynard Keynes that a free government could (and should) seek to guide its economy with a combination of fiscal and monetary moves. The Kennedy/ Johnson Administrations did just that. The economy responded well. And the United States was launched on what became the longest boom period in its entire history.

What that success also did, however, was to give Government officials the confidence that they could do almost anything with the economy. In fact, of course, they could not. Even though the Keynesian theories worked, there were other considerations that played a role. So, before too long, the economy went from a happy boom stage into an ominous period.

This section deals with the period between 1965, the healthiest peak of the boom, and 1968, the end of the Johnson Administration, a time when everyone knew things had gone amiss. The first article is one that *Time* magazine ran at the peak of enthusiasm over Keynes. It explains the theories (and the man behind them) that were used to achieve the boom. The second selection, an article from *Business Week,* describes a confrontation President Johnson had with the aluminum industry. Even in 1965 inflationary pressures were threatening. To contain them the President instituted wage-price guidelines. The object was to ensure that neither wages nor prices would be raised more than a national estimate of productivity gains. In 1965 that figure was 3.2 percent.

While the guidelines were voluntary, President Johnson frequently found that he had to use the influence of his office to persuade an industry to hold the price line. This ritual, which the second article touches on, soon came to be known as "jawbone" economics.

The third selection is from a 1966 *Life* editorial. It notes that even though the economy is still healthy, the heavy demands of war in Vietnam are beginning to take a toll. It warns that inflation is creeping up and that there are other signs of trouble ahead.

The final article in the section is a 1968 *U.S. News & World Report* piece which documents how President Johnson miscalculated the economy. The President had anticipated that the United States could have both "guns and butter"—that is, it could conduct the war in Vietnam without making any special sacrifices in the home economy. It just didn't work out. And an economy that was already precariously perched was being pushed further off balance.

"WE ARE ALL KEYNESIANS NOW" [1]

The ideas of economists and political philosophers, both when they are right and when they are wrong, are more powerful than is commonly understood. Indeed the world is ruled by little else. Practical men, who believe themselves to be quite exempt from any intellectual influences, are usually the slaves of some defunct economist.—The General Theory of Employment, Interest and Money

Concluding his most important book with those words in 1935, John Maynard Keynes was confident that he had

[1] From article in *Time*. 86:64-7B. D. 31, '65. Reprinted by permission from *Time,* the weekly newsmagazine; © Time Inc. 1965.

laid down a philosophy that would move and change men's affairs. Today, some twenty years after his death, his theories are a prime influence on the world's free economies, especially on America's, the richest and most expansionist. In Washington the men who formulate the nation's economic policies have used Keynesian principles not only to avoid the violent cycles of prewar days but to produce a phenomenal economic growth and to achieve remarkably stable prices. In 1965 they skillfully applied Keynes's ideas—together with a number of their own invention—to lift the nation through the fifth, and best, consecutive year of the most sizable, prolonged and widely distributed prosperity in history.

By growing 5 percent in real terms, the United States experienced a sharper expansion than any other major nation. Even the most optimistic forecasts for 1965 turned out to be too low. The gross national product leaped from $628 billion to $672 billion—$14 billion more than the President's economists had expected. Among the other new records: auto production rose 22 percent, steel production 6 percent, capital spending 16 percent, personal income 7 percent and corporate profits 21 percent. Figuring that the United States had somehow discovered the secret of steady, stable, noninflationary growth, the leaders of many countries on both sides of the Iron Curtain openly tried to emulate its success.

Basically, Washington's economic managers scaled these heights by their adherence to Keynes's central theme: the modern capitalist economy does not automatically work at top efficiency, but can be raised to that level by the intervention and influence of the government. Keynes was the first to demonstrate convincingly that government has not only the ability but the responsibility to use its powers to increase production, incomes and jobs. Moreover, he argued that government can do this without violating freedom or restraining competition. It can, he said, achieve calculated prosperity by manipulating three main tools: tax policy, credit policy and budget policy. Their use would have the effect of strengthening private spending, investment and production.

From Mischief to Orthodoxy

When Keynes first propagated his theories, many people considered them to be bizarre or slightly subversive, and Keynes himself to be little but a Left-wing mischief maker. Now Keynes and his ideas, though they still make some people nervous, have been so widely accepted that they constitute both the new orthodoxy in the universities and the touchstone of economic management in Washington. They have led to a greater degree of Government involvement in the nation's economy than ever before in time of general peace. Says [Johnson's] Budget Director Charles L. Schultze: "We can't prevent every little wiggle in the economic cycle, but we now can prevent a major slide."

A slide, of course, is not what the United States Government's economic managers have been worrying about in 1965; they have been pursuing a strongly expansionist policy. They carried out the second stage of a two-stage income-tax cut, thus giving consumers $11.5 billion more to spend and corporations $3 billion more to invest. In addition, they put through a long-overdue reduction in excise taxes, slicing $1.5 billion this year and another $1.5 billion in the year beginning January 1 [1966]. In an application of the Keynesian argument that an economy is likely to grow best when the government pumps in more money than it takes out, they boosted total Federal spending to a record high of $121 billion and ran a deficit of more than $5 billion. Meanwhile, the Federal Reserve Board kept money easier and cheaper than it is in any other major nation, though proudly independent Chairman William McChesney Martin at year's end piloted through an increase in interest rates—thus following the classic anti-inflationary prescription.

Why They Work

By and large, Keynesian public policies are working well because the private sector of the economy is making them work. Government gave business the incentive to expand, but it was private businessmen who made the decisions as to whether, when and where to do it. Washington gave consumers a stimulus to spend, but millions of ordinary Americans made the decisions—so vital to the economy—as to how and how much to spend. For all that it has profited from the ideas of Lord Keynes, the US economy is still the world's most private and most free-enterprising. Were he alive, Keynes would certainly like it to stay that way.

The recent successes of Keynes's theories have given a new stature and luster to the men who practice what Carlyle called "the dismal science." Economists have descended in force from their ivory towers and now sit confidently at the elbow of almost every important leader in Government and business, where they are increasingly called upon to forecast, plan and decide. In Washington the ideas of Keynes have been carried into the White House by such activist economists as Gardner Ackley, Arthur Okun, Otto Eckstein (all members of . . . [Johnson's] Council of Economic Advisers), Walter Heller (its former chairman), MIT's Paul Samuelson, Yale's James Tobin and Seymour Harris of the University of California at San Diego.

First the US economists embraced Keynesianism, then the public accepted its tenets. Now even businessmen, traditionally hostile to Government's role in the economy, have been won over—not only because Keynesianism works but because Lyndon Johnson knows how to make it palatable. They have begun to take for granted that the Government will intervene to head off recession or choke off inflation, no longer think that deficit spending is immoral. Nor, in perhaps the greatest change of all, do they believe that Government will ever fully pay off its debt, any more than General

Motors or IBM find it advisable to pay off their long-term obligations; instead of demanding payment, creditors would rather continue collecting interest.

To a New Stage

Though Keynes is the figure who looms largest in these recent changes, modern-day economists have naturally expanded and added to his theories, giving birth to a form of neo-Keynesianism. Because he was a creature of his times, Keynes was primarily interested in pulling a depression-ridden world up to some form of prosperity and stability; today's economists are more concerned about making an already prospering economy grow still further. As Keynes might have put it: Keynesianism+the theory of growth= The New Economics. Says Gardner Ackley, chairman of the Council of Economic Advisers: "The new economics is based on Keynes. The fiscal revolution stems from him." Adds the University of Chicago's Milton Friedman, the nation's leading conservative economist, who was presidential candidate Barry Goldwater's adviser on economics: "We are all Keynesians now." ...

The US economy [at the end of 1965] is moving into a new stage. Production is scraping up against the top levels of the nation's capacity, and Federal spending and demand are soaring because of the war in Vietnam. The economists' problem is to draw a fine line between promoting growth and preventing a debilitating inflation. As they search for new ways to accomplish this balance, they will be guided in large part by the Keynes legacy.

That legacy was the product of a man whose personality and ideas still surprise both his critics and his friends. Far from being a Socialist Left-winger, Keynes (pronounced *canes*) was a high-caste Establishment leader who disdained what he called "the boorish proletariat" and said: "For better or worse, I am a bourgeois economist." Keynes was suspicious of the power of unions, inveighed against the perils of inflation, praised the virtue of profits. "The engine which drives enterprise," he wrote, "is not thrift but profit." He condemned the Marxists as being "illogical and so dull" and saw himself as a doctor of capitalism, which he was convinced could lead mankind to universal plenty within a century. Communists, Marxists and the British Labour party's radical fringe damned Keynes because he sought to strengthen a system that they wanted to overthrow.

Truth and Consequences

Keynes was born the year Marx died (1883) and died in the first full year of capitalism's lengthy postwar boom (1946). The son of a noted Cambridge political economist, he whizzed through Eton and Cambridge, then entered the civil service. He got his lowest mark in economics. "The examiners," he later remarked, "presumably knew less than I did." He entered the India Office, soon after became a Cambridge don. Later, he was the British Treasury's representative to the Versailles Conference, and saw that it settled nothing but the inevitability of another disaster. He resigned in protest and wrote a book, *The Economic Consequences of the Peace,* that stirred an international sensation by clearly foretelling the crisis to come.

He went back to teaching at Cambridge, but at the same time operated with skill and dash in business. The National Mutual Life Assurance Society named him its chairman, and whenever he gave his annual reports to stockholders, the London Money Market suspended trading to hear his forecasts for interest rates in the year ahead. He was also editor of the erudite British *Economic Journal,* chairman of the *New Statesman and Nation* and a director of the Bank of England.

Keynes began each day propped up in bed, poring for half an hour over reports of the world's gyrating currency and commodity markets; by speculating in them, he earned a fortune of more than $2 million. Money, he said, should be valued not as a possession but "as a means to the enjoyments and realities of life." He took pleasure in assembling the world's finest collection of Newton's manuscripts and in organizing London's Camargo Ballet and Cambridge's Arts Theater. Later, the government tapped him to head Britain's Arts Council, and in 1942 King George VI made him a lord.

Part dilettante and part Renaissance man, Keynes moved easily in Britain's eclectic world of arts and letters. Though he remarked that economists should be humble, like dentists, he enjoyed trouncing countesses at bridge and prime ministers at lunch-table debates. He became a leader of the Bloomsbury set of avant-garde writers and painters, including Virginia and Leonard Woolf, Lytton Strachey and E. M. Forster. At a party at the Sitwells, he met Lydia Lopokova, a ballerina of the Diaghilev Russian ballet. She was blonde and buxom; he was frail and stoop-shouldered, with watery blue eyes. She chucked her career to marry him. His only regret in life, said Keynes shortly before his death of a heart attack, was that he had not drunk more champagne.

The Whole Economy

The thrust of Keynes's personality, however strong, was vastly less important than the force of his ideas. Those ideas were so original and persuasive that Keynes now ranks with Adam Smith and Karl Marx as one of history's most significant economists. Today his theses are the basis of economic policies in Britain, Canada, Australia and part of continental Europe, as well as in the United States.

Economics is a young science, a mere two hundred years old. Addressing its problems in the second half of its second century, Keynes was more successful than his predecessors in seeing it whole. Great theorists before him had tried to take a wide view of economic forces, but they lacked the twentieth century statistical tools to do the job, and they tended to concentrate on certain specialties. Adam Smith focused on the marketplace, Malthus on population, Ricardo on rent and land, Marx on labor and wages. Modern economists call those specializations "microeconomics"; Keynes was the precursor of what is now known as "macroeconomics"—from the Greek *makros,* for large or extended. He decided that the way to look at the economy was to measure all the myriad forces tugging and pulling at it—production, prices, profits, incomes, interest rates, government policies.

For most of his life, Keynes wrote, wrote, wrote. He was so prolific that a compendium of his books, tracts and essays fills twenty-two pages. In succession he wrote books about mathematical probability (1921), the gold standard and monetary reform (1923), and the causes of business cycles (1930); each of his works further developed his economic thinking. Then he bundled his major theories into his magnum opus, *The General Theory,* published in 1936. It is an uneven and ill-organized book, as difficult as Deuteronomy and open to almost as many interpretations. Yet for all its faults, it had more influence in a shorter time than any other book ever written on economics, including Smith's *The Wealth of Nations* and Marx's *Das Kapital.*

Permanent Quasi Boom

Keynes perceived that the prime goal of any economy was to achieve "full employment." By that, he meant full employment of materials and machines as well as of men. Before Keynes, classical economists had presumed that the economy was naturally regulated by what Adam Smith had called the "invisible hand," which brought all forces into balance and used them fully. Smith argued, for example, that if wages rose too fast, employers would lay off so many workers that wages would fall until they reached the point at which employers would start rehiring. French economist Jean Baptiste Say embroidered that idea by theorizing that production always creates just enough income to consume whatever it produces, thus permitting any excesses of demand to correct themselves quickly.

Keynes showed that the hard facts of history contradicted these unrealistic assumptions. For centuries, he pointed out, the economic cycle had gyrated from giddy boom to violent bust; periods of inflated prosperity induced a speculative rise, which then disrupted commerce and led inexorably to impoverished deflation. The climax came during the depression of the 1930s. Wages plummeted and unemployment rocketed, but neither the laissez-faire classicists nor the sullen and angry Communists adequately diagnosed the disease or offered any reasonable remedies.

By applying both logic and historical example to economic cycles, Keynes showed that the automatic stabilizers that economists had long banked on could actually aggravate rather than prevent a depression. If employers responded to a falloff in demand by slicing wages and dumping workers, said Keynes, that would only reduce incomes and demand, and plunge production still deeper. If bankers responded to a falloff in savings by raising interest rates, that would not tempt penniless people to save more—but it would move hard-pressed industrialists to borrow less for capital investment. Yet Keynes did not despair of capitalism as so many other economists did. Said he:

The right remedy for the trade cycle is not to be found in abolishing booms and keeping us permanently in a semislump; but in abolishing slumps and thus keeping us permanently in a quasi boom.

Management of Demand

The key to achieving that, Keynes perceived, is to maintain constantly a high level of what he called "aggregate demand." To him, that meant the total of all demand in the economy—demand for consumption and for investment, for both private and public purposes. His inescapable conclusion was that, if private demand should flag and falter, then it had to be revived and stimulated by the only force strong enough to lift consumption: the government.

The pre-Keynesian "classical" economists had thought of the government too. But almost all of them had contended that, in times of depression, the government should raise taxes and reduce spending in order to balance the budget. In the early 1930s, Keynes cried out that the only way to revive aggregate demand was for the government to cut taxes, reduce interest rates, spend heavily—and deficits be damned. Said Keynes:

> The state will have to exercise a guiding influence on the propensity to consume partly through its scheme of taxation, partly by fixing the rates of interest, and partly, perhaps, in other ways.

A few other economists of Keynes's time had called for more or less the same thing. Yet Keynes was the only one with enough influence and stature to get governments to sit up and pay attention. He was the right man at the right time, and his career and fame derived largely from the fact that when his theories appeared the world was racked by history's worst depression and governments were desperately searching for a way out.

Contrary to the Marxists and the Socialists, Keynes opposed government ownership of industry and fought those centralists who would plan everything ("They wish to serve not God but the devil"). While he called for conscious and calculated state intervention, he argued just as passionately that the government had no right to tamper with individual freedoms to choose or change jobs, to buy or sell goods, or to earn respectable profits. He had tremendous faith that private men could change, improve and expand capitalism.

Perhaps Immoral

Like any genius, Keynes had plenty of faults and shortcomings. Even his admirers admit that he could be maddeningly abstruse and confusing. MIT's Paul Samuelson, for example, thinks that Keynes downplayed the importance of monetary policy. His few outright critics feel that, while he knew how to buoy a depression-stricken industrial economy, he offered little in the way of practical information about how to keep a prosperous modern economy fat and secure. Keynesian theories are certainly unworkable in the underdeveloped nations, where the problem is not too little demand but insufficient supply, and where the object is not to stimulate consumption but to spur savings, form capital and raise production.

Such critics as former US Budget Director Maurice Stans still worry that Keynes makes spenders seem virtuous and savers wicked, and thus subtly threatens the nation's moral fiber. Other doubters contend that earlier obscure economists originated some of the ideas that Keynes popularized, and that all he did was wrap them up in a general theory. But even his several detractors bow to his brilliance, use the macroeconomic terms and framework that he devised, and concede that his main theories have largely worked out in practice. . . .

Congress adopted the Keynesian course in 1946, when it passed the Employment Act, establishing Government responsibility to achieve "maximum employment, production and purchasing power." The act also created the Council of Economic Advisers, which for the first time brought professional economic thinking into close and constant touch with the President. Surprisingly it was Dwight Eisenhower's not-notably-Keynesian economists who most effectively demonstrated the efficacy of Keynes's antirecession prescriptions; to fight the slumps of 1953-54 and 1957-58, they turned to prodigious spending and huge deficits.

J.M.K. & L.B.J.

Still, Keynesianism made its biggest breakthrough under John Kennedy, who, as Arthur Schlesinger reports in *A Thousand Days,* "was unquestionably the first Keynesian President." Kennedy's economists, led by Chief Economic

Adviser Walter Heller, presided over the birth of the New
Economics as a practical policy and set out to add a new
dimension to Keynesianism. They began to use Keynes's
theories as a basis not only for correcting the 1960 recession,
which prematurely arrived only two years after the 1957-58
recession, but also to spur an expanding economy to still
faster growth. Kennedy was intrigued by the "growth gap"
theory, first put across to him by Yale economist Arthur
Okun (. . . a member of the Council of Economic Advisers),
who argued that even though the United States was prosperous, it was producing $51 billion a year less than it really
could. Under the prodding and guidance of Heller, Kennedy thereupon opened the door to activist, imaginative
economics.

He particularly called for tax reductions—a step that
Keynes had advocated as early as 1933. The Kennedy Administration stimulated capital investment by giving businessmen a 7 percent tax kickback on their purchases of new
equipment and by liberalizing depreciation allowances.
Kennedy also campaigned for an overall reduction in the
oppressive income-tax rates in order to increase further both
investment and personal consumption. That idea, he remarked, was "straight Keynes and Heller."

Lyndon Johnson came into the presidency worrying
about the wisdom of large deficits and questioning the need
for a tax cut, but he was convinced by the Keynesian economists around him, and hurried the measure through Congress. The quick success of the income-tax cuts prompted
Congress to try a variant: the reduction . . . of excise taxes
on such goods as furs, jewelry and cars.

Nowadays, Johnson is not only practicing Keynesian economics, but is pursuing policies of pressure and persuasion
that go far beyond anything Keynes ever dreamed of. In
1965 Johnson vigorously wielded the wage-price "guidelines"
to hold wages and prices down, forced producers of aluminum, copper and wheat to retreat from price hikes by threat-

ening to dump the Government's commodity stockpiles, and battled the nation's persistent balance-of-payments deficit with the so-called voluntary controls on spending and lending abroad. Some Keynesians believe that these policies violate Keynes's theories because they are basically microeconomic instead of macroeconomic—because they restrict prices, wages and capital movements in some parts of the economy but not others. Businessmen also complain about what they call "government by guideline" or "the managed economy," but not with total conviction. Business, after all, is booming, and besides, the Government is a big customer with unbounded retaliatory powers.

Imitation Behind the Curtain

While the United States has been accepting the idea of more and more Government intervention within the bounds of private enterprise, many other nations are drifting away from strong central controls over their economies and opting for the freer American system. Britain's ruling Labour party has become practically bourgeois, and this year scrapped almost all notions of nationalizing industry; West Germany's Socialists have long since done the same in an effort—so far unsuccessful—to wrest power from the free-enterprising Christian Democrats; and traditionally Socialist Norway in 1965 voted a conservative government into power for the first time in thirty years.

Piqued by the ideas popularized by Soviet economist Evsei Liberman, the command economies of Communist Europe are openly and eagerly adopting such capitalist tenets as cost accounting and the profit motive. East Germany, Czechoslovakia and other formerly Stalinist satrapies are cautiously granting more powers to local managers to boost or slash production, prices, investments and labor forces. State enterprises in Poland, Hungary and Rumania . . . [have] closed deals to start joint companies in partnership with capitalist Western firms.

Near the Goal

The United States right now is closer to Keynes's cherished goal of full employment of its resources than it has ever been in peacetime. Unemployment melted during 1965 from 4.8 percent to an eight-year low of 4.2 percent. Labor shortages, particularly among skilled workers, are beginning to pinch such industries as aerospace, construction and shipbuilding. Manufacturers are operating at a ten-year high of 91 percent of capacity, and autos, aluminum and some other basic industries are scraping up against 100 percent. Contrary to popular belief, industrialists do not like to run so high because it forces them to start up some of their older and less efficient machines, as many companies lately have been obliged to do.

The economy is beginning to show the strain of this rapid expansion. For the first time in five years, labor costs rose faster than productivity in 1965: 4.2 percent versus 2.5 percent. Consumer prices last year jumped 1.8 percent, and wholesale prices rose 1.3 percent, the first rise of any kind since 1959. This is already threatening the nation's remarkable record of price stability. The economy cannot continue its present growth rate at today's productivity level without serious upward pressure on prices.

Growth Versus Stability

The economic policies of 1966 will be determined most of all by one factor: the war in Vietnam. Barring an unexpected truce, defense spending will soar so high—by at least an additional $7 billion—that it will impose a severe demand upon the nation's productive capacity and give body to the specter of inflation. Keynes feared inflation, and warned that "there is no subtler, no surer means of overturning the existing basis of a society than to debauch the currency." Once chided for undertipping a bootblack in Algiers, he replied: "I will not be party to debasing the currency."

The immediate problem that Vietnam and the threat of inflation pose to Washington's economic planners is whether they should aim for more growth or more stability. Labor Secretary Willard Wirtz argues that the Government should continue pushing and stimulating the economy, even at the risk of some inflation, in order to bring unemployment down to 3 percent. Treasury Secretary Henry Fowler's aides argue just as firmly that the Government should tighten up a bit on spending and credit policy in order to check prices and get the nation's international payments into balance.

The man whose counsel will carry the most weight with Lyndon Johnson and who must make the delicate decisions in the next few weeks is the President's quiet, effective and Keynesian-minded chief economic strategist, Gardner Ackley. "We're learning to live with prosperity," says Ackley, "and frankly, we don't know as much about managing prosperity as getting there."

The Sword's Other Side

Prosperity will bring the Government an extra $8.5 billion in tax revenues in the next fiscal year, and that means the United States can afford to boost its total Federal spending by $8.5 billion without causing significant inflationary pressure. If spending bulges much higher, the economists can fight inflation by brandishing the other sides of their Keynesian swords. Though Keynes spoke more about stimulus than restraint, he also stressed that his ideas could be turned around to bring an overworked economy back into balance. Says Walter Heller:

It should be made entirely clear that Keynes is a two-way street. In many ways we're entering a more fascinating era than the one I faced. Essentially the job is to maintain stability without resorting to obnoxious controls as we did in World War II and Korea.

. . . Economists in and out of Government are much more bullish than they were a year ago. The economy is not only running close to optimum speed, but has no serious excesses and few soft spots. Says Economic Adviser Okun: "It's hard to find a time when the economy has been closer to equilibrium than it is today." Orders are rising faster than production; wages are rising faster than prices; corporate profits are now rising faster than the stock market, even though the Dow-Jones average has jumped more than four hundred points since mid-1962 and last week closed at an all-time high of 966. Businessmen plan in 1966 to increase capital spending 15 percent; auto-makers and steel-makers expect to top this year's production records. Ackley and his colleagues anticipate that the gross national product will grow another 5 percent in real terms during 1966, to $715 billion—or perhaps more.

The Feeling Is Mutual

More meaningful than breaking records is the fact that the US economy is changing for the better. In Lyndon Johnson's profit-minded Administration, Government planners have come to appreciate the importance of helping private business to invest in order to create jobs, income and demand. Johnson knows that he must have a vigorous economy to support his Great Society programs as well as the war in Vietnam and the United States's reach for the moon. To further that aim, he has more day-to-day contact with businessmen than any President since Hoover; he telephones hundreds of them regularly and invites scores to the Oval Room to hear their opinions. Under the atmospherics of the Johnson Administration, the United States has a Government whose economic policies are simultaneously devoted to Keynesianism, committed to growth, and decidedly pro-business.

Businessmen, for their part, have come to accept that the Government should actively use its Keynesian tools to promote growth and stability. They believe that whatever happens, the Government will somehow keep the economy strong and rising. With this new confidence, they no longer worry so much about the short-term wiggles and squiggles of the economic curve but instead budget their capital spending for the long-term and thus help to prolong the expansion.

If the nation has economic problems, they are the problems of high employment, high growth and high hopes. As the United States enters what shapes up as the sixth straight year of expansion, its economic strategists confess rather cheerily that they have just about reached the outer limits of economic knowledge. They have proved that they can prod, goad and inspire a rich and free nation to climb to nearly full employment and unprecedented prosperity. The job of maintaining expansion without inflation will require not only their present skills but new ones as well. Perhaps the United States needs another, more modern Keynes to grapple with the growing pains, a specialist in keeping economies at a healthy high. But even if he comes along, he will have to build on what he learned from John Maynard Keynes.

THE SOMETIME GUIDEPOSTS [2]

President Johnson . . . [in November 1965] carefully gauged business reaction to his successful jab at the aluminum price rise. Despite the tough enforcement of his anti-inflation wage-price guideposts, he believes his business consensus is still intact.

Nevertheless, he has assigned several aides the task of developing machinery for communicating more effectively with industry and labor on the guideposts. The idea is to find a means that's less abrasive and dramatic than the periodic confrontations that have taken place to date.

The officials involved want to avoid anything that has the slightest taint of formal wage and price controls. A special effort will be made to convince construction unions and

[2] Article "Will the Guideposts Hold?" *Business Week*. p 35-6. N. 20, '65. Reprinted from the November 20, 1965 issue of *Business Week* by special permission. Copyright, 1965 by McGraw-Hill, Inc.

contractors that they have an obligation under the guideposts. Construction wage agreements, arrived at locally, have
exceeded the limit.

Test Period

The Administration's effort is a preparation for crucial
tests ahead for the Johnson concept of government by consensus. The use of guideposts will broaden and increase,
since aides think it's the best method to maintain stability
short of direct controls. Yet, guideposts work only by consensus. Thus, as Johnson's need to preserve the consensus
becomes greater, the task of using guideposts becomes more
difficult.

Right now, businessmen accept the use of Government
pressure on prices. But they are disgruntled at the philosophy
of selectivity they feel is behind it in this and other areas.
Many businessmen feel that general curbs, such as tight
fiscal or monetary policy, have the advantage of putting all
competitors on an equal footing. Under the selective approach, they feel, they have to make decisions without knowing what the Government reaction will be.

But the guidepost philosophy is being questioned in
Washington as well as in business circles. . . . Senator Philip
A. Hart (Democrat, Michigan), chairman of the antitrust
subcommittee, sent a letter to Attorney General Nicholas
deB. Katzenbach urging a probe of aluminum and other
"concentrated industries."

Yet Hart's reasoning on the wage-price guideposts could
have been penned by any executive: "You and I know that
the Administration's success on this particular issue should
not establish this as the wisest or most successful method of
dealing with industry pricing policies over the long run."

The Future

At the Federal Reserve Board, which has some faith in
the new wage-price guidepost policy, officials are already

looking to the day when the Johnson Administration may face a choice between using old-fashioned monetary medicine or compulsory controls over prices.

But before these thinkers have their day, businessmen will see more use of Government by guideline—and in more areas than prices:

Foreign investment: Corporations soon will be asked to curb their capital outflows overseas in a more effective way.

Bank rates: Despite rising interest rates in the markets, basic bank rates are being held down by the widely spread word that the Administration does not believe the market has correctly assessed the business outlook.

Bonds: At a simple word from the Treasury Department last week, New York investment bankers agreed to postpone more than $250 million in bond underwritings scheduled for Canadian borrowers.

Prices: Aluminum and now copper have demonstrated that the Administration is stepping up its efforts to keep prices under control as the climate for increases warms.

Chain Reaction

The trouble is, one point of selection tends to breed another. The wage-price guideposts of January 1962 were designed to reduce the need for monetary policy in fighting inflation. This followed from the Kennedy Administration's first "selective" decision of January 1961: to combat the dollar drain by "twisting" interest rates—holding short rates high, long rates stable.

The twist led to another move to distort markets—the interest equalization tax [a tax on anyone outside the United States who wants to borrow money in the United States] as a way of discouraging foreign borrowing in this country, without raising interest rates. Already it has been supplemented by the year's voluntary program to slow bank lending abroad.

Adjustment

But, Government officials moan, selectivity spirals. Banks could not be asked to "contribute" without asking corporations. Corporations will be asked to do more. This is feeding back to the bank program, because corporations claim the bank curbs cut down on the availability of export financing. Treasury is trying to determine whether this is true or not. If it is, the rules may be changed again.

Moreover, businessmen and bankers complain they can't be expected to carry the whole burden. So, under pressure, the Government is once again turning to the tourist as the possible next point of selection.

In prices and wages, the question is the same: Where does selection stop? Vaguely, Government officials think it is at the point where psychology, or anticipatory pricing, borrowing, and stockbuilding leave off and "real" market forces take over.

Wage Problem

In wages, who will judge the market forces? Since summer, US unemployment has been dropping faster than Administration officials would expect in relation to the gains in gross national product. So far they find a number of "nonmarket" reasons for this—but the worry remains that at least some of this unexplained drop is due to market forces.

Moreover, if the Administration expects to hold its business consensus, it will have to make a strong demonstration on the wage side.

The first opportunity for a demonstration may come in the setting of the 1966 guideposts. The wage guidepost was 3.2 percent this year and last. For next year, it will rise to 3.6 percent—and Administration officials want badly to change the basis of figuring it so that it will not appear as a new target for wage increases. If the Government lowers the numbers, the unions will scream; if it doesn't, business may do the screaming.

In prices, will President Johnson take on "real" market forces? It will long be debated whether the aluminum price rise was a result of market forces. Wall Street investors had been demanding that the industry raise its earnings. Yet experts doubted the price rise would stick.

For the time being, perhaps, the rule of thumb is the one laid down . . . by Commerce Secretary John T. Connor. The kinds of price and wage rises that the President is deeply concerned about, he said, are "dramatic, symbolic events that could ignite the fireworks of inflation."

DARK CLOUDS AHEAD [3]

The US economy, still hale after what MIT economist Paul Samuelson happily calls "a real Methuselah of an expansion" fifty-nine months old, is bumping its head against the ceiling. The problem is no longer how to sustain a high rate of growth, but how to prevent inflation. This threat is more real than it has been for a decade, in large part because of Vietnam. Unless current peace feelers unexpectedly result in a truce, the already high cost of the war there will continue to grow.

Prices have started going up, which is hardly news to shoppers. The consumer price index rose 1.5 percent during 1965, compared to an annual average of 1.3 percent between 1958 and 1964. Even more significantly, wholesale prices climbed 2 percent in the past year, following seven years of virtual stability. Food was the biggest villain—bought any beef lately?

Our economy is now at full stretch, or very near to it, and the devices which worked so well in prodding it into that condition are beginning to be counterproductive. The tax cuts, special relief for industry, heavy Government spending and easy monetary policies employed by the Kennedy

[3] Editorial, "1966; Booming But Look Out." *Life*. 60:4. Ja. 7, '66. Reprinted by permission from *Life* Magazine, © 1966 Time Inc.

and Johnson Administrations have paid off with surging and apparently unstoppable private demand. Such demand is fine so long as the economy can supply the goods, but otherwise, look out! An overstrained economy and unsatisfied demand mean higher costs and higher prices or, in other words, inflation.

Right now only the first twinges of strain are beginning to be felt, but they are coming at crucial points. Many industries are operating at capacity. Wages are rising—4.2 percent last year—but productivity is not keeping pace. The real danger is a labor shortage. In November unemployment hit an eight-year low of 4.2 percent of the total work force. Considering that this equals some 3 million workers, the situation still sounds pretty serious, but the statistic exaggerates the actual availability of useful labor. Excluding construction workers usually employed seasonally, only 1.9 percent of skilled workmen were unemployed; only 2 percent of all heads of families; long-term unemployment (15 weeks or more) fell below 1 percent. Actual shortages have developed in some categories. Out of 150 major labor areas in the country, only 19 are now listed as having substantial unemployment. A year ago there were 30.

Nobody knows for sure just how far unemployment can be reduced before labor shortages start pushing wages and costs upward. Some say 4 percent, others say 3 percent. Labor Secretary Willard Wirtz would like to see expansionary policies continued until unemployment falls to 3 percent and is willing to accept in return a degree of inflation as a necessary evil. He undoubtedly has in mind the persistent unemployment among Negroes (8.4 percent) and teen-agers (13 percent). But in view of the wooliness of unemployment statistics, and the terrible cost of making a mistake, his course would be a dangerous one.

Fortunately Wirtz doesn't appear to have much support in a Washington where most of those concerned are trying to put together a Federal budget as uninflationary as possible. Without a truce in Vietnam the war there will boost defense spending by $7 to $10 billion during the next fiscal year. Nobody is proposing economies in that quarter. Instead, cutbacks are likely and desirable in some of the Great Society programs which for political reasons are unlikely to be abolished.

The President will probably aim for a budget totaling between $110 and $112 billion (up from $99.7 billion this year, which actually led to an expenditure of $105 to $107 billion). If he can hold to this level, and if the economy generates the sort of revenue increase it is expected to, the overall deficit should be under the current year's $7.5 billion. But if Vietnam costs swell still more, a tax increase is a mid-year possibility. Johnson should not hesitate to request it, nor should he boggle at using other anti-inflation weapons when and if they are necessary. Certainly we can live with higher taxes if need be. And the country is fortunate that the Federal Reserve Board made its sensible decision to raise the bank rate when it did, notwithstanding the President's protestations of disappointment. President Johnson and the economy will get the benefit of the Fed's anti-inflationary move, while politician Johnson could take an easy-money stance.

In spite of the threat of inflation, as we move into 1966 the giant US economy appears to be generally in top form and ready for another record-breaking year. This is in part due to the wise choices of the President and his economists over the past few years, choices which may well prove harder to make in the months ahead. But most of the credit must go as usual to our efficient and effervescent economy itself which, while paying the bills for Vietnam and building a Great Society at home, still looks as though it has plenty of energy left to grow.

FAILURE OF A POLICY [4]

Reprinted from *U.S. News & World Report*.

Vietnam is forcing some second thoughts about the idea that war could be won under a "Do Not Disturb" sign at home. Goal of "business as usual" in the United States in the midst of faraway combat is going by the board. Policy looked good on paper, but—

"Taps" appears to be sounding for one policy on which President Johnson has rested his first full term in the White House.

The policy: to fight a war—to have "guns" in abundance —and at the same time to have "business as usual," giving people all the "butter" they want.

Ever since 1965, when the decision was made to go into Vietnam with a major military operation, the plan in Washington has involved an effort to mix guns and butter.

That effort today is being reassessed.

A war that was supposed to be something like the Indian wars in the United States, or the border wars in which Great Britain was involved in an earlier day, has turned into one of the really big wars of American history.

The fortunes of this war—fought on a part-time basis— have not been favorable to the United States. There are some signs, including seizure by North Korea of a US naval vessel, that this war in Asia may yet expand beyond Vietnam. Even now, Russia is furnishing the enemy in North Vietnam with sophisticated modern weapons, oil products and other supplies valued, according to latest Allied intelligence, at about $6 billion a year, and rising.

Domestic Troubles

Neither is the "Great Society" at home thriving, although its costs continue, on the basis of budgeted spending, to head skyward.

[4] Article, "Guns and Butter—Failure of a Policy." *U.S. News & World Report*. 64:27-9. F. 12, '68.

Promises of help for the cities, help for the poor, help for schools, help for housing have generated expectations that the Government apparently cannot begin to fulfill without a massive increase in spending above that planned.

While budgeted spending is to reach $186 billion in the year beginning July 1 [1968], of which $109 billion is for nonwar purposes, nobody seems to feel that the dollars involved will be enough to please the cities or the minority groups and others interested in Federal handouts.

Of the $109 billion for nonmilitary spending, $59 billion is strictly for butter—for "Great Society" programs.

From the last full year of John F. Kennedy's presidency through the year ahead, for which President Johnson has just budgeted, welfare-state types of spending have risen by nearly $33 billion, or 125 percent. On the basis of comparison with past periods, that appears as a lavish serving of butter.

The military, including the war itself, has not been so lavishly served with the guns it regards as necessary to fight a war successfully.

Military spending in the Johnson years, including spending on war, has risen $27 billion, or 54 percent. That's the guns portion of the White House policy, compared with the butter portion for "Great Society" spending—up $32.8 billion.

In terms of money, the people in the field doing the fighting have been somewhat less favored than those back home wanting to enjoy a better life.

This policy of holding down on guns in wartime in order to give butter to the people at home, on the basis of progress reports in the war, is being described as a failure. Military services find themselves short of "guns"—the men, planes, big weapons and ships—all of the needed things, other than atomic weapons, to meet threats that may develop outside Vietnam. Also, the military services have been complaining for years that they were being denied the weapons and manpower needed to bring the war in Vietnam to a successful conclusion.

In other words, as the military services see it, the US policy has been rough on those called on to fight a war, but quite pleasant for the more numerous individuals back home who are enjoying a life far removed from the strife and strain of a battlefield.

A Look at Spending

Other results have flowed from the guns-and-butter policy.

In a time of war, plus "business as usual" at home, plus large and expanding welfare programs, the total impact has caused a vast outpouring of dollars from Washington. During the years of the Johnson Administration, spending has risen from the $111.3 billion of the last Kennedy year to the budgeted $186.1 billion in fiscal year 1969. That is a rise of $74.8 billion, or more than two thirds in a span of six years.

This large amount of money from Washington—a good part of it calling for matching expenditures on the part of states and cities—has boosted the economy. Business activity and employment have been at high levels.

With what amounts to full employment, unions have found themselves in a favorable position to demand and— often after strikes—get large increases in pay and in fringe benefits. Employers, in turn, with costs then higher, have been under pressure to raise prices.

Part of the guns-and-butter policy—with its "business as usual" theme—has called for avoidance of formal controls over wages or prices or credit.

Wage-price inflation—called cost-push inflation—has been the result. Prices, and with them the cost of living for average families, are in a strong rise at this time.

In 1965, when war was expanded, the President's economic advisers and others recommended an increase in income taxes. This recommendation was repeated in 1966.

Mr. Johnson backed away from an action that many considered politically unpopular.

Also, as costs of war rose, dollars poured into the world to pay for goods purchased abroad or to support troops abroad. The hoard of dollars in the hands of foreigners rose toward $30 billion. Many of these holders of dollars became concerned about the soundness of their dollars and demanded gold in exchange. The result was that this country's gold supply shrank steadily, even dramatically. Barely $1.7 billion of "free gold" remains to satisfy potential claims of $30 billion.

Owners of these $30 billion held abroad—largely central banks of major nations—have urged that United States start to put its financial house in order. There was insistence that —as their price for continuing to hold dollars rather than demanding gold—the U.S. raise taxes, raise interest rates to discourage borrowing, and make other moves to show ability to live within its means.

The Dollar in Difficulty

Late in 1967, when Britain faced bankruptcy and devalued the pound, the US dollar was in critical straits.

It was at this point that the guns-and-butter policy— "business as usual" during a major war—began to be in trouble.

The first controls of a wartime nature, designed to bulwark the dollar, came early in the year. Those controls applied to investments by US businessmen in Western Europe and some other parts of the world. They directed that a fixed portion of earnings abroad by business be returned to this country.

President Johnson, at the same time, called for Congress to enact a tax on travel abroad by Americans. The President wants a penalty to apply to Americans who take trips and spend money outside the Western Hemisphere. Foreign travel has resulted in a net loss of nearly $2 billion a year, adding that total to the net dollar holdings of foreign nations.

Mr. Johnson, too, is asking Congress to impose a small special tax on imports, and to provide some form of tax concession to stimulate exports. Major nations in Europe now impose special taxes on US products that seek to get into their markets.

In Congress, there is growing sentiment for action to bring back formal controls on installment credit—fixing the size of down payments and the term for repayment of loans.

A Boost to Inflation

The President on February 1 [1968] moved to reestablish wage-price guidelines that would be applied on a semivoluntary basis. A committee of Cabinet members would meet with labor and business leaders to shape a policy. The trouble is that wage settlements now being reached far exceed any guidelines that Federal planners would be expected to call reasonable, with the result that inflation pressures already are found to be out of hand.

Wage and price controls by law are not being considered at this juncture. However, if war does broaden, either by an outbreak in Korea or by involvement of Laos, Thailand and Cambodia, formal controls might be forced.

President Johnson now is insistent that a tax surcharge of 10 percent be applied as soon as possible to incomes of individuals and corporations.

Again, a policy of guns and butter—without higher taxes —means badly unbalanced Government books. In the year to end June 30, Mr. Johnson estimates, they will be out of balance by $20 billion. They will be at least that badly out in the year that follows, he predicts, unless taxes are raised.

Congress, however, is not convinced that a tax rise would be more desirable than a cutback of spending for butter.

At the time of the Korean War—a smaller one than the Vietnam war—the United States emphasized guns and de-emphasized butter. There were wage-price controls. Use of credit was controlled. The country organized itself for war and veered away from "business as usual."

Military leaders of the United States never have been happy about war on the mainland of Asia. When the decision was made to move in with regular US forces, they advised that this war would be difficult and require many troops. Their advice and recommendations all along have been discounted by civilian leaders of the Defense department who had the ear of the President. The Joint Chiefs of Staff, as a result, have been dissatisfied throughout over the size of the forces on which they could draw and the equipment assigned to them.

In the early days of the Vietnam war, US pilots were forced to fly World War II planes because of a civilian decision that jets were not suited for Vietnam. The enemy, from the first, has been underestimated by virtually everyone in the President's inner circle of civilian advisers.

Mr. Johnson now is warning, however, that his estimates of military spending may have to be raised. When and if that happens, some of the "butter" in Federal programs may have to give way. As it is, the President no longer refers publicly to a "Great Society"—which is being tripped up by war.

III. THE CRISIS

EDITOR'S INTRODUCTION

By the first half of 1971 Richard Nixon had been in office more than two years. And if one had listened to his officials then, one might have felt that all the economic problems that the Johnson Administration had created were on their way to being solved.

But were they? Close scrutiny shows that not only were they not solved, they were being compounded. The problems in 1968 involved inflation but not unemployment. In 1971 both unemployment and inflation were rampant. What is more, the problems at home were worsening the situation abroad. The dollar was constantly under attack and US trade was becoming less and less vigorous.

In short, in 1971 the US economy was in trouble and headed for crisis.

Selections in this section look at the major problem areas at that time. Not surprisingly they were the very same areas that the President's New Economic Policy was aimed at later that year. But at the time the President and his advisers tried to keep a public image of self-assured control over the entire situation.

The section begins with an interview with George P. Shultz, the director of the budget, who steadfastly maintained that President Nixon's economic game plan was right on target. The next article, however, indicates how serious inflation had become. There follows an article that looks at rising unemployment. The fourth piece in the section documents a dollar crisis that flared up in late spring. The fifth recounts the efforts then being made to get the deteriorating US balance of trade on a more favorable footing.

ECONOMIC POLICY ON COURSE [1]

Reprinted from *U.S. News & World Report.*

The basic strategy of economic policy and its current tactical implementation are generally on course, and economic policy can benefit from application of the old nautical phrase, "Steady as you go."

For we are going forward with expansion of the economy as the war in Vietnam continues to wind down and as the pressures of inflation diminish in their intensity.

But also with each passing day the pressures mount to alter the course and to steer not by the compass but by the wind, tossing caution to the wind in the process. I can assure you that these counsels meet strong resistance from the President.

Of course, there are problems:

There are uncertainties to be monitored and adjusted for in the tactics of economic policy as new data become available. There are changes in the structure of demand and supply in the marketplace which must be taken into account. Unemployment is too high, and there are pockets of unemployment—created mainly by the shift from war to peacetime production—that must be treated directly.

But beyond these issues what are the broad objectives of the President's economic policy?

One strategic purpose of this Administration has been to slow a rapidly escalating inflation without inducing a downturn in economic activity.

Another has been to stop the Government budget from creating instability, which it had been doing, and get the budget onto a more sustainable basis, which is what we are doing now.

[1] Article entitled " 'Economic Policy on Course,' Says Top Nixon Aide," taken from transcript of address to the Economic Club of Chicago, April 22, 1971, by George P. Shultz, director, Office of Management and Budget in the Nixon Administration. *U.S. News & World Report.* 70:55-7. My. 10, '71.

A third has been and is to create the conditions for steady economic expansion in a way that nourishes the freedom and innovative spirit of management, labor and individuals —in a way that does not involve the takeover of the economy by Government.

Now, let's look at the results so far.

Inflation has begun a turn downward after a relatively mild slowing of the economy. It has taken longer than we hoped and unemployment has been higher than we wanted, but the progress is unmistakable.

The consumer price index, for example, has declined in its rate of increase from over 6 percent in the first half of 1970 to a little under 5 percent in the second half of 1970 to about 2.7 percent in the first quarter of 1971. This is the lowest quarterly increase since the second quarter of 1967.

A balance in the budget at full employment has been attained and held for all three Nixon years after three years of rapidly rising and ultimately tremendous deficits at full employment, thereby removing a destabilizing Government influence from the economy and replacing it with a steadying influence.

And now the economy is moving forward, having registered a solid advance of 6.5 percent in real gross national product in the first quarter of this year, with the upward movement clearly and substantially stronger and more broadly based toward the end of the quarter than at the beginning.

Yet there are real differences in approach to economic policy today, and we would do well to recognize the disagreements and clarify the arguments.

There is a school of thought that our economy has changed to such an extent that the free-market economy will no longer work well enough. In order to achieve stability, this school says, Government must do much more to manage the private sector. Some members of this school believe that more Government management is needed not only temporarily to cure our current inflation but indefinitely.

It is time to challenge the basic premise that the economy has changed drastically over the past decade. "Times have changed" is a truism that is hard to refute, but let us see what has changed and what has not.

A principal argument that has been used to justify this seeming newness is that corporations and labor now have a great deal more market power than they previously had.

In fact, however, there is little evidence that the power of business has grown—has become more concentrated or monopolistic in recent times. Studies of horizontal integration, which use concentration ratios and rates of return, find little evidence of a secular increase in this indicator of monopoly. Likewise, a study of vertical integration, which uses sales to value-added ratios, finds no evidence for a secular trend. Monopoly power does not appear to be on the rise.

When conglomeration was in vogue a few years ago, the specter was raised of a dozen supercorporations dominating the business scene. But because conglomeration did not provide a magic formula for management or financial success, that threat has receded.

Waves of conglomerate activity have been experienced in the US economy before. As before, the aftermath of the recent wave has been its reversal. Antitrust enforcement was a factor, but the free market itself provided the main self-cleansing force. The trend in business today is toward more competition, not less, and the successful conglomerates have often been the agents of this sharper competition.

Only in an atmosphere of false boom—of an economy superheated by Government—covering up errors of business judgment can inefficient aggregations of enterprise prosper. We have now seen what happens when Government stops racing the economic engine beyond its capacity to perform: The wheeling and dealing gives way to a more fundamental and more healthy form of competition among business enterprises.

But what about organized labor? Has it grown in power so markedly in recent years that new regulations are needed in the labor market and in collective bargaining?

Let us look at the Government sector of the economy. Here we see both rapid growth in union membership and rapid growth in employment, with the proportion rising from about 12.6 percent to about 18.2 percent of the Government labor force over the years from 1956 to 1968. It is noteworthy, but perhaps not surprising under the circumstances, that wage rates have risen especially rapidly in this sector of the economy.

In my judgment, the problems of employer-employee relations in Government will deserve and will command more and more attention in the years ahead. Certainly we are far from a resolution of the fundamental problems involved, and they are problems that will affect not only wages and costs—taxes—in the public sector but the private labor market as well. This is indeed a new factor in the picture.

In the private nonfarm sector of the economy, by sharp contrast, union membership grew only slightly—not nearly so fast as employment—so that its proportionate importance declined from about 38 percent to about 32 percent of this labor force.

Lack of growth does not mean a lack of issues about present arrangements in the labor market. But it seems fair to say the issues are not newly created. It cannot be argued that the current inflation is associated with rising union strength.

Broad statistics on the increase in average hourly earnings of private nonfarm workers show a level of increase that must be reduced if we are to have an extended period of price stability. At the same time they tend to confirm the picture of no basic change in the arrangements of labor markets.

The rise in wages and benefits over twelve-month spans has moved largely within a narrow band between 6 and 8

percent for about five years. There are differential movements by industry, with nonunion areas, such as trade,
moving up more sharply when labor markets were at their
tightest and reacting more quickly to the current slack.

It may be noted that conditions in labor markets did not
ease greatly until mid-1970. Conversely, fixed-term contracts
tend to produce a slower response in union rates when the
labor market tightens, but to project that response—unfortunately, sometimes at an unwarranted and unwise level—on
into a period of changed economic circumstances. This is,
however, a well-known phenomenon, identifiable throughout the post—World War II period.

Another well-known movement is also under way—one
that has created great difficulty in the fight against inflation
but which will now provide us some help. The top of a
boom and a time of slowing economic activity are always
times when the growth of output per man-hour—productivity—also slows. But, as output rises again, productivity does
so as well and initially at a rate above its long-term average.

Output Per Man-Hour on the Rise Again

A little-noted but very important aspect of the first-quar-
ter results was the appearance again of this predictable development: Productivity rose at a rate better than 5 percent
after three years of below-average growth. This shift will
make a dramatic difference in unit costs of labor and is a
hopeful factor insofar as inflation is concerned.

But that is not the main point here. The point is that
events are proceeding generally in accord with what might
be expected on the basis of past experience.

There are special problems:

High expectations for performance of the economy create
a dynamic of their own. We have already noted the area of
Government employment. The construction industry has
long been in difficulty and may well be helped out of at least
some of its problems through efforts now being made with

stimulation from the President. And there are a number of other industries—notably transportation—where high wage settlements pose difficult cost problems.

The steel industry is very much on our minds. The problem here is not one of setting an inflationary wage pattern: Steel is at the end of the round, not the beginning. Nor is the industry so large and important that it can force a generally higher cost level on the economy.

The problem is the reverse: The industry is weak, beset with competition from substitute materials, losing ground in world markets and showing a rate of return that can hardly impress investors. These problems will be facing labor and management whatever the outcome of their wage bargaining and would be badly aggravated by a settlement that extends fixed, high increases into future years.

The answer to these problems is not more-severe import quotas, for these will only put American steel users in a poorer and poorer competitive position at home as well as abroad.

Management and labor have a common and severe problem here. Working together with a common goal, they can make a big difference in cost per ton, even without major changes in technology. Perhaps Government can help. Certainly a union that produced a Clint Golden and a Joe Scanlon [former officials of the Steelworkers Union] can draw upon its traditions for constructive alternatives.

We need leadership from the industry to produce a program that combines fair wages and competitive cost through high productivity. In this direction, there is a chance for secure jobs—important to young and older workers alike— and of adequate returns for the capital necessary to the long-run health of the industry.

Two other problem areas deserve special note:

Economic activity in 1970 was substantially disrupted by strikes, which occurred with relatively high frequency. Strikes are unfortunate. Peaceful settlements are certainly to be preferred, and we may expect 1971 to be somewhat more peaceful than its predecessor. But we must also remember that strikes occur most often when an economy is shifting its gears.

Last year, when the brakes were applied to inflation, profit margins narrowed, making it difficult for companies to meet the rising demands of labor—demands often reflecting the absence of any gain in real earnings during the prior contract term. The result was conflict. But the fact of this conflict is not evidence that our system is breaking down; it is evidence that the system is working—reacting, as it must, to the end of a spiraling rate of inflation.

Over the past two decades we have engaged in more and more trade with the rest of the world. The high returns from this increase in trade have been shared by both Americans and foreigners. In addition, competition from abroad has served to protect the consumer in the United States.

The share of the economy represented by trade in goods and services has increased from about 9 percent to over 12 percent of gross national product since 1950, with exports growing from about 5 percent to 6.5 percent of the gross national product and imports from a little over 4 percent to about 6 percent.

But this increased trade—especially the imports—has posed severe problems in many industries and imposed inequities in some cases.

A "Hard-Nosed Review" of Foreign Trade

The whole area of international economic policy deserves careful, hard-nosed and comprehensive review. That review is going forward now under the aegis of the new Council on International Economic Policy created last February [1971] by the President's executive order.

The President, who has traveled to sixty-seven countries over the past twenty-four years, is determined that when

American business goes abroad its interests will be strongly represented and advocated by our Government.

Perhaps the most troublesome problem from the standpoint of economic policy generally is the area to which I am the closest: the Federal budget. The upward thrust built into this gigantic flow of spending is awesome, and there is a continuous and continuing threat that outlays will develop a momentum carrying them well beyond full-employment revenues. Tempting though the immediate prospect of such free spending seems to be, it is bad news for the long-run prospects of the economy. Inflation or a tax increase follow in its wake.

For fiscal year 1971, despite a deficit we now estimate at about $19 billion, outlays will be held just within full-employment revenues—but only because of the President's willingness to veto apparently popular spending bills and of the willingness of a sufficient number of Congressmen to stand with him.

Fiscal year 1972 will not start for another ten weeks, and Congress has barely started its work on this budget. Yet actions so far—other things remaining as in the President's budget—already carry the deficit above $15 billion and outlays to a level well above full-employment revenues.

We desperately need a steadiness, a sense of balance and longer-term perspective in our budget policy. The years 1971 and 1972 are certainly important to this Administration, but we must operate also with an eye to 1973 and beyond.

Do we have the ability—perhaps a better word is "guts" —to hold a steady course on the budget? I can assure you of a strong effort from this Administration.

The President has been earning the reputation for credibility and perseverance the hard way. When he came into office he said he would slow the increasing momentum of inflation. Others said the inflationary thrust could never be contained without a virtual takeover of economic activity or a major depression. It was—and without either.

The decisions were not easy to make. The cutbacks required to balance the full-employment budget and the degree of monetary restraint necessary to slow the inflation were not popular. But now we can see a reduction of the rate of inflation.

A portion of the battle against inflation is now over; time and the guts to take the time—not additional medicine —are required for the sickness to disappear. We should now follow a noninflationary path back to full employment, assessing developments as we go and ready to provide stimulation as needed. But the temptation is there to go overboard on excessive stimulation. These pressures exist on both the monetary and budgetary fronts. We must again provide the steadiness to resist these pressures.

The effects of balanced stimulation appear to be taking hold: Interest rates have fallen sharply, and, as is usually the case, new housing starts have increased substantially. As you all have also read recently, the increase in gross national product from the fourth to the first quarter was the largest absolute increase in history. Although we can't recover from an auto strike every quarter, we expect solid increases in output for the remainder of the year.

These facts, along with a policy of "steady as you go," have been accompanied by an unprecedented rise in the stock market. It was just about a year ago that the President suggested that it might be a good time to buy stocks. Stocks are up about 30 percent from the time he made that statement.

The facts reviewed here do not suggest a sharp departure from prior experience. Perhaps the only significant departure is the "steady as you go" policy. . . .

Federal Controls in the Free-Market System

Government does have the responsibility to remove artificial props to wages and prices when the free-market system is abused. And in selective cases—in a critical industry or in an especially flagrant situation—Government should be willing to be the catalyst in achieving voluntary stabilization and, when necessary, to help restructure the bargaining process.

But we will not be drawn into a series of steps that will lead to wage and price controls, rationing, black markets and a loss of the effectiveness of the free economic system.

A single theme runs through everything this Administration does: In foreign policy, our Government will help others help themselves where they are willing to bear the major portion of their own defense and where it is in our national interest to help. In domestic policy, the Federal Government is moving to help people more, in a way that returns power and responsibility to states and localities. And in economic policy, the Federal Government will seek to create the climate in which a free economy can expand steadily and solidly without domination by Government.

INFLATION SHREDS THE DOLLAR [2]

Ever since last year's [1970] mild recession President Nixon has clung tenaciously to his Administration's economic game plan for business recovery, firmly resisting the counsel of those who find his formula one part too little and two parts too late. In particular, despite repeated urgings by his old economic mentor, Dr. Arthur Burns, Federal Reserve chairman, he has flatly rejected an "incomes policy" that would directly influence wages and prices. Instead, Mr. Nixon has bet on the considerable power of fiscal and mone-

[2] From "Inflation Scores on the Game Plan." *Newsweek.* 78:59-61. Ag. 16, '71. Copyright Newsweek, Inc., August 16, 1971. Reprinted by permission.

tary measures to expand the lagging economy and on gentle use of the jawbone to slow the inflationary wage-price spiral.

But by last week, it was all too clear that the Administration cure for the nation's economic health—if it is taking at all—has left the patient too shaky for the President to ignore insistent demands for sterner remedies. To be sure, he strongly reiterated his opposition to Washington-prescribed controls on wages and prices. But Mr. Nixon opened the door ever so slightly by telling reporters he would "consider" with an "open mind" a wage-price review board, provided Congress can convince him in hearings that such a body would not stifle economic growth.

Actually, President Nixon's move was a neat bit of political footwork calculated to widen his options and draw him closer to his harshest economic critics, an increasing number of whom are from his own party. Just hours before his mild concession at a news conference, in fact, an ideologically diverse group of fifteen Republican senators announced sponsorship of a bill to create a three-man commission. The commission would be empowered to research and publish guidelines for noninflationary wage-price decisions and report to the President settlements it considered unjustified. *Newsweek*'s Rich Thomas learned further that the proposal was sent for comment and polishing to none other than Arthur Burns himself, who performed those tasks and returned it to its sponsors with his blessing. "It's time," proclaimed Connecticut Senator Lowell P. Weicker, Jr. [Republican], one of the bill's backers, "to move the ball out of the economic end zone." And last week's developments offered precious little evidence that the ball would advance of its own accord:

After down-to-the-wire negotiations, a costly steel strike was averted, but at the cost of a highly inflationary settlement. Less than twenty-four hours after United Steelworkers President I. W. Abel announced contract terms to his cheering local union leaders in Washington, U.S. Steel kicked off the biggest price increase in the industry's history—about 8 percent across the board.

With considerable help from Assistant Labor Secretary W. J. Usery . . . the United Transportation Union settled its twenty-month dispute with the nation's major rail carriers after a series of selective strikes that bruised the still-tender economic recovery. Again, the settlement was inflationary. As a result, higher freight rates are considered a certainty.

The Labor Department reported that unemployment edged up two tenths of 1 percent to 5.8 percent in July on a seasonally adjusted basis. But Republicans and Democrats differed sharply in their interpretation of this politically sensitive barometer. George Shultz, director of the Office of Management and Budget, said the unemployment level continued to show improvement since 160,000 fewer people were unemployed. However, the unemployment percentage increased because of a larger number of people looking for work, prompting Democratic National Chairman Lawrence F. O'Brien to chastise "the Nixon Administration's head-in-the-sand approach to the nation's economy."

The industrial wholesale price index, a major economic barometer, jumped seven tenths of 1 percent in July, the largest monthly rise in fifteen years.

The West Coast dock strike dragged into its seventh week, with only skimpy signs of settlement in sight. The strike's effects are mounting steadily, particularly among citrus exporters and lumber importers.

July sales of American-made automobiles moved up 4.3 percent in July, but the increase was dwarfed by a remarkable 22.9 percent leap in the foreign-car sector.

Stock prices slid, responding to the inflationary impact of the steel and rail settlements and reflecting the growing uncertainty among investors. The Dow Jones industrial average dropped an alarming 14.89 points last Tuesday alone [August 10, 1971] and closed the week at 850.62, its lowest level since January.

All this added up to a grim panorama of economic dislocation that Republican congressional incumbents find unnerving and Democratic critics observe with barely disguised glee. And nowhere did the gloomy picture come into sharper focus than in the steel situation.

Abel went to the bargaining table knowing full well his membership would not stand for anything less than the 31 percent boost over three years that the USW got from the aluminum and can industries earlier this year. But even a short strike was repugnant to an Administration deeply concerned about consumer—and voter—confidence. So when bargaining began to lag with just one day left before a scheduled walkout, President Nixon sent Labor Secretary James Hodgson into action. And after meetings with both sides and a twenty-four-hour delay of the strike deadline, an agreement finally was reached: a hefty $1 increase in hourly wages over three years, including for the first time a guaranteed 25-cent cost-of-living adjustment. "I could not have done better," an ebullient Abel told his members, and most agreed.

Costly Settlements

R. Heath Larry, the industry's chief negotiator, was hardly so enthusiastic, and with good reason. In its first year alone, the contract will cost the nine major steel makers $650 million, some $137 million more than those companies earned in all 1970. Thus, even though he called the settlement "enormous," President Nixon last week took pity on the industry and its sorry state and announced he would not seek a rollback of steel's record price hike.

Surprisingly enough, though, there were some long-range bright spots in the steel picture. For the first time, the union agreed to help improve the industry's perilously low productivity rate and said it would not block technological change. "In the next five years, this could mean the loss of 200,000 jobs," a top USW official said. "But we are resolved to do this. We are going to try to convince the workers that their futures depend on steel becoming more competitive."

Still, the steel settlement and price increase that followed clearly had the ring of inflation. In fact, unless it is offset by other movements, the 8 percent boost in steel prices alone will move the wholesale price index up nearly three tenths of 1 percent in August. Already, the multiplier effect of the steel settlement has become evident in the auto industry; three days after terms of the new contract were announced, General Motors Corporation announced price increases of about 4 percent on its 1972 models, which undoubtedly will be the eventual pattern for Ford Motor Company and Chrysler Corporation as well.

The rail settlement was no more promising to inflation fighters. True, the Administration was able to avoid congressional action to end the strike, economic disaster was averted and a mechanism for eliminating archaic work rules and featherbedding was established—but all at an enormous price. For while the productivity improvements granted the railroads will take years to surface, the union's mammoth 42 percent wage and fringes boost over 42 months begins immediately. As a result, said one rail spokesman, "an application for an increase in basic freight rates sometime soon is almost inevitable."

And Nixon economic planners face still further gloomy prospects. Once again, commercial banks are considering an increase in the prime lending rate from which most interest charges are scaled upward. Democratic members of the powerful Joint Economic Committee probably will propose a series of fiscal stimulants—including tax cuts and increased Federal spending—to bolster the economy. And perhaps most ominous of all, contracts covering 80,000 workers in the bituminous coal industry expire October 1, and miners in president W. A. (Tony) Boyle's United Mine Workers union are hungry. A strike there could have a crushing effect on any economic recovery—and a lush settlement could add further to the nation's inflationary woes. "Whether they settle or strike," summed up one White House official last week, "we are terribly worried about what might happen in coal."

UNEMPLOYMENT GROWS [3]

Reprinted from *U.S. News & World Report.*

As unemployment in the United States clings stubbornly close to 6 percent of the labor force—

Fresh controversy is boiling up over this long-standing question: Will it ever be possible to provide jobs for all the people who want to work?

The issue has plagued Government and business for at least a quarter century, ever since Congress passed the Employment Act of 1946.

That law declared, among other things, that it was Federal policy to promote "maximum employment."

But it set no benchmark as to how high unemployment might go before it became a threat to the economy.

Over the years, the term "maximum employment" has been freely translated as "full employment"—still with no firm consensus as to what is "full."

Now, with business recovery lagging, and pockets of unemployment as high as 9 percent to more than 12 percent in some communities, the job outlook is shaping up as a crucial issue in the 1972 political campaign.

Signs of concern show up in such developments as these:

President Nixon, reversing a previous stand, signed legislation early in July to let the Federal Government spend $2 billion over two years to underwrite 150,000 state and local public-service jobs. Mr. Nixon said the measure will have "an immediate effect in areas of high unemployment" such as southern California.

[3] From "Jobs for All: Any Time Soon?" *U.S. News & World Report.* 71:30-2. Ag. 2, '71.

AFL-CIO President George Meany attacked the Administration's whole economic strategy and called for far heavier Federal spending for public works. Mr. Meany said he "doesn't buy" the idea that "full employment is not attainable," and noted that unemployment was as low as 3.4 percent of the work force as recently as January 1969.

Democrats in Congress have made barbed comments about the job problem. House Speaker Carl Albert, of Oklahoma, claimed that "unemployment is approaching breadline proportions." Senator Henry M. Jackson, of Washington, declared that the real rate of unemployment is "at least 8 percent, not around 6 as the Administration claims," and added that "official statistics show only the tip of the iceberg." Senator Hubert Humphrey, of Minnesota, said that current figures disguise "a disastrous rate of unemployment."

Defending the Administration's program, Treasury Secretary John Connally said that "policies the President is going to follow are . . . designed to try to reduce the number of unemployed as quickly as he can." Mr. Connally added that an unemployment rate as low as 4 percent of the work force has never been "the norm" in years past.

A University of Michigan survey found that only 14 percent of those questioned felt the Government was doing a "good job" of controlling unemployment and inflation. Some 28 percent called the effort "poor."

Basic Disagreement

Complicating all the furor over today's unemployment problem is broad disagreement among economists, Government officials and labor authorities on several basic points: Is the system for counting the unemployed an accurate one? Can the Government stimulate business enough to increase jobs without courting disastrous inflation? Are there quirks in the unemployment picture now that differ from those in previous recession-and-recovery periods?

Some officials insist that the goal of "full employment" is itself a myth, since no one has ever defined the term.

They point to the fact that only in periods of forced-draft production associated with wartime or postwar booms has the annual rate of joblessness fallen below 4 percent— even though it has dropped lower than that in particular months. . . .

Two special factors show up in the present unemployment situation.

One is the high rate of joblessness among veterans returning from Vietnam. In the April-June quarter of 1971, the unemployment rate for veterans aged twenty to twenty-four was 12.4 percent, compared with 9.5 percent for nonveterans of the same ages.

The second problem centers on high unemployment among skilled technicians, scientists and engineers and among well-paid professional people.

Cutbacks in aerospace programs, for example, have intensified job troubles in such cities as Seattle and Tacoma, Washington; in Wichita, Kansas, and in Los Angeles, San Diego and other cities in California.

The job market for teachers and professors, particularly among recent college graduates, is very tight. Many young people intent on teaching careers, for which they were educated, are having to take whatever jobs they can find.

Many experts believe the job squeeze is temporary, and that a return to normal economic activity will automatically provide needed jobs.

A study by the Labor department . . . gives a glimpse of the nation's job pattern in 1980.

This survey anticipates 15.3 million additional jobs by that time, mostly in services, government and trade.

Keeping Count

How does the Government determine the number of people who are unemployed at any one time?

A spokesman for the Federal Bureau of Labor Statistics gives this explanation:

Each month the Census Bureau, on behalf of the Labor department, surveys a statistical sample of 50,000 households.

To be listed as unemployed, an individual must report that he is available for work, that he has not worked for pay during the previous week, even as much as an hour, and that he has actively sought work within the past four weeks.

Those who are on temporary layoffs from regular jobs also are counted as unemployed, even though they have made no effort to find other work. So are persons who have been assured jobs within the next thirty days, but who are not yet working.

Persons away from regular jobs because of vacations, strikes, illness or personal reasons are counted as employed. All part-time workers are listed as employed, regardless of the number of hours they worked.

BLS has a second category covering so-called hidden unemployment, but officials say this is less precise and is compiled only quarterly.

This category consists of "discouraged" workers—individuals who say they would take a job if they could get one, but who no longer are actively seeking employment. BLS estimated this group at 700,000 during the second quarter of 1971, up 100,000 from the similar period a year ago.

BLS officials also point out that some industrial nations count the unemployed in much different fashion than is the case in the United States.

For example, in England, registration with a Government job office is necessary to be counted as jobless. A study some years ago noted that when the unemployment rate in the United States was 5.5 percent, seasonally adjusted, the jobless rate in England was only 1.6 percent. However, if the US system had been used, the British rate would have been 2.4 percent.

What of the future?

Four nationally known economists, interviewed by *U.S. News & World Report*, estimated the current rate of unemployment at about 6 percent and indicated it would hold close to that for the rest of 1971. Down the road several years, however, they forecast a brighter outlook for jobs. Among their comments—

Professor Otto Eckstein of Harvard University, a member of the Council of Economic Advisers under President Johnson:

We can get back to full employment. I expect this will happen by 1973. By then, the unemployment rate should be down to 4.25 or 4.5 percent, which we think the country can live with.

Nat Goldfinger, AFL-CIO director of research:

It is certainly feasible to get full employment if the Administration wants it. I think Secretary Connally is dangerously wrong in saying the Government cannot effect that. If the Government sets the policies and adopts the required measures, we can have full employment. It's as simple as that.

Robert R. Nathan, private economic consultant in Washington:

I believe it is entirely possible to get the unemployment rate down to 3 or 3.5 percent, which is essentially full employment. This is simply a matter of employing enough fiscal and monetary measures to stimulate the economy. But the problem is that this generates great inflationary pressures, and the Administration has not been willing to take the measures necessary to cope with these pressures on wages and prices.

Martin Gainsbrugh, of the Conference Board in New York:

With as much slack as we have now in the labor force and in industrial capacity, concern over the rise in inflation should take second place to concern over unemployment. I believe full employment should be our prime target. And I believe it is feasible to attain, with unemployment held down to 4 or 4.5 percent as the optimum rate for a society such as ours.

We could be moving toward that goal by 1972, given the appropriate fiscal stimuli. And we could reach the 4 to 4.5 percent level by the middle of this decade if we carry through.

THE DOLLAR IN CRISIS [4]

For the fifth time in just three years, the world was caught up this week in a major monetary crisis. Foreign exchange markets all across Europe closed in the face of a massive inflow of dollars, and US tourists and businessmen on the continent were forced to scratch for takers of their greenbacks.

In many ways it was the most perilous crisis of all—certainly the worst since the weekend in March 1968, when harried central bankers had to rush off to Washington to deal with a panicked flight from all currencies into gold. Foreign exchange markets closed then, too, and stayed closed until the central bankers finally created the two-tier gold market: one market for themselves and the other just for speculators.

It will probably take a major realignment of the world's key currencies to restore peace to the international monetary arena this time—either a devaluation of the US dollar in relation to gold, which is most unlikely, or a revaluation of other currencies, which is very likely what will happen.

The Germans, hit hardest by the dollar flood, were to reveal their plans after a Friday cabinet meeting. The guessing at midweek was that Germany would simply let the mark "float" for a time against the US dollar, much as it did late in 1969. The mark would presumably float up—by maybe 5 percent or so—and Germany would have a revalued currency without having to come right out and say so.

Once the mark is allowed to float vis-à-vis the dollar, other currencies might either be out-and-out revalued or be allowed to float as well. Switzerland, Holland, Belgium, and Austria all were hit hard by dollar inflows this week; all were seen at midweek as potential candidates for revaluation. Another likely candidate is the Japanese yen—probably the most undervalued currency of all these days.

[4] Article, "Hot Dollars Spark a Global Crisis." *Business Week*. p. 16-17. My. 8, '71. Reprinted from the May 8, 1971, issue of *Business Week* by special permission. Copyright, 1971 by McGraw-Hill, Inc.

US Stand

Treasury Secretary John B. Connally tried his hand at pouring oil on the waters. There will be no change in the present value of the dollar, said Connally . . . [on May 4, 1971]—meaning no change in the current $35-an-ounce official price of gold. But the United States would issue more special securities aimed at sopping up some of the billions of US dollars that have built up in the hands of private and government banks abroad. The Treasury and the Export-Import Bank have each brought back $1.5 billion from overseas through such offerings, and now there will be more of them. Finally, said Connally, "measures to improve the balance of payments will remain of high priority."

Yet no one in Europe really paid very much attention to Connally. What jars European financial men is the nagging fear that the crisis is going to linger on no matter how many special securities the United States sells abroad. They are afraid that the outcome of this week's flare-up will not be lasting monetary peace, but only a tenuous truce.

The United States would gain a short-run victory if other currencies do revalue. That is precisely what this country has been advocating as a cure to an overvalued dollar. Yet as Europeans were quick to point out this week, it could prove a costly victory.

Wide Split

The old pattern of close monetary cooperation that successfully cooled down each crisis in the late 1960s has been badly frayed. There is anger at the United States for not doing more to reduce a balance-of-payments deficit that has grown mammoth over the past two years—and anger at the United States for letting interest rates fall so low in this country that money was sucked overseas by the higher rates there.

The other Common Market countries are dismayed that Germany might take unilateral action just a month before all the European Economic Community countries are to take an important step toward monetary union by narrowing the margins within which their currencies can fluctuate against one another. "If the Germans go off on their own," said one European, "then we don't have a community."

Most serious is the split between Germany and France over monetary matters. Finance Minister Valéry Giscard d'Estaing made clear on Wednesday that France was not going to float the franc, no matter what Germany does. The monetary system built twenty-seven years ago at Bretton Woods, New Hampshire, was based on fixed exchange rates and, said Giscard, "France is sticking to the rules of Bretton Woods."

However, there was not much that Germany could have done this week except to stop buying dollars. The dollar inflow was not merely big—it was staggeringly big. Some $1.2 billion poured into the country on Tuesday alone. Another $1 billion rushed in during just one hour on Wednesday morning. The German central bank, the Bundesbank, must pay out marks to buy up those dollars, and, with a domestic inflation rate of around 5 percent, the last thing Germany needs is a flood of new marks entering the economy. On Wednesday morning the Bundesbank simply quit buying dollars. In fast order, the central banks of Switzerland, Belgium, Holland, and Austria—each on the receiving end of the dollar inflow—followed suit. Only Britain, France, and Italy kept buying dollars on Wednesday.

Some hot money moved into gold—though not the way it moved into gold three years ago. Still, the London free market price did jump by nearly 50 cents per ounce on Wednesday to close the day at $40.13, which is the highest it has been since October 1969.

Of course, money has been moving into Germany, and into Switzerland as well, for some weeks. Around $1 billion moved into Germany and $300 million into Switzerland in one three-day span early in April. But this week was different.

No longer could governments soothingly describe the money flows as merely the mechanical consequence of interest rates that are higher in Europe than in the United States. This time it was pure speculation, a bet that the world's money managers would have to change the value of their currencies to reflect the weakness of the dollar.

Placing the Blame

Obviously, the United States gets some blame. The US balance-of-payments deficit amounted to a staggering $5 billion in this year's first quarter. The Federal Reserve has been trying to narrow the payments gap by pushing up interest rates here while Europeans push them down. Still, there is concern abroad that the Nixon Administration has paid less attention than it should have to the huge payments gap and to the decidedly overvalued look of the dollar.

What galls bankers elsewhere in Europe is the conviction that it was Germany—or more precisely Karl Schiller, Germany's loquacious economics minister—that really started money moving in the first place by openly flirting with the possibility of a realignment of currency values. Said a top official at one European central bank: "We can't blame the United States for this. It's Schiller's fault, and it's up to the Germans to stop the crisis."

Schiller really started the pot boiling last week by arguing with his Common Market partners that, since the United States was not going to oblige by devaluing the dollar, they should let their currencies float against the dollar. In other words, since the dollar will not be brought down in value, European currencies should be allowed to move up in value. The French quickly vetoed that suggestion because it would recognize that the free world was on a de facto dollar standard. But foreign exchange markets in Europe trembled just the same.

The pot boiled more furiously last Monday when a group of German economic institutes issued a joint report suggesting that the mark should either float or be revalued. Said one of the economists: "We do not exclude that this report will provoke more speculation." It did, especially after Schiller called the report "worthy of further consideration."

By Wednesday morning it was a full-blown crisis—the "Schiller crisis" as central bankers outside Germany called it. And now the money managers, in Germany and elsewhere, must seek a solution, and a quick one. Foreign exchange markets will be flooded anew with dollars should they attempt to reopen before the question of currency values is dealt with.

In the end, of course, Schiller may get precisely what he has been pumping for—a broad realignment of currency values. "He may be forcing us to do just what he has been asking us to do," observed a European central banker on Wednesday.

In fact, Schiller may wind up with more than he has bargained for. If the short run does produce a floating mark, and maybe some other floating currencies, the longer run may produce new limits on the freedom of currencies to move back and forth across international frontiers at will. No matter what solution Europeans achieve now, the world may well be moving toward a new era of exchange controls and aggressive economic nationalism.

TRADE BALANCE WORSENS [5]

The world economy, and the American role in it, is changing faster than ever before. Fifteen years ago, the United States accounted for nearly one third of the $32 billion trade of industrial countries. Last year [1970] the total soared to more than $200 billion, but the US share dropped to one fifth. Japan has emerged as a formidable industrial

[5] From article, "The U.S. Searches for a Realistic Trade Policy." *Business Week*. p. 64-70. Jl. 3, '71. Reprinted from the July 3, 1971, issue of *Business Week* by special permission. Copyright, 1971 by McGraw-Hill, Inc.

competitor. The exports of Common Market countries, if Britain joins, will be more than double those of the United States.

These trends will continue. They reflect the tremendous industrial upsurge of Western Europe and Japan, and more recently, a speedup in the economic growth of developing countries from Brazil to Taiwan.

Now the Administration, Congress, businessmen, and labor unions are all beginning to recognize that the changed situation requires new international economic policies. The competition for markets at home and abroad is already fierce. It will get tougher. And it is becoming a hot political issue because labor and management in such industries as shoes and textiles are discovering that their domestic markets are not safe, and they are shouting for protection.

The US technological lead in many industries has narrowed or disappeared. Wage and price inflation have weakened the ability of some American producers to compete in international markets. Trade with major partners such as Canada and Japan has swung sharply into deficit, and the overall US trade balance has deteriorated. This week, for the first time since 1950, the Commerce department announced that the United States exported less than it purchased from abroad in two consecutive months. A trade deficit totaling $420 million in April and May raised the possibility that the United States could run a deficit for the entire year—something that has not happened since 1893. Because earnings from trade no longer offset heavy dollar outflows for travel, foreign investment, and military spending, the dollar is under attack.

Now these problems are becoming so urgent that President Nixon is convinced that US commercial interests and other economic ties with foreign countries must play a larger role in the formulation of US foreign policy. To help plan economic strategy, Nixon last January created a new, high-level Council on International Economic Policy, the counterpart in economic affairs of the National Security Council. To be executive secretary of this interagency unit at a $42,500 yearly salary, he picked Peter G. Peterson, former head of Bell & Howell Company. Peterson also serves as chief White House adviser on foreign economic policy. Working with a small staff in the ornate old White House annex and consulting with other Government agencies, Peterson is starting to sketch basic policy guidelines and laying the groundwork for eventual legislative proposals aimed at strengthening the US position in world trade, investment, and finance. In briefing sessions, Peterson is telling businessmen, congressional leaders, and labor union officials that the United States is at a "watershed" in trade policy.

At issue, more basically, is what kind of economy the United States will have in the future. American industry can become more competitive, and thus continue to participate in the growth of a rapidly expanding world economy. Or it can withdraw behind the shield of protectionist measures, and thus cut itself off from world markets. Nixon is determined to compete for the US share of international trade.

I know that the President sees the post-Vietnam world as both more economic and more competitive [Peterson says]. And we will be more vigorous in pursuing our economic interests. As we move into the decade we will see our foreign policy and foreign economic policy moving more closely together.

In former years [he adds], a lot of our thrust was on building a world economy because it served our security objectives. As the world has changed and our economic position has changed, our policy balance should change.

An example was US acceptance, in the 1960s, of the Common Market's protectionist farm policies, which hurt American agricultural exports. Now the United States is leaning hard on Western European governments to keep the door open to American products.

Partly, this shift in emphasis reflects success in achieving some basic US foreign policy goals of earlier years: a liberal international trading system, a closeknit and prosperous international economy, and the economic strength and political stability of Western Europe and Japan. Partly, and more urgently, it is a response to Congress, labor unions, and businessmen demanding that affluent US allies observe stricter reciprocity in trade and investment, and that they shoulder a fairer share of defense burdens.

President Nixon is expected to reflect such concerns in a speech on international economic policy sometime this month. Before then, he will receive a three-hundred-page report from a twenty-seven-man Commission on International Trade & Investment Policy, headed by Albert Williams, chairman of the executive committee of International Business Machines Corporation. Among other things, the report is expected to call for major international economic negotiations with Europe and Japan, covering trade, investment, and monetary relations, in order to head off a threatened drift into a trade war.

Meantime, the international economic policy debate within the Administration covers a wide range of topics:

Trends in trade, the balance of payments, and multinational investment

Potential problems in economic ties with the Common Market, with Japan, and with developing countries

Supplies of raw materials and fuel for US industry, which is becoming increasingly dependent on foreign sources. By 1980, Peterson says, the United States will run a trade deficit of $12 billion to $15 billion in oil alone.

In Peterson's view, international economic relations are inseparable from domestic economic policies, and the agenda is weighted with such questions as the impact of technology on US industry, inflation, capital investment, and productivity.

"We are not just dealing with trade problems," Peterson explains. "Trade is the result of a lot of things you do. When you look at trade, you are often looking at the symptoms."

Bringing into focus the Administration's thinking in these areas is perhaps Peterson's most delicate task. After all, he is not the only official advocating solutions for America's trade problems. Commerce Secretary Maurice Stans, for instance, is promoting proposals such as tax and investment incentives for strengthening the US trade position. And Treasury Secretary John Connally is attracting a lot of attention by urging a "get-tough" policy with foreign countries that discriminate against US products and with Latin countries that are putting the squeeze on US investors.

What is likely to emerge from this debate in the near future is more aid to US exporters, such as expanded Export-Import Bank credit, and more pressure on Europe and Japan to knock down barriers to US exports and investment. US officials have been hinting to the Japanese that the yen should be revalued, a move which would help American exports to that country and take the edge off the Japanese sales drive in the United States. Proposals that are considerably more far-reaching have been made, entailing an expanded Government role in planning and guiding parts of the US economy.

While any action this year, or indeed before the 1972 elections, is unlikely, certain possibilities are being discussed seriously enough:

Subsidies or tax credits might be granted to maintain America's vital technological lead.

Antitrust rules could be eased to help companies meet foreign competition.

The Government could vastly expand aid to US manufacturers and workers hurt by imports.

All these schemes have one problem in common: They would have to get through Congress. And protectionists in Congress are always on the lookout for trade bills which they can transform into "Christmas trees" festooned with import quotas, especially while the US economy is in the doldrums. . . .

Skeptics about the Administration's approach to trade policy can be found . . . among businessmen, economists, and labor leaders. "Complaints about imports will die down to a great degree as the economy improves and as we pull military personnel back from Vietnam and elsewhere," predicts Robert W. Cornell, chairman of Cleveland's Parker-Hannefin Corporation, a $211 million manufacturer of hydraulic equipment. John Corcoran, president of Consolidation Coal Company, a subsidiary of Continental Oil Corporation, opposes such things as trade adjustment assistance, tax incentives for exports, and liberal export credit. "The problem is that we are pricing ourselves out of world markets," he says. "We are not treating the root of the problem. We have got to control inflation." He adds that "we are only kidding ourselves in the long run" by propping up US industry with artificial financial structures.

Major labor unions are not much impressed by long-range strategies to strengthen US companies' competitive position in world markets. They worry about loss of jobs and call for quotas to keep out foreign products. Elizabeth Jager, chief international economist for AFL-CIO, pooh-poohs the Administration's approach. "It is all theoretical, and we have to live with real people," she says. "The tragedy is I think they believe it might work."

But at least one aspect of the Administration's policy is showing some results: its get-tough line with foreigners. Politically, of course, this is popular as well. The harder line on abuses and inequities in trade actually began under President Johnson, who slapped special "countervailing duties" on products such as steel transmission line towers and sorghum that received export subsidies from European governments. Johnson also began subsidizing some US farm exports to offset Common Market dumping.

Under Nixon, the Treasury has tightened enforcement of the US antidumping law against imports of Japanese television sets and other products. By threatening retaliation against such European exports as Volkswagens, the United States blocked a move by the Common Market to impose a high tax on soybeans, a major US export. In what looked like a case of diplomatic overkill, Connally even suggested recently that the United States withdraw the Sixth Fleet from the Mediterranean because the Common Market was discriminating against US citrus fruits in favor of those from Spain and Israel. Now the Common Market has offered a compromise.

Japan is one of the main targets of US pressures because of its quotas on imports, its curbs on American investment, and the pervasive "Japan, Inc." partnership between government and business, which gives Japanese companies some of the competitive advantages of a huge cartel. Now the Japanese are moving to ease some of the trade problems with the United States.

There is some doubt, though, that the Administration can get much tougher without provoking retaliation abroad. The United States has its share of barriers to trade, including quota limitations on such products as oil, meat, dairy products, cotton textiles, and steel, which comprise one fourth of all US imports. In a trade war, particularly with the expanding Common Market, the United States could lose more than it gained. One official who warns against going too far is Theodore Gates, the President's Assistant Special Representative for Trade Negotiations, who in previous years argued within the Administration for a stronger defense of US commercial interests. Now he cautions: "Tough talk is not the answer to our problems. If the big trading nations concluded that we were reversing our liberal trade policies, they could and would make their own arrangements and leave us out."

The United States can use its military and political support for its allies as a lever to extract economic concessions. But in the long run, the price for such gains might be some sacrifice of US influence abroad. C. Fred Bergsten, former

Nixon adviser on foreign economic policy, believes that there is a "strong risk that trade policy will come to dominate overall foreign policy disastrously." One example is the political strain that could develop between the United States and Japan if protectionists in the Senate carry out their threat to hold up ratification of the treaty on the return of Okinawa unless the Japanese accept their demands on curbing textile exports to the United States.

While demanding more equitable treatment for US exports, the Administration also hopes to make American products more attractive to potential customers abroad by providing more export credit through the Export-Import Bank. The Senate has approved a big increase in Ex-Im's lending authority and, more important, has removed the bank's operations from Federal budget restrictions. The House is expected to follow suit. Congress also looks virtually certain to lift the ban on Ex-Im financing for sales to Communist countries.

With the new lending authority, Ex-Im President Henry Kearns expects to provide $2 billion worth of additional export credit in the first year and several times that much in following years. Currently the bank finances and insures $4 billion worth of sales annually. Not everyone in the Administration is enthusiastic about expanding Ex-Im's operations. Federal Reserve Chairman Arthur Burns and Hendrik Houthakker, retiring member of the Council of Economic Advisers, suspect that many sales generated by export credit would have occurred anyway. Their favorite target is Ex-Im's financing for exports of big aircraft which can be bought only in the United States.

But among businessmen, considerable support exists for more export financing. Says William S. Brewster, chairman and chief executive of Boston's USM Corporation, a diversified machinery maker: "Export credit is extremely important. In heavy machinery, price is not always the most important factor, it is the payment terms that count."

None of these measures to spur exports and clear away barriers to US products in international markets will give more than temporary help, though, unless US industry keeps its competitive edge in trade. One of the goals of policy must be "economic growth to pay for the improved quality of life that we all want," says Peterson. "And in a world economy that kind of growth requires, I believe, a renewed dedication to the fundamental idea that we are going to be competitive and all that implies: more and better technology, newer plants, more stress on productivity."

Technology is one of the keys to competitiveness, Peterson and others in the Administration firmly believe. Economist Michael Boretsky, an assistant to Commerce Secretary Stans, has been working for the past eighteen months on an analysis of US trade based mainly on technological inputs. The US maintains a modest trade surplus in farm products, mainly because of its rich farmlands and advanced farming methods. In oil, minerals, and other raw materials, the United States is becoming, increasingly, a have-not nation. Ten years from now, Boretsky predicts, the United States will be importing 50 percent of its raw materials, compared with 30 percent at present. A healthy trade balance, he points out, depends heavily on the US lead in "technology-intensive" products such as aircraft, machinery, and computers. American makers of such products still have the lion's share of world markets, despite the competitive disadvantage of paying the world's highest wages. "We sell the 747 not because of price but because it is unique," Boretsky observes. But for other manufactured goods, the US technological edge has narrowed. In such products, the US trade balance is plunging into a deep deficit.

Peterson, Stans, and others conclude that the United States needs to spur more research and development in order to maintain a strong trade position. But no clear Administration program for stimulating more and better R&D has yet evolved. White House Science Adviser Edward E. David, Jr., says only that incentives to private industry "perhaps" are needed.

Stans is closer to producing a package of specific proposals. A number of ideas are under study:

Tax credits for added research by companies, or for certain kinds of R&D

Quasi-public R&D corporations that would do research in such fields as new energy sources, and would auction off the results to private industry

New rate structures to encourage more R&D by utilities and other regulated industries

Such proposals are highly controversial. They encounter considerable skepticism as to how much they would achieve. Says Milton Harris, former chief of research at Gillette Company: "I think the major flaw is attributing so much of economic growth to R&D. A lot of things contribute: capital, labor, productivity. If you could do something in labor you could have a greater input than with all your R&D." Other businessmen doubt that R&D subsidies could be administered fairly. And Robert M. Adams, vice president for research at 3M [Minnesota Mining & Manufacturing] Company, doubts the workability of tax credits. He recalls that 3M tried to take advantage of a Canadian tax credit scheme introduced in 1967. "They put so many restrictions on such research that they made it almost impossible to do it," he says. "We found we just couldn't live with it and went back to spending our own money."

Even more controversy is likely to be stirred by suggestions for relaxing antitrust regulations so that US companies can compete more effectively against foreign rivals that are under less constraint. Stans made a strong plea for a more relaxed antitrust policy last week in testimony before the congressional Joint Economic Committee's panel on foreign economic policy, chaired by Representative Hale Boggs (Democrat, Louisiana). He cited Japan's computer manufacturers and the German machine tool industry as examples of foreign competitors that pool R&D.

But Richard W. McLaren, chief of the Justice department's antitrust division, is cool to such ideas, and Stans conceded that the Administration may not make any legislative proposals. "It may be that, if there are other ways of helping the trade balance, we will dismiss antitrust," Stans told the committee.

Even if the United States manages to restore a healthy overall trade balance, US companies, workers, and entire communities will still face a growing problem of adjustment to the increasingly rapid shifts in the pattern of international trade. The accelerating pace of technological change, improved communications, and faster transport are speeding the invasion of international markets by new products and suppliers. The swift takeover of a big part of the US desk-top calculator market by Japanese electronic machines is just one example. As a result, manufacturers have less time than in former years to adjust to rising foreign competition. In New England alone, some ninety footwear makers have closed down and an estimated 25,000 jobs have been lost in the last three years—though it is hard to tell just how many of these are the result of imports and how many are the victims of the business slowdown.

One answer to the problem, as an alternative to import protection, is aid to companies hurt by imports, to help them modernize, reequip, or shift to other products, combined with retraining and extended unemployment benefits for workers.

We need a more comprehensive adjustment program that reflects the world of higher technology and faster change that we live in [Peterson says]. Time is very important. We must do a better job of dealing with the important human and social problems created by rapid adjustment.

The Administration is asking for $200 million for adjustment assistance in the coming fiscal year. Stans figures that as much as $500 million to $1 billion may be needed in future years.

Labor's view is expressed by Elizabeth Jager, who dismisses the program as "funeral benefits."

But Nathaniel Samuels, Deputy Under Secretary of State for Economic Affairs, explained the rationale of the program in testimony before the Boggs committee.

The basic question facing all nations in this era of rapid technological advance is how continually to reorient resources so as to derive the benefits of this advance while minimizing the disruptive effects to particular segments of the economy [he said]. Certainly the solution is not to perpetuate high-cost and noncompetitive segments through subsidy and highly protectionist policies that were so unsuccessful in the past.

Such proposals, of course, imply more planning and a more active role for the Government in the economy. Indeed, Peterson and others in the Administration are clearly impressed by the achievements of Japan through close cooperation between business and government.

This kind of world implies more goal-setting [Peterson says]. I'm not for a Japanese transplant. But in a high-technology world that is changing fast, we ought to ask, "What kind of planning for the future is appropriate, given the kind of economic system we have?"
In all this, let's not make the mistake of downgrading this country. We have great resources in dollars, technologies, people, a tradition of competitiveness and inventiveness. The task is how to apply them in such a way that, by the end of this decade, this country is still a world leader—and the right kind of leader.

IV. WHAT WENT WRONG?

EDITOR'S INTRODUCTION

It was now the middle of 1971. Two Presidents—Johnson and Nixon—had known that since 1966 the economy was becoming unbalanced. Maybe Mr. Johnson had been preoccupied with Vietnam and other problems. But, surely, Mr. Nixon had ample time to solve these economic problems before they reached crisis stage. Why hadn't he done so? What had gone wrong?

This section deals with those questions. The first article is by Melville Ulmer, a frequent contributor to the *New Republic*. Mr. Ulmer argues that the Nixon Administration had failed to use the right fiscal and monetary policies and had thus bumbled its way into the crisis. The next article is by former Treasury Under Secretary for Monetary Affairs Robert Roosa, whose argument is that the Administration misinterprets the nature of the inflation it is dealing with. This is "cost-push" inflation, he says, and the remedies applied by President Nixon are those needed to put down a "demand-pull" inflation. (Demand-pull means that demand is so great it forces prices up because buyers bid among themselves. Cost-push inflation occurs when sellers constantly keep raising prices without any relationship to demand.)

The third article, by the political commentators Rowland Evans, Jr., and Robert D. Novak, deals with still another interpretation—the political one. It would be reassuring to assume that the welfare of the nation, or the majority of its people, is the only factor that goes into top-level decision making about the economy. In fact, however, the top-level decision makers are politicians, and their decisions invariably contain "political realities." Accordingly, this article takes a look at some of the political realities that have shaped the handling of the economy.

Each of the articles in the section notes that the crisis at hand is unusual in that both inflation and unemployment are present. And both Mr. Ulmer and Mr. Roosa make the recommendation that wage and price controls are one way of breaking out of the trap.

The final article in the section is a fascinating blow-by-blow account of how President Nixon finally came to share the same point of view, and how, once he had decided on the course of action, he quickly put together the vast program that now goes under the banner of the New Economic Policy.

THE WRONG POLICIES WERE USED [1]

Old ideas seldom fade away, in economics. More commonly they explode, sometimes with a blast strong enough to unseat governments. Herbert Hoover was a devotee of the theory that capitalism is self-equilibrating, that depressions can cure themselves, and quickly. That idea, which survived the test of time for 150 years or more, exploded with a reverberation that shook the country from October 1929 until November 1932. President Nixon pledges allegiance to the "new" or Keynesian economics, which has been gospel for the last thirty-five years. If a political time bomb is embedded in that theory, too, as I believe, it could go off in November 1972. For the fatal flaw of the new economics, whatever its merits may be, is its inability to provide full employment and stable prices at the same time.

Ever since the end of World War II we have faced the same central problem: the closer our economy draws toward the full employment level, the faster prices tend to rise.

[1] Article entitled "Applied Nixonomics: The Inflation/Unemployment Seesaw," by Melville J. Ulmer, free-lance writer on economics. *New Republic.* 164:15-18. Ap. 24, '71. Reprinted by permission of The New Republic, © 1971, Harrison-Blaine of New Jersey, Inc.

Moving in the opposite direction, the more we dampen prices, the more unemployment deepens. Keynesian economics simply determines the direction of the pendulum's swing. Thus when inflation threatens, the Keynesian formula calls for some combination of tight money, higher taxes, and/or reduced government expenditures. This reduces demand, usually retards the price rise, but always increases unemployment. When unemployment threatens, the formula calls for easy money, lower taxes, and/or higher government expenditures. This stimulant raises demand, lowers unemployment, but also lifts prices again.

Like a mindless automaton, one Administration after the other has fought inflation (usually when the price rise mounts to an annual rate of 3 or 4 percent) by creating unemployment, and then fought unemployment (usually when it swells to 6 or 7 percent of the labor force) by creating inflation. Here are the zigs and zags, Truman through Nixon.

Truman

Expansionary Zig: 1946-1948. Unemployment is reduced from 5 percent to 3.5 percent of the labor force, but inflation explodes, spurred by abandonment of wartime price controls.

Contractionary Zag: 1948-1949. Inflation is checked but unemployment swells from 3.5 to 7.9 percent.

Expansionary Zig: 1949-1952. Unemployment is cut to less than 3 percent but consumer prices mount at an annual rate of more than 4 percent.

Eisenhower

Contractionary Zag: 1953-1954. Inflation is brought nearly to a halt but unemployment moves back to about 6 percent.

Expansionary Zig: 1955-1957. Unemployment is pressed down to 4 percent but prices start moving up again.

Contractionary Zag: 1957-1959. The attempt to check inflation provokes most severe recession of postwar era and unemployment zooms to nearly 8 percent in spring of 1958.

Kennedy-Johnson

Expansionary Zig: 1961-1968. Economy recovers slowly at first but then gathers force with Vietnam war adding impetus. Unemployment drops from nearly 7 percent in 1961 to 4.5 percent in 1965 and then to 3.3 percent at the end of 1968. Inflation also gathers force with the annual price rise reaching more than 4 percent.

Nixon

Contractionary Zag: 1969-1970. Unemployment is raised from 3.3 percent at the end of 1968 to 6.2 percent by the end of 1970. Only slight success in retarding price rise, from a bit above a 6 percent annual rate in 1969 to a bit below 6 percent in 1970.

Insofar as it differs from that of his predecessors, Mr. Nixon's plight is suggested in the last sentence. All the less attractive elements of a contractionary zag were present during the past year—a decline in output, a plummeting stock market, high interest rates, joblessness, and diminished sales and profits. But following the longest inflationary expansion in recent history, the upward pressures on prices were extraordinarily stubborn, a fact that poses special problems—economic and political—for the year ahead.

If the Administration yields to popular demand and provides an authoritative fiscal push to the economy, the inflationary forces that are still alive could rise to a fury unmatched since the all-out economic effort of World War II. Among other things, the nation's weak balance of international payments could be disastrously upset, with worldwide repercussions. On the other hand, to extend the economic slowdown with widespread unemployment could expose the Administration to charges of a callous disregard for our innumerable social problems, including especially the fate of those on the lower rungs of the economic ladder. More than 70 percent of the unemployed in 1970 were unskilled or semiskilled workers with little or no financial resources to tide them over—one important reason for the spectacular rise in welfare costs and the financial difficulties of the states and cities during the past twelve months. The output lost because of deliberately induced recession—the difference between what the nation *did* produce in 1970 and what it *could* have produced at full employment—amounted to $45 billion, or twice the monetary cost of the Vietnam war that year.

The answer of Mr. Nixon and his economic advisers to this dilemma is an appeal to what may be called the *economic law of opposites*. Since January 1969, there has been a marked disparity, regular and reliable, between what the Administration said it would do and what would happen on the one hand, and what it did do and what actually came to pass on the other. In the present instance the Administration proclaimed its intention, beginning well before the November 1970 election, to pursue a vigorously expansive fiscal policy. In line with this, the Council of Economic Advisers startled most authorities outside the Government by predicting a 9 percent increase in the gross national product, as great a one-year jump as any in the last two decades.

But following the law of opposites, the actual fiscal policy pursued since last fall has been restrictive rather than expansionary, and business activity, as developed through this early spring, has shown little sign of an exuberant expansion. The Federal budget presented to Congress at the start of this year [1971] called for a reduction in the nation's deficit, despite confusing references to what the figures would show if calibrated on a "full employment" basis. Federal Government expenditures during the three months ending this past February amounted to $49 billion, a 5 percent decline from the preceding three months. The withholding of appropriated funds for urban development, loudly protested by the nation's mayors, is part of the calculated policy of parsimony—a policy, it must be emphasized, that is just the opposite of the one that has been advertised. Hence, industrial production has remained weak even after the artificial stimulus it received from "makeup" purchasing following the General Motors strike; the latest figure for February showed a decline. Housing starts flattened out disappointingly this winter, though they were the lone bright spot in the economic picture during the second half of 1970. The rise of personal income in February was the smallest since last October, when the GM strike bit into earnings. After correction for price changes, retail sales this winter were below last year's. Although Federal Reserve Board chairman Arthur Burns has dutifully provided the nation's financial institutions with ample reserves, the effect thus far on output has been negligible; no way has been discovered for driving businessmen into the banks to borrow. At best, the outlook suggests a slow, desultory rise in production in the months ahead with a continuation of unemployment not much below its recent level of 6 percent. The expected payoff, from the Administration's point of view, would be a further and more pronounced dampening of inflation.

President Nixon was politically scarred once by recession, or thinks he was, in the election of 1960. No doubt he has other plans for November 1972. Indeed, only an Administration bent on destruction would fail to open up the fiscal valves in time to provide a substantial lift to the economy well in advance of Election Day. Congress has already taken a first important step toward that objective by passing a 10 percent boost in Social Security benefits, with payments to begin this June, while deferring the compensating increase in Social Security taxes. With Administration urging, Congress could probably be induced to restore the tax credit on business investment, which would give profits in general and the capital goods industries in particular a lift. But aside from any inadvertent help he may receive from his political adversaries, the President has ample latitude to accelerate the expenditure of already appropriated funds, such as those currently withheld from the cities. That he will do so is as certain as anything else in economics, provided the economy is still lagging later this year. The Council of Economic Advisers has predicted that the unemployment rate will be down to 4.5 percent by mid-1972, just before the impending flow of oratory, and this is one Administration forecast (perhaps its first) that may violate the erstwhile economic law of opposites.

Assuming that a robust business expansion is engendered in time for the spring or summer of 1972, after more than two years of excessive unemployment, what about prices? Will they not be rising once again, very likely accelerating to the end of the year, and confronting the victorious President, whoever he may be, with the recurrent task of applying the brakes, or bluntly, inducing another recession? Aside from its nasty overtones of immorality, isn't the practice of fighting inflation with unemployment merely a temporary, self-defeating retreat from the problem itself? All our economic history, of which a portion was sketched above, says that it is. The economy, as we have seen, has moved up and down endlessly, and neither the Republican nor the Democratic party has confronted the basic task of how to get us off the seesaw. Republicans have been more tolerant of unemployment; Democrats have been more tolerant of inflation. But there, in stabilization policy at least, the difference ends. For those who cannot move or see beyond the traditional Keynesian theory of forty years ago, the objective of full employment *without* inflation must remain a mirage.

Not so for others, let us hope, who are not so tied to the policies of the past. Here, in brief outline, is what could be done.

Public Service Employment. An economy that operates at breakneck speed for any appreciable length of time generates a head of steam that inevitably presses on the price level. Occasional cooling-off periods are essential. The problem is that economic slowdowns, even mild ones, throw people out of work, particularly though not exclusively the unskilled and the disadvantaged. One solution is to provide guaranteed public service jobs for all who are able to work. With the vast multiplicity of public needs in environmental control and conservation, care of the aged, medical assistance, recreational facilities, public housing, sanitation and urban renewal, it would be a triumph of bureaucratic non-achievement if most of the new public employees were not assigned to socially useful work. Furthermore, on-the-job training could help the unskilled move up the employment ladder. Most important, if the cost of these public jobs were met fully by current taxation, full employment could be maintained without inflating the economy. Legislation for public service jobs along these lines has been proposed by Senator Gaylord Nelson (Democrat, Wisconsin) and Congressmen James O'Hara (Democrat, Michigan) and William Steiger (Republican, Wisconsin).

Wage-Price Controls. Monopolistic corporations and powerful unions have shown they can boost prices and wages even when business is slack, as in 1970. Some other favored groups (physicians, for example) have also been successful, through price hikes, in getting a larger share of the pie. The only check for this brand of inflation, which does not yield to mild business setbacks or recession, is a national standard for regulation of prices, wages, and other incomes, enforced voluntarily where possible, but backed by mandatory controls when voluntary cooperation is absent. An uneasy halfway house to that kind of control is "jawboning," which President Nixon once scorned but is now viewing with considerable tolerance. The Administration several weeks ago established wage guidelines for the building trades. But experience has shown that partial voluntary systems for checking prices and wages collapse under pressure, as "jawboning" did in 1966, and at best they have had only a minor influence. A more comprehensive and systematic scheme with provision for enforcement is required, and is available. Temporary authority for mandatory wage-price controls was enacted by Congress last year and was recently renewed.

Flexible Fiscal Controls. The tools now used to regulate the nation's overall level of business activity, principally tax changes and alterations in Government spending, are blunt and cumbersome. Congressional hearings and debate on such proposed changes sometimes occupy a year or two or more. One way to achieve greater speed and flexibility is through a system of refundable taxes, or compulsory loans. Briefly, the compulsory loans and their subsequent repayment would be invoked by presidential order, within limits set by Congress, and would be operated in connection with a special stabilization trust fund, so that money paid into it would be held in escrow or "sterilized." The loans would appear as positive, refundable taxes, and the repayments would appear as negative taxes, in our regular income tax returns. Each loan would be repaid with interest at the end of three years, unless earlier redemption were ordered by the President. Hence loans and repayments could be used to build up purchasing power, or reduce it, as required. In contrast with our lumbering, often ineffectual fiscal efforts of the past, this system would work with push-button speed whenever necessary.

Given the Nixon Administration's reflexive reaction to institutional innovations and intellectual adventure in general, the immediate prospect for the three-point plan just outlined, or some reasonable variant, is not much brighter than that for nationalization of the AT&T [American Telephone & Telegraph Company]. Although the public service employment proposed in the Nelson-O'Hara-Steiger bill provided for little more than a modest pilot study, it was briskly vetoed by President Nixon. Equal treatment has been promised for the even more modest public service employment act just passed by the Senate under the sponsorship of Senators Nelson and Jacob Javits (Republican, New York). Despite a growing disposition to intervene in special cases (such as steel and construction), the White House has persisted in opposing systematic national wage-price controls because "they treat symptoms and not causes, can never be administered equitably, and are not compatible with a free economy." When this three-point plan in its entirety was suggested to the Nixon Administration, shortly after it came to office, the reaction of Council of Economic Adviser Herbert Stein was: "We want no more WPAs." [The Works Progress Administration was the major agency set up during the Depression to provide jobs for the unemployed.—Ed.] As this writer mentioned at the time, most of us want no more recessions and inflations.

COST-PUSH OR DEMAND-PULL? [2]

Despite repeated official assurances of its early demise, inflation remains alive and rampant. Indeed, after so much discouragement, quite a few voices are saying that, given the political and social realities in the United States, nothing much can be done about inflation, and therefore we will just have to learn to live with it. But something *can* be done, provided that those who make the political decisions are prepared to supplement, though certainly not supplant, conventional monetary and fiscal policies with additional methods for reaching the forces that inflate costs and prices. Courageous political decisions are needed because the Administration's fiscal and monetary policies for fighting inflation have entailed unacceptably high costs in lost output, unemployment, the international standing of the dollar, and confidence, at a time of acute and growing national needs.

Any prescription of remedies must start with the consideration that inflation is not only a statistic but also a state of mind. Statistically, the diligent number watchers can

[2] From "A Strategy for Winding Down Inflation," by Robert V. Roosa. *Fortune.* 84:70-3+. S. '71. Reprinted by permission of *Fortune* magazine; © 1971 Time Inc. Mr. Roosa, a partner in Brown Brothers Harriman & Co., was formerly a vice president of the Federal Reserve Bank of New York and from 1961 to 1965 Under Secretary for Monetary Affairs, Treasury Department of the United States.

point to some progress. Through the first half of 1971 the rate of increase in most prices has seemingly stopped rising. But that still leaves prices going up at 4, or 5, or even 6 percent a year. And the inflation mentality, having shown signs of receding around the turn of the year, was insidiously reviving by midyear.

That mentality is hardly a measurable quantity, to be sure; it appears most convincingly in the eye of the skeptical beholder. Its surface manifestations—fits and starts in consumer spending, mounting demands for wage increases, precautionary marking up of administered prices and interest rates—are not readily distinguishable from the early signs of a sound economic expansion. But there is a difference in the fever running through the marketplaces of the nation. The mood is apprehension, not confidence. Every businessman, every union leader, and everyone who purchases a loaf of bread, a restaurant meal, a theatre ticket, a light bulb, or a power mower will recognize that difference, or sense it. Responsible political leadership quite understandably reacts, as President Nixon did during his midyear economic reassessment at Camp David, by withholding further stimulants to recovery in order to minimize the risk of further stimulating inflation.

For those who prefer to appraise the economy's condition through cold figures, rather than a subjective rendering of forces apparent in the marketplace, the performance of wholesale commodity prices has also been flashing a warning. They advanced by less than 1 percent during the last six months of 1970, establishing a base for some eventual slackening in the rise of other prices in 1971. But they began moving faster in the first half of this year [1971], and by the middle of the year were advancing at an annual rate of almost 5 percent.

At least equally arresting has been the pace of advance in wages and fringe benefits since early 1969, when the new Administration made clear that it would hold to a deliberate hands-off policy with respect to wages and prices. Man-hour compensation advanced more than 7 percent on average in both 1969 and 1970 (in the private economy, excluding farms), while the average rise in productivity was barely 1 percent. Compensation rates have already risen as much again in 1971. Several major industries—apparently discouraged when General Motors had to raise its labor costs 30 percent over three years, even after a two-month strike—have agreed to even larger increases.

During the first quarter of this year [1971], to be sure, productivity, at least in manufacturing, began advancing at an annual rate of 5 percent. But there is little basis as yet for viewing that speedup as more than a transient byproduct of continued underutilization of capacity. If the recovery of 1971 continues to meander, the scope for raising productivity will soon be exhausted. Progress from there will require more productivity-raising investment. And that for the present is stagnant. In real terms, plant and equipment investment is declining, not rising.

Rekindled Apprehensions

There is in fact great perplexity and doubt throughout the business community, among the men who make the crucial investment decisions on which rising productivity over the years ahead must depend. Having admired the Administration's courage in risking the man-made recession of 1970 while moving to halt the inflation, businessmen generally have become disillusioned and dispirited as prices and costs have gone on rising this year. In view of the shift in Administration policy from restraint to expansion several months ago, businessmen, and no doubt workers and consumers as well, are understandably apprehensive. If the rekindling of the economy is successful, can a fresh burst of inflation be avoided? If the rekindling fails, will not the defensive efforts of unions and companies to protect their individual positions by raising wage demands or prices result in stagnation or renewed decline in the economy as a whole?

It is because such doubts are so widespread that the inflation mentality is permeated with foreboding this time, rather than with speculative exhilaration. In moving from the demand-pull of the later 1960s to the present cost-push phase, inflation has apparently set in motion new forces of caution and containment that promote the continuance of the inflation itself. In the second quarter of 1971 the rate of savings out of disposable personal income was running at 8.4 percent—more than a third higher than the long-run average. Yet consumer prices were still going up rapidly.

Many are asking whether the inflation can ever be stopped before the distortions it creates have produced widespread breakdown—a "natural" depression as contrasted with a self-imposed recession. Paradoxically, that very state of mind explains why the inflation itself, so far as its practical implications are concerned, cannot be said to be slowing down—however the slight month-to-month variations in some statistics may wishfully be interpreted.

Can We Have "Stabilized" Inflation?

Partly, no doubt, because it has proved unexpectedly difficult to get back to the approximate price stability of the early 1960s, some are now asking whether the objective is really so important. If labor and consumers and business could look forward with reasonable confidence to an environment of 4 or 5 percent annual inflation, what would be wrong with that?

To begin with, the very possibility of stabilized inflation is far from clear. Inhuman strains would be placed upon the men responsible for diagnosing the economy and prescribing just the right doses of fiscal and monetary stimulus. And certainly there would be great danger of irregular speedups leading toward a galloping inflation. In such an event, the Government would probably have to turn for a time to direct controls over many or most prices and wages.

Even if stabilized inflation of 4 or 5 percent a year is possible, however, it may still not be desirable, or even tolerable. No sharp dividing line can be drawn, of course, between acceptable and unacceptable rates of inflation. General price increases of 5 or even 6 percent may be tolerable for brief periods in an economy as complex as ours, provided they serve the fundamental economic purpose of price increases—to evoke additional output, contain demand, and thereby lead to their own correction. But the only hard evidence available, the experience of the past dozen years or so, suggests that in the US economy continued inflation in a 4 or 5 percent range would erode, and perhaps even totally disintegrate, the orderly processes of production, distribution, and the rendering of services.

The contrast between the noninflationary years of 1958-1965 and the inflationary years of 1966-1971 provides at least a clue. From early 1965 to mid-1971, hourly earnings of production workers in manufacturing, for example, rose 36 percent, but in real terms, adjusted for inflation, these earnings rose barely 1 percent a year. Indeed from 1969 onward, as nominal earnings of manufacturing production workers rose nearly twice as much as in the noninflationary years, real earnings advanced by less than one half of 1 percent annually.

What has been happening is evident enough. Once price rises reach a critical range—which seems to be somewhere between 3 and 5 percent for the American economy—labor becomes caught up in a pattern of imitation. Each union, large or small, must do as well as any other that by any conceivable standard may be considered comparable. Indeed, to be on the safe side, each tries to do just a little better than the others. No group can be satisfied any longer to have its wages and benefits determined by what the employer can afford on the basis of last year's, or even today's, prices for his products.

Responsible labor leaders feel as inextricably caught up in the vicious circle of cost-push inflation as do responsible businessmen. All know that they are trapped in a pattern, which no one, acting alone, can break, regardless of how strongly the President or anyone else may exhort one sector or another, on its own, to reach a noninflationary settlement within the bounds of productivity gains. Instead, it is assumed that in the inflationary atmosphere the employer will have to raise his prices to cover whatever the latest labor contract provides. This is the self-propelling nature of a cost-push inflation, once it has been ignited.

Nor do the profits of manufacturers fare any better in this process. While wage costs in dollars were rising rapidly, the proportion of revenues left over for return on equity (and for encouraging new investment) was dropping. Indeed, the rate of return on stockholders' equity for manufacturing corporations dropped from above 14 percent in 1966 to below 9 percent in the first quarter of 1971. Thus in the manufacturing sector, for which data are more nearly complete and current than for the remainder of the economy, the real earnings of labor have stagnated and the profit margins of business declined since 1965, even though in the late 1960s wages and sales in current dollars may have given an appearance of abounding prosperity. There need be little wonder, then, that the employment of production workers in manufacturing, having increased nearly 13 percent from 1958-59 to 1965-66, actually declined slightly in the past five years.

The "New Services State"

Of course, declining profitability and manufacturing employment can be explained in part by the recession in the economy in the last two years, and by inflationary pressures generated by growth in the services and Government sectors. These pressures in turn have contributed to stagnation in the employment of production workers by adding to the cost of hiring qualified entry-level workers. Indeed, the shift in the economic structure to services and public employment may already have made Professor Galbraith's "new industrial state" an anachronism. The need now is for an understanding of the "new services state."

Another aspect of the inflationary distortion has been apparent in US foreign trade. Excluding military aid, the United States maintained a surplus of exports over imports averaging close to $4 billion a year from 1958 to 1965, as measured in 1958 (i.e., constant) prices. As inflation rose into the 4 to 5 percent range, the trade surplus steadily declined in real terms, and for a time in 1968 and 1969, and again this year the United States ran a real trade deficit.

Even more menacing than the actual trade deterioration itself, however, is the version of the inflation mentality that is now penetrating foreign markets. Concern over whether the United States can stop the momentum of inflation is arousing fear for the future of the dollar throughout the foreign financial markets—in which the dollar has so long served as the steadiest unit of account in common use among many countries.

A full analysis of manufacturing performance and foreign trade would have to go much deeper into the intricate interplay of influences at work, but the general implications are nonetheless quite clear. At a 4 to 5 percent rate of inflation, material costs and labor costs rise at an increasing rate, while manpower unemployment and plant underemployment increase. At these high overall levels of cost and price advances, a relatively free-market-oriented economy—viewed as if it were a single company—is literally pricing itself out of its markets, at home and abroad. When prices are pushed up by costs—rather than by increases in demand—the physical volume of output and sales can scarcely be expected to maintain earlier rates of gain. There seems to be something about a low-grade inflationary fever that creates imbalances among the organic parts of the American economy—imbalances that are not necessarily self-correcting.

A Trade-Off That Won't Work in Reverse

The current inflation, having reached a self-propelling stage, apparently persists because everyone, employee and employer alike, reacts naturally and normally by taking individual protective action against an overall rate of price advance that no individual group feels able by itself to influence or control. The economy is no longer organized, if it ever was, in such a way that the overall performance of prices —the parameter to which each sector must adjust—can be wound down by Government action that affects only the demand side of the economy.

The prevailing theory, held with courageous tenacity by the Nixon Administration, and indeed by most economists for many years, maintains quite the contrary, that the limitation of total demand by Government can effectively reduce the pace of inflation. This conviction has been put into the economics textbooks in terms of the "trade-off" between the rate of unemployment and the rate of increase in prices (the famous Phillips curve). And the formulation is certainly not altogether wrong. When the Vietnam inflation began, and probably until some time late in 1968 or 1969, the principal cause of the inflation was an excess of Government-stimulated demand. Unemployment was declining, and prices were indeed rising. An earlier curbing of the excess demand (which the Federal Reserve tried unsuccessfully to do alone through monetary restraint in 1966) could almost certainly have stopped the inflation.

But this approach is simply not adequate for all conditions all of the time. President Nixon has been relying on the theory and the techniques appropriate for curbing President Johnson's inflation. The Nixon inflation has become predominantly of another kind.

In these circumstances, no matter how much embroidery there may be around Professor Phillips' curve in academic journals, the reverse path—more unemployment, lower prices—simply is not there, at least not within the time intervals and unemployment levels that are socially tolerable in a modern economy. Either the curve takes a quite different course on the way down, or there are wide discontinuities in it, or it is, at least for practical purposes, only a one-directional guide. Whatever the theorists may decide, the Administration has in practice abandoned further constricting of demand and is casting hopeful glances toward the possible lagging effect of last year's restraint on this year's price level. The deflationary potentials of such a lag, however, have certainly not become apparent in any of the 1971 claims for wage increases, or in the continued upward movement of prices. Until the President's August 15 speech, as this article went to press, something had clearly been wrong with the Administration's assumptions.

It seems plain that powerful new conditions, acting together, are undermining the assumption that rates of rise in wages or prices will flexibly respond to restraints on demand and increases in unemployment. One of the new conditions, of course, is the changed composition of the labor force itself, and the consequent mismatching between the skills that are needed and those that are available. Another array of complications comes from the rigidities created by the increasing instances of quasi-monopoly power exercised by companies or unions in the setting of prices, or wages, or guarantees of employment or markets. Also, the building of fringe benefits and cost-of-living escalators into wage contracts has resulted in a kind of deferred cost-push inflation. And yet another factor has been the undue reliance on restrictive monetary policy to limit demand, with the perverse result of making interest rates themselves a major cost-push force.

Over time, Government may be able to do something about some of the imperfections in markets, for example, by coordinating person-by-person information on the unemployed with job-by-job information on vacancies, by offering better employment counseling and manpower retraining, and by liberalizing union entrance requirements and work rules. But to a great extent the pressures that have kept price advances from slowing down in the face of larger unemployment have come from processes of change and advance that cannot, and presumably should not, be altered—the shift toward services, the rising proportion of skilled employees in much of industry, the growth of fringe benefits, Social Security, and indeed the public commitment to maintain employment opportunities and a minimum income.

The markets in which wages and prices are determined today are far removed from the free markets of classical tradition. Yet the American economy is, in form and objectives, a market-oriented economy, and virtually everyone wants to keep it that way. The confusion comes from assuming, for such purposes as winding down the inflation, that all of the essential conditions for a fully flexible market economy exist.

How to Break Out of the Circle

Even if the economy could be made more competitive and flexible overnight, one persistent force would almost certainly continue to propel cost-push inflation. Once the pattern of imitation begins, the criterion for wage increases becomes what the employees of other companies have just obtained, rather than what one's own employer can afford, considering the current prices he's getting for his products. Thus the momentum builds up. For employers will mark up their prices, adding to the material and capital costs of other businesses. By relaxing its own earlier restrictive policies, Government will help to assure that total demand accommodates the higher prices. Unless some other counterforce is found, the consequences already described will persist. Profits will be under pressure. Investment will remain slack. Productivity will fail to show sustained gains. Unemployment will remain high. And individual prices will be raised mainly in order to defend the status quo for every sector, rather than, through selective movements, to direct resources into increasingly productive uses. The need, clearly, was to find some way, consistent with the general objectives of a free market—where Government does not set individual wages and prices—to break the momentum of the kind of cost-push that prevailed in mid-1971.

The absolutely essential condition in any remedial action is that each major segment of business and labor must feel that it is subject to the same constraint as every other segment. No one can afford to be "caught out" as the naive victim of an appeal to public responsibility that others have not heard or heeded.

NIXONOMICS AND THE WHITE HOUSE [3]

Nixonomics means that all the things that should go up —the stock market, corporate profits, real spendable income, productivity—go down, and all the things that should go down—unemployment, prices, interest rates—go up.—Lawrence F. O'Brien, chairman of the Democratic National Committee, on May 21, 1970

In early April 1969, Richard Nixon called Representative Wilbur D. Mills [Democrat] of Arkansas, chairman of the House Ways and Means Committee, to the White House to reveal his plans for fiscal austerity. He had managed to cut some $4 billion, the new President informed Mills, from Lyndon Johnson's last and "uncuttable" budget. No member of Congress was more disturbed than Mills by the way

[3] Article: "Nixonomics: How the Game Plan Went Wrong," by Rowland Evans, Jr., and Robert D. Novak, syndicated columnists and authors of several books on politics, as it appeared in *Atlantic Monthly*. 228:66-80. Jl. '71. The article is taken from *Nixon in the White House: The Frustration of Power*, by Rowland Evans, Jr., and Robert D. Novak. Random House. '71. Copyright © 1971 by Rowland Evans Jr. and Robert D. Novak. Reprinted by permission of Random House, Inc.

Federal spending had gone out of control under Johnson, and he was pleased by the reduction. But he wanted more—say another $4 billion?

"Oh, no! We can't do that," said Nixon. "We can't cut so deep that we start a recession."

Mills was puzzled. As he understood it, Nixon's economic strategy—or "game plan" as it was known, in deference to the football-loving President—called for slowing down inflation in 1969 at the regrettable expense of some temporary unemployment. Thus, Nixon seemed to be saying that he was willing to slow down the economy enough to cause some unemployment but not enough to cause a recession. To Mills, this ambivalence made no sense. On the question of how much to slow down the economy, the ambivalence was deeply ingrained, born not of mere skepticism of economic orthodoxy but of two deeply embedded, conflicting impulses that Nixon carried with him into the White House.

Early in 1968, before the series of heart attacks that were to end his life a year later, General Dwight D. Eisenhower discussed the first impulse candidly. "I think Dick's going to be elected President," he told one of Nixon's political advisers, "but I think he's going to be a one-term President. I think he's really going to fight inflation, and that will kill him politically." To Eisenhower as well as to most orthodox Republicans, that would be the worthy sacrifice of a courageous political martyr. For the old General there was no higher imperative for a new Republican President than to curb the torrent of inflation that had been loosed on the economy since full US intervention in the Vietnam war in 1965. To them, at stake was nothing less than the value of the dollar, the role of the United States as a great power, and the very quality of life in this country. To save all this, entailed sacrifice. Attempting a reduction in the rate of inflation from 1953 through 1960 (considerably less virulent than the present siege), President Eisenhower's economic policy induced three recessions; these had three disastrous consequences for the Republican party. First came the Democratic landslide in the elections of 1958, which ended the previous postwar pattern of a virtually even balance between the parties in Congress and established huge Democratic majorities (which persisted even when Nixon was elected President a decade later). Second was the election of Democrat John F. Kennedy for President in 1960. Finally, and perhaps worst of all, the Republican image, formed in the days of Herbert Hoover, as the party of bad times was reinforced in the voters' minds. Now, eight years later, blessed with not a fraction of Eisenhower's unlimited popularity, Nixon would have to take more unpopular actions to fight a worse inflation. The resulting unemployment, business slowdown, and stock market decline almost surely would prevent his reelection in 1972, Eisenhower speculated. But considering the deeds he would be performing in the service of his nation, Eisenhower felt the sacrifice not only would be worthwhile but would assure Nixon a place in history.

Nixon, too, regarded inflation as something more than a campaign issue handy for attacking the Democrats. Some two weeks before the election of 1968 in a paid address over the CBS network, Nixon declared: "Inflation penalizes thrift and encourages speculation. Because it is a national and perverse force—dramatically affecting individuals but beyond their power to influence—inflation is a source of frustration for all who lack great economic power." That is, in Nixon's diagnosis, inflation was a virus affecting not just the health of the economy but the frame of mind of the entire country. He fully agreed with the assessment by Theodore White as the Nixon Administration took office that "inflation, in the past four years of American life, has ravaged our standards of behavior." There was, then, reason to suspect that General Eisenhower's assessment was correct.

There was also, however, a conflicting impulse in Nixon. During that difficult decade after his defeat in 1960, aides and close friends had heard Nixon say privately time after

time that had President Eisenhower only taken his and
Arthur Burns's advice early in 1960 and moved rapidly toward stimulating the economy, he—not Jack Kennedy—
would have been elected President. The implication, not
quite stated flatly, was that Richard Nixon, if he had the
power, would never again go into a presidential election
with the economy in a state of deflation.

The closest Nixon came to putting this view on the public record was in a passage from *Six Crises,* his autobiograph-
ical work published in 1962. Nixonologists in the world of
business cited the passage to their colleagues as the true test
of what they could expect in the next few years. After telling
of Burns's failure in 1960 to convince Eisenhower to act,
Nixon writes this memorable assessment of the election that
year, unable fully to restrain his bitterness:

> Unfortunately, Arthur Burns turned out to be a good prophet.
> The bottom of the 1960 dip did come in October and the economy
> started to move up again in November—after it was too late to
> affect the election returns. In October, usually a month of rising
> employment, the jobless rolls increased by 452,000. All the speeches,
> television broadcasts, and precinct work in the world could not
> counteract that one hard fact.

Here, then, was the source of the ambivalence perceived
by Wilbur Mills in April 1969. Should Nixon be the self-
abnegating statesman sacrificing his personal future to save
the republic from inner rot, or the pragmatic politician
finally removing from the Republican party the curse of
Herbert Hoover? Whether or not this ambivalence was ap-
preciated by Richard Nixon in his own inner thoughts, it
did not surface in the early meetings on the economy in his
new Administration.

Those meetings were concerned almost exclusively with
the problem of inflation which had dropped the value of the
1957-1959 dollar to 81.1 cents as Nixon took office. Presiding
occasionally at meetings of the Cabinet Committee on Eco-

nomic Policy, of the Quadriad, and of the Troika,* Nixon made obvious his deep commitment to curbing inflation. Nixon as President could engage his full attention on only three or four large items at one time, and inflation was the only domestic issue that had that level of presidential attention as his Administration began. In private conversations with his staff, Nixon asserted he must deal rapidly and decisively with two principal crises: the Vietnam war and inflation. Furthermore, those few members of his economic team who also had served President Eisenhower noted with satisfaction that Nixon had an incomparably more sophisticated grasp of economics than did the General.

But that scarcely qualified Nixon as an economist. "This is not his long suit," "this is not his cup of tea," "this is not his background," are the remarkably similar assessments of Nixon the economist by three separate members of his economic team. More serious than lack of technical competence, however, was Nixon's lack of emotional commitment. Though he intellectually understood the seriousness of inflation, the Dismal Science did not capture his imagination as did the Vietnam war, détente with the Soviets, or rehabilitation of the Western Alliance.

Given these deficiencies in both his knowledge of and interest in economics, his first-string economic team, the Quadriad, was of peculiar importance. For the first year of Nixon's presidency, this was the Quadriad:

William McChesney Martin, sixty-two, chairman of the Federal Reserve Board (then completing his eighteenth and last year in charge of the nation's central bank). Martin (a nominal Democrat) had not for some years been the dynamic proponent of economic conservatism that he was dur-

---

* The Quadriad consists of the four top economic officials of the Government: the chairman of the Federal Reserve Board, the Secretary of the Treasury, the director of the Bureau of the Budget, and the chairman of the President's Council of Economic Advisers. The Troika consists of the three top economic officials of the Administration: The Quadriad less the chairman of the Federal Reserve Board, an independent official serving a fixed term and not a member of the Administration

ing the Eisenhower and Kennedy Administrations and was now a somewhat dispirited lame duck. He had no personal relationship with Nixon and did not develop one.

David Kennedy, sixty-three, Secretary of the Treasury. Named on the recommendation of banking interests and Wall Street men, this distinguished Chicago banker, unskilled in macroeconomics, conceived of himself more as manager than policy maker. His relations with Nixon were scarcely any more intimate the day he left the Treasury than the day he entered.

Robert Mayo, fifty-two, director of the Bureau of the Budget. After nineteen years as a career government economist at the Treasury, he joined the banking business as a subordinate to David Kennedy, who recommended him to Nixon for the Budget Bureau. In the Government, too, Mayo seemed more Secretary Kennedy's subordinate than Nixon's. Not in recent memory had a Budget Director been more distant from the President.

Paul McCracken, fifty-three, chairman of the President's Council of Economic Advisers. This cool, unflappable, unfailingly gracious economics professor from the University of Michigan had been a member of the Council in Eisenhower's second term and was so well regarded professionally that despite his conservatism, his appointment was hailed by liberal economists. Recommended for the post by Arthur Burns, he was to be the principal author of Nixon's economic game plan and the dominant member of the Quadriad through 1969. But he, too, would never achieve an intimate relationship with the President. McCracken was the essence of the pedagogue, his presentations to the President having the bloodless quality of professorial lectures in Economics 100. As McCracken unfolded historical background and explored every conceivable side of the subject, Nixon's eyes would glaze over. McCracken bored him stiff.

In contrast to the rest of Nixon's domestic policy team, the Quadriad was older, more professionally qualified, better known to the outside world, and more distinguished generally. But it was also less dynamic and less able to penetrate the Haldeman-Ehrlichman Berlin Wall. There was in the Quadriad no John Mitchell, Melvin Laird, Patrick Moynihan, George Shultz, or John Volpe who, for one reason or other, could enchant, convince, or pester the President into accepting his point of view or, at least, actively engage Nixon's interest.

Present at the White House as Counsellor to the President, of course, was an economist who *was* an old Nixon intimate: Arthur Burns (who did sometimes sit with the economic team as "the Quadriad Plus One"). But Burns was eager not to be looking over the shoulder of Paul McCracken, the man he had recommended, and felt his post as Counsellor required as much devotion to noneconomic as economic questions in the domestic area.

With these men, Nixon knew that inflation was a crisis ripping at the innards of America. But he lacked consuming interest in the subject, and his economic team neither stimulated nor influenced him. What nobody could realize in January 1969, was that inflation would prove to be Nixon's most intractable problem (far worse than Vietnam), would lead to wrenching Republican disappointments in the 1970 midterm elections, and by 1971 would make General Eisenhower's prediction of a one-term presidency seem very real indeed.

In 1942, four years before he ran for Congress and ten years before he was elected Vice President of the United States, Richard Nixon spent ten months in wartime Washington as a lawyer for the Office of Price Administration. It was an experience which seared his soul, as he revealed early in his presidency, on February 14, 1969, while attempting to give an inspirational address to personnel at the Treasury. Speaking without a text, Nixon wanted to establish empathy with the bureaucrats by recalling the days when he was one himself. What came out, however, was more melancholy reminiscence than nostalgia:

> I was once a P-3 when they had that. Some of you will re-member that. A P-3 lawyer in the OPA in 1942 was a very low form of life, I can assure you.
>
> I remember then the task that I had of preparing form letters and also preparing congressional mail to be signed by the President of the United States on tire rationing.
>
> It seemed to me to be a very boring job at times.

Dick Nixon, P-3 lawyer, was then twenty-nine, working in a dead-end bureaucratic job in Tempo D, a dreary wooden shack left over from World War I—without money, without family connections, without much in the way of prospects, and certainly without political ambition. His own unhappy condition might be one reason he carried from OPA such an uncharacteristically dogmatic opposition to wage and price controls of any kind. Although the wartime OPA in retrospect had been given generally high grades for its per-formance of a difficult and onerous but necessary task, Nixon's personal recollection was otherwise. In private con-versations over the years, he talked of the corruption, the cheating by the public, and the unhappy consequences when a government seeks to control the private economic decisions of private citizens.

Nixon the supreme pragmatist was inflexible about eco-nomic controls; however much his interest might flag in dis-cussion of other economic questions, his enthusiastic advo-cacy on this point was constant. Nor was Nixon adamant simply against outright Government controls. He was equally opposed to a return to the policy instituted by Presi-dent Kennedy in 1961: voluntary guideposts issued by the Government to limit wage and price increases—what is called an incomes policy in Great Britain and Canada. The guide-posts had been plowed over and abandoned in the infla-tionary surge of 1966 following President Johnson's full-scale intervention in Vietnam. But late in 1968, Johnson's

Cabinet Committee on Price Stability recommended a return to official guideposts (based on a maximum 5 percent wage increase in 1969), and Hubert Humphrey almost surely would have followed the recommendation had he been elected. But a guideposts policy would work, Nixon believed, only if the Government used muscle to enforce it—as when John F. Kennedy forced the steel industry to roll back a price increase in 1962. That, to Nixon, was nothing more than mandatory wage-price controls without statutory sanction. Finally, Nixon ruled out even those admonitions by a President and other Federal officials called "jawboning," used by Kennedy-Johnson officials both in conjunction with a guideposts policy and after the guideposts had been abandoned.

Fatefully, Nixon's prejudices happened to coincide perfectly with the expert opinion of his advisers. The entire Quadriad plus Burns agreed with Nixon's opposition to controls, to an incomes policy, to jawboning. This further coincided with the prevalent opinion in the business community, which had so rapturously given its support to Nixon against Humphrey. Following the eight prosperous years of the Kennedy-Johnson era uninterrupted by a genuine recession, business was riding high in January 1969. With its goal of quick profits and an ever expanding economy, business wanted nothing more than to be left alone by the Government. That is precisely what Nixon's campaign promised business, and to be left alone meant not only easing Federal control of regulated industries (including the stock exchange) but also a moratorium on nagging about higher wages and higher prices.

Consequently, there had been no previous great debate, either inside or outside the new Administration, when Nixon told his first press conference on the morning of January 27:

I do not go along with the suggestion that inflation can be effectively controlled by exhorting labor and management and industry to follow certain guidelines. I think that is a very laudable objective for labor and management to follow. But I think I am aware of the fact that the leaders of labor and the leaders of management, much as they might personally want to do what is in the best interests of the nation, have to be guided by the interests of the organization they represent.

So the primary responsibility for controlling inflation rests with the national Administration and its handling of fiscal and monetary affairs.

With those comments, the new President was reflecting a view widely held not only by his own advisers but by economists generally: the inflation roaring wildly in January 1969 was essentially caused by the Federal Government. The record of the Federal Reserve Board in controlling the nation's money supply in the second half of the 1960s was a sorry one. Having choked off the money supply as an anti-inflation device in 1966 so tightly that it produced a serious slump in housing and construction (called by some a "mini-recession"), the central bank started pouring out money too quickly and too generously in 1967 and thereby spoon-fed a new inflation. The Federal Reserve's culpability, however, did not approach Lyndon B. Johnson's. Refusing to ask Congress for a tax increase to finance the Vietnam war when he intervened in 1965, President Johnson piled up huge inflationary budget deficits climaxed by $28.4 billion in red ink for the year ending July 1, 1968. To compensate for these governmental excesses, the Nixon game plan was to hold down the money supply by means of monetary policy and achieve a budget surplus through fiscal policy.

But the business community interpreted Nixon's comments of January 27 in slightly different fashion. What it thought Nixon was saying was this: Fighting inflation is our business, not yours; you fellows have no responsibility to do anything in the way of self-restraint. Even before Nixon's January 27 press conference, businessmen were being told authoritatively that Washington was now laissez-faire on prices. Dr. Pierre Rinfret, an influential economic consultant in New York in close touch with the Nixon team, advised his clients to raise their prices and raise them *now*; because everything else was going up, they would get no backlash from Washington, and besides, the responsibility for fighting inflation was the Government's, not theirs. So, unwittingly, Nixon's abandonment of jawboning helped to generate the inflationary psychology he was trying to control and imposed a still greater burden on the Government's monetary and fiscal policy.

Monetary policy was no immediate problem. William McChesney Martin and the rest of the Federal Reserve Board had instituted a tight-money regime in 1968 and were keeping the screws tightened.

Fiscal policy was another matter. As he entered the White House, Nixon was undecided about requesting an extension of the 10 percent income tax surcharge proposed by President Johnson in 1967 and finally passed by Congress in 1968. Burns and the Quadriad were unanimous in advising Nixon that letting the surtax lapse (along with its $10 billion a year in revenue) was sheer madness. But Nixon had his doubts. He was on record with a somewhat wishy-washy commitment during the 1968 campaign to repeal the surtax, and a great many Republican candidates for Congress had made a stronger commitment. Besides, Nixon was not happy about the LBJ label on the surtax. But in the end, he reluctantly agreed to propose reenactment.

There still remained the more difficult basic problem of putting a rein on Federal expenditures, bloated by the Vietnam war. The results were disclosed by the President in a message to Congress on April 12. The expenditure estimate of $195.3 billion contained in Johnson's final budget (for the fiscal year ending July 1, 1970) was spurious, the Nixon men found. The more realistic figure was $196.9 billion. The President then reduced this by $4 billion, to give him a projected surplus of $5.8 billion, which Nixon quickly labeled the largest surplus in eighteen years and the fourth largest in history. Seemingly, Nixon had moved quickly and masterfully to bring the budget under control; a step toward victory in his fight against inflation.

In truth, however, the budget balancers in the Administration were defeated. Arthur Burns, in particular, felt that Nixon had lost the golden opportunity to check Federal spending. He realized that the highly publicized budget cuts were largely cosmetic without seriously drawing back long-range spending programs. As Budget Director, Mayo tried to bring the budget into line but failed. Part of the trouble stemmed from the inability of Mayo, the gentlemanly ex-Treasury bureaucrat, to force deep cuts in expenditures on Nixon's department and agency heads, who now were championing the causes of their new bureaucratic constituencies. But the blame cannot be placed solely on Mayo. Many of his most important initiatives to cut expenditures were not backed up by the President. The reduction of $1.1 billion for the Pentagon would have been still larger had Nixon sided with Mayo instead of Laird. Nor was the space exploration program cut to Mayo's specifications. Nixon overruled Mayo's attempt to eliminate the costly supersonic-transport (SST) subsidy program. And he lost his argument with the President that the proposed new program of income maintenance for the poor, whatever its long-range savings, was fiscally irresponsible in the short range.

Mayo's failure is traceable in part to the peculiarities of the Nixon presidency. A stolid fellow lacking the ability to entrance Nixon, Mayo had no standing in the White House. He could not compete with a Pat Moynihan persuading the President to support income maintenance, or a John Volpe drumming up arguments for the SST. His only budget-cutting ally in the White House was Arthur Burns, who was having his own trouble influencing the President. Indeed, before long Mayo lost all physical contact with Nixon. By late 1969, he was getting his instructions from the President via John Ehrlichman and relaying his proposals to the President via John Ehrlichman—an unprecedented ignominy for a Budget Director that he should not have tolerated.

Beyond personalities, however, there was also Nixon's fear as expressed to Wilbur Mills that too great a budget reduction would induce a whopper of a recession. The result was a policy enunciated by Dr. McCracken as "gradualism" —gradually reducing inflationary pressures by moderate, not precipitate, pruning of Federal spending. That McCracken and just about every other Nixon adviser (with the conspicuous exception of Burns) agreed that gradualism was the proper antidote testifies to how badly they underestimated the force of inflation.

McCracken's concept of the power of gradualism was succinctly described by Hobart Rowen in his column in the Washington *Post* on March 22:

At some point . . . probably suddenly and without advance notice, big and little people are going to decide that prices (including the price of money) are too high.

At that point (and Mr. Nixon's people hope it will arrive soon), plant expansion projections will ease off, consumers will start to save a little more and spend a little less, and the exaggerated pace of the economy will settle back to earth.

On March 22, 1969, Richard Nixon seemed to have put all his own faith in the game plan of gradualism. Four months later the chilling doubts set in.

Pierre Rinfret, a flamboyant Canadian-born economist, was an early Nixon-for-President enthusiast, and joined the team of advisers at Mission Bay, California, making campaign strategy following Nixon's nomination for President in the summer of 1968. After the election, a Nixon aide sounded out Rinfret on the possibility of his becoming a member of the President's Council of Economic Advisers, but Rinfret replied that he would not give up his lucrative New York—based consulting firm for any Federal post. Although McCracken and the other Council members tended to look down their noses at his professional credentials, Rin-

fret remained in close and amiable contact with several figures in the Administration, including Arthur Burns.

But by July 3, Rinfret had become so disaffected that he
distributed to clients of his firm a two-page confidential
memorandum titled "We Accuse" which said: "We accuse
this Administration of incompetence."

In attempting to curb inflation, charged Rinfret, the Administration (in collaboration with the Federal Reserve
Board) was promoting "the current mood of economic and
financial terror." In Pierre Rinfret's view, the Administration had started badly and was steadily getting worse. "We
accuse the Administration of totally miscalculating the need
for advance economic planning before it got into office and
for being totally unprepared once it did. It went into office
with slogans and little else." Most of all, it erred in thinking
"that inflation could easily be turned off" and therefore did
not sufficiently cut Federal spending. Instead, it was risking
a financial panic by relying on the Federal Reserve Board's
tight-money policy as the first line in the war against inflation. The Administration was "fostering, abetting and creating inflation while it has advocated deflation" because "the
first thing it did was to announce the abandonment of the
wage and price guidelines, which created 'open sesame' on
prices and wages."

Rinfret's harsh language typified the startlingly rapid
turn of sentiment against Richard Nixon in the business
community during those first five months. On July 3, the
President's ratings in the polls were still high, the peace
movement had not stirred, and the Democrats had scarcely
pinked him. But his supporters in the world of business had
turned against him with the ferocity of a friend betrayed.
Under the man they had supported for President, the business climate was becoming a bad dream: stock market down
and falling; interest rates up and rising; money so tight that
some businessmen were unable to operate; a recession on
the horizon; and finally, that precious commodity, business

confidence, failing. And yet, all this had not brought an end to inflation. On June 11, David Kennedy, using language more candid than that of other members of the Quadriad, told a meeting of the Advertising Council in Washington that the nation was on the brink "of a runaway inflation."

Kennedy's candor was unusual. According to the Nixon party line, the game plan was working and everybody should be patient. But by the time of Pierre Rinfret's broadside, Nixon's economic team—though probably not Nixon himself —knew it had underestimated inflation, and so far had not brought it under control. The further cold reality was that current policies would produce a moderate recession in 1970 whether or not they stopped inflation. The Nixon Administration faced the nightmare of *simultaneous* inflation and recession for the first time in modern economic history.

At the White House, Arthur Burns was clearly less than pleased with McCracken, the man he chose to be the President's chief economic adviser. He confided to friends that McCracken was talking too much publicly about stopping inflation and not talking hard enough privately about cutting back on Federal spending. Burns fought for greater budget austerity and in August came up with a notable success. He won Nixon's approval for an immediate cutback of 75 percent in all Federal construction, including the massive interstate highway program. To Burns, the shock value of this move might just jolt the inflationary psychology still gripping the nation. One political obstacle, however, was the predictable outrage of the state governors, now overwhelmingly Republican. To deal gently with the governors, announcement of Nixon's move was delayed until the first week in September, when they would all be together at their annual national conference in Colorado Springs, Colorado. Burns would be there to do the explaining.

What followed was one of those strange attacks of indecisiveness, compounded by failure of communications, that sometimes undermined the best domestic intentions of Richard Nixon.

Nixon arrived in Colorado Springs on the afternoon of September 1, 1969, from his beach house at San Clemente, California, where he was spending much of the summer. Scheduled to address the governors' black tie banquet at the Broadmoor Hotel that night, the President might have taken the opportunity to slip the governors the bad news about the construction cutback and urge them to keep a stiff upper lip for the good of the republic. Instead, Nixon delivered a conventional jeremiad against social welfare spending under Johnson during the past five years ($250 billion that had "reaped a harvest of dissatisfaction, frustration and bitter division") without revealing his new plans for austerity, and returned to San Clemente that night.

The reason he left without mentioning the cutbacks was that his politically conscious advisers persuaded him of the adverse impact on the governors from such talk. Vice President Spiro T. Agnew, only seven months out of the governorship of Maryland and now playing a liaison role with his former colleagues, told the President the governors were far more worried about recession than inflation and would rise up in wrath against a flat-out cutback. He was backed by Volpe, who as governor of Massachusetts had led a delegation to the White House in 1967 to protest a highway-construction freeze imposed by Lyndon Johnson. Agnew's alternative: delay the cutback on Federal grants to the states for six months, until April, giving them a chance to inventory federally financed projects and to select which ones to cut back.

With Air Force One shuttling the President back and forth between California and Colorado, with key officials of the Government scattered across the continent between Washington, San Clemente, and Colorado Springs, the difficulty in communications at top levels of the Administration was compounded. Agnew thought he had Nixon's agreement to the six-month delay. The White House thought no such thing. On the afternoon of September 2, Agnew privately briefed the governors about the impending cutback plans, adding that there would be a six-month reprieve on Federal-state projects. In Colorado Springs, when Arthur Burns learned about Agnew's retreat, he was furious. Now, having promised the governors a six-month reprieve, there could be no immediate cutback, the essential shock value had disappeared, and worst of all, the press and the politicians would believe that Nixon did not have the stomach to deal courageously with inflation. That bothered Burns the most.

Two days later at San Clemente Nixon issued a statement ordering an immediate 75 percent cutback in new Federal construction. In view of Agnew's intervention, he temporized about Federal grants to states, urging state and local governments "to follow the example of the Federal Government by cutting back temporarily on their own construction plans." He warned that he himself would reduce Federal grants an undetermined amount "if the response proves insufficient," but even in that event, said the President, "the states and localities will, of course, be given due notice, so that they can adjust their affairs properly." Predictably, the state and municipalities did not heed the President's admonition; predictably, the President did not make good on his threat, even with the Agnew formula included. So ended still another effort by Arthur Burns for a drastic slowdown in Federal spending.

Even before that defeat, however, Burns concluded that this Administration was not going to curb Federal spending enough to hold down inflationary pressures. By August, he had come to believe something else was necessary, and that something else was an incomes policy—a return to wage-price guideposts rejected by Nixon on January 27. Throughout his career as an economist, Burns, like most conservatives, had opposed the concept of an incomes policy. He firmly believed that mandatory Government controls on wages and prices were incompatible with a free society and that an incomes policy was but a way station to controls. In the late summer of 1969, however, Burns was changing his mind. He noted that an incomes policy had been instituted in Canada, the Netherlands, and the United States (the Kennedy era guideposts), and had not been followed by controls. For Burns, at age sixty-four popularly considered one of the most doctrinaire conservatives in the Administration, to have abandoned his position reflects just how anxious he felt. Burns had allied with him a good part of the Cabinet concerned with economic policy: Kennedy, Romney, Volpe, Postmaster General Blount, but not McCracken or the rest of the Council of Economic Advisers. And, most important, not the President.

In an October 17 radio address to the nation on inflation, the President rejected an incomes policy, rejected any substantial change in his economic game plan, and rejected any suggestion of failure. "We are not going to change our game plan at the end of the first quarter of the game, particularly at a time that we feel we are ahead," he said. Recalling yet again his experience with the OPA in World War II ("rationing, black markets, regimentation"), he rejected not only direct controls but the guideposts that Burns had been urging on him—describing guideposts as "putting the Government into the business of telling the workingman how much he should charge for his services or how much the businessman should charge for his goods." The President's dogmatism on the wage-price question had not been diluted by nine months of failure. He even reiterated his objection to jawboning: "Instead of relying on our jawbone, we have put some backbone in Government's determination to hold the line for the consumer." In fact, however, he did engage in a very benign form of jawboning. Pledging that the Government would stick to a strict anti-inflationary policy, Nixon asserted that "by responding to the changed conditions," labor and management "will be following their self-interest and helping the national interest as well." This was a perceptible departure from his January 27 implication that labor and management had no stake in the national welfare, but it was far from what Burns wanted.

Even that minimum of jawboning was forgotten little more than a month later. On November 27, the Administration assembled some 1600 top-rank American business leaders to hear Nixon and his economic team give an off-the-record briefing at Washington's Sheraton Park Hotel. Not a word urging price restraint came from the President or anybody else. It was the same old line: The Government means business about curbing inflation. "Those who bet on inflation will lose their bets, but those who bet on a cooling off will win, because we're committed," said the President.

There was one attempted change in the game plan in the closing months of 1969. In August, just when Burns was changing his mind about an incomes policy, a campaign against the tight-money policy of the Federal Reserve Board was being waged by an influential Republican economist outside the Government: Professor Milton Friedman of the University of Chicago. In his column in *Newsweek,* in discussions with key figures in the Administration, and even in one telephone conversation with William McChesney Martin, Friedman argued that the Federal Reserve had now kept the money supply choked off for so long that further restrictions threatened a severe recession. Friedman's arguments made no impact on Martin or other members of the Quadriad, but he did pick up one influential disciple, George Shultz, Friedman's former colleague at Chicago and now a rising figure in the Administration. Shultz took the view that Friedman had studied the money supply with greater care and perception than anybody in the Administration had and deserved to be listened to. After taking this line in private conversations through the early autumn, Shultz surfaced with it in Nixon's presence at a mid-October meeting of the Cabinet Committee on Economic Policy.

There was no immediate support for Shultz at that meeting, but it was not long in coming. By November, McCracken believed the tight-money policy must be ended (though, for public consumption, he denied it lest he give the impression the Administration was backing away from the fight against inflation). In a meeting of the Quadriad, McCracken asked William McChesney Martin what the prospects were for loosening the money screws. Martin, scheduled to be replaced on January 31 by Burns, was unresponsive. But the Federal Reserve did switch to a less restrictive policy late in the year—far too late in the opinion of many economists.

Thus, 1969 ended with the President's economic game plan disintegrating, his advisers split, and the economy failing. By year's end, the value of the 1957-1959 dollar had slipped from 81.1 cents when Nixon took power to 76.7 cents. And though inflation was not curbed, unemployment was rising fast, and a recession loomed. Yet there was no sense of crisis in the Oval Office. Buoyed by his continued high popularity, by his successes abroad, and by scattered off-year Republican election victories, Richard Nixon could not focus on the specter of economic crisis confronting him. Economic policy continued to be made in a casual manner with little regard for consequences. The tax bill he signed to end the year on December 30 was proof enough of that.

When Nixon early in 1969 joined the swelling demand for tax reform, there was little thought of economic consequences. Tax reform concerned equity. It was not part of the fight against inflation. Yet in pursuing tax reform, the Administration could not avoid making vitally important economic decisions. But instead of approaching this task judiciously, it made these decisions in slapdash fashion, with rueful consequences. What happened is another story, but in the end, at a time when Nixon was trying his best to fight inflation and avoid recession, he had signed a bill that was *both* inflationary (because it increased personal exemptions, and thus deficit spending) and recessionary (because it repealed the investment tax credit first sponsored by President Kennedy in 1962). This had happened because the President's economic team concentrated on the economic aspects of tax reform only belatedly, and then in a haphazard manner that proved totally ineffective. Throughout the late summer and autumn when the Democratic Congress was transmuting tax reform into tax relief, the President was remote from the struggle, ineffective and irresolute. Then came his unfulfilled threat to veto an out-of-balance tax bill. By allowing his bluff to be called, the President had suffered a loss of prestige almost as great as he would have if Congress had overridden one of his vetoes.

On the evening of January 30, 1970, Richard Nixon's first press conference of the new year was opened by Douglas B. Cornell of the Associated Press, whose question graphically revealed how much the economic outlook had changed in the month since the President had signed the tax bill:

> Mr. President, for several days I have been collecting some headlines that sort of point up the question I would like to put to you. . . .
> "Big firms' 1969 profits down." "Dow average hits new low for three years." "GNP rise halted." "Ford joins GM and Chrysler in work cutbacks." "Wholesale prices show sharp rise." "U.S. Steel will raise sheet prices February 1."
> The question is: How, sir, do you assess the possibility that we may be in for perhaps the worst possible sort of economic conditions—inflation and a recession?

Indeed, key economic indicators—industrial production, personal income, business sales, real Gross National Product —were down. So was the slumping stock market. Unemployment was on the rise. But at the same time, interest rates and prices continued to climb. Dr. Walter Heller, chairman of the Council of Economic Advisers in Kennedy-Johnson days, had a name for this combination of bad economic news never before experienced in America: Nixonomics.

McCracken, Kennedy, and Treasury Under Secretary Dr. Charles Walker, who spent 1969 promising that an end to inflation was just around the corner, now not only reiterated those promises but pledged as well that there would be no recession—their credibility undermined by every unfulfilled promise. Nixon joined the parade of sunshine talkers. In answer to Cornell's press-conference question, he said:

> Our policies have been planned to avoid a recession. I do expect that the present rate of inflation, which was less in the second half of 1969 than in the first half, will continue to decline and that we will be able to control inflation without recession.

Specifically, the President promised that three days later, he would offer a bare-bones budget for the fiscal year ending July 1, 1971. The new budget, he promised, "will be a major blow in stopping the inflation psychology." That budget, in fact, was a much more serious attempt at austerity than his first one a year earlier, and that represented a major, though temporary, victory for Arthur Burns.

Late in December 1969, Budget Director Mayo had reported to the President at San Clemente that there was no possible way to cut expenditures deeply enough to balance the new budget. But there simply had to be a balanced budget. Everybody in the Administration now agreed with Milton Friedman that the Federal Reserve Board's tight-money policy must be loosened or the economy would strangle. But Dr. Burns, who would replace William McChesney Martin as chairman at the Federal Reserve on January 31, had made clear he could not countenance an easier monetary policy unless *fiscal* policy were tight—that is, at the bare minimum, a balanced budget. With Mayo pleading inability to cut expenditures enough, new revenue would be needed for a balance. The Treasury came up with a $4.5 billion painless tax package: a speedup in estate- and gift-tax collections and higher excises on liquor, tobacco, and gasoline. Nixon promptly bought the package.

But not Arthur Burns. To make fiscal policy properly tight enough was not only a matter of a balanced budget but of a *properly* balanced budget, he told the President, and not a budget balanced through some patchwork tax gimmicks. The implication was clear. There would be no easing of policy at the Federal Reserve unless the last drop of blood was squeezed out of expenditures. Nixon had already made up his mind to go the Burns route when he returned to Washington from San Clemente in time for a January 13 meeting of the Cabinet. Although it lasted three and one-half hours, it was a *pro forma* affair. Mayo pleaded that the budget was uncuttable, supported by Kennedy. Burns's position was voiced with great passion by his usual acolyte, George Romney, who exhorted his colleagues to cut even deeper into their own budgets and capped his plea by an astonishing sermon calling on all members of the Cabinet, *and* the President, to take a 25 percent pay cut. "This is going to make me as popular as a skunk at a Sunday school picnic," he said, and he was right. Soon after the meeting, Nixon ordered anguished department heads to make still greater cuts to achieve a Burns-style balance. When the budget was sent to Congress on February 2, it called for a $1.3 billion surplus.

Arthur Burns had demonstrated that, blessed with the massive power of the Federal Reserve System, he now had leverage with the President that he never had as Counsellor. But the victory was one year too late. Nixon, Burns, and everybody else sitting around the Cabinet table on January 13 refused to face the grim reality that there was no possible way to balance the budget, either the Mayo-Kennedy way or the Burns-Romney way. The economic rot of recession was at so advanced a stage that tax receipts were already falling precipitately, which explained why the fat $5.6 billion budget surplus projected by Nixon in his first budget for the year ending July 1, 1970, had disappeared and would end up as a $2.8 billion deficit. As for the 1971 budget, the

$1.3 billion surplus bullied through by Burns never had a chance. The recession-induced loss of revenue would, instead, create a deficit to rival Lyndon Johnson's worst.

The President would not admit it, but the game plan was dead. Even before Burns formally replaced Martin, the tight-money policy at the Federal Reserve was quietly abandoned; Burns in charge made sure that the badly needed money kept flowing into the banking system. By early spring, it was obvious that a massive budget deficit, in excess of $15 billion, was in the works (though Administration officials still piously denied it). If a recession loomed and neither the Federal Reserve nor the budget was now being used to fight inflation, what could be done? More and more, Nixon's economic team was doing what would have been inconceivable a year earlier—looking hard at an incomes policy.

Burns's move to the Federal Reserve Board had not stopped him from lobbying for an incomes policy, vigorously supported by Romney. By May, the combination of rising unemployment and rising inflation led to a desperate attempt to change the game plan toward adopting a modest incomes policy. The President had decided to deliver an address to the nation on the economy in mid-June, and this could be the vehicle for a major turn in policy.

Arthur Burns led off the campaign on May 19 with a major policy speech to the American Bankers Association's Monetary Conference in Hot Springs, Virginia, urging a form of voluntary controls as the only way to fight inflation without risking "a very serious business recession." Second- and third-level officials of the Treasury and the Budget Bureau, meeting with their counterparts from the Council of Economic Advisers (in groups called Troika II and Troika III), began pressing for an incomes policy. On May 28, Dr. Walker went on NBC's *Today* show to say he saw "merit" in a bill by Senator Jacob Javits [Republican] of New York that would instruct the Council of Economic Advisers to analyze and publicize wage and price decisions to spotlight inflationary increases—the rudimentary start of an incomes policy.

On June 5, Maurice Mann, a professional economist and political independent who had been recruited by Mayo from the Federal Reserve Bank of Cleveland to become Assistant Budget Director, addressed a Washington meeting of the Rural Electric Cooperative Association and brought out what was happening inside the Administration. Speaking without notes, Mann described the Government economists as divided into two camps—one camp for continued tight fiscal and monetary policy, the other camp for attacking inflation with an incomes policy because the present policy was "an abysmal failure." Mann left no doubt he was in the second group. Not until he had finished speaking did he realize that a reporter, Murray Seeger of the Los Angeles *Times,* was present.

Hobart Rowen, business and financial editor of the Washington *Post,* read Seeger's story on the Los Angeles *Times* news wire and cornered Mann two days later at the District of Columbia Bankers Association's annual convention in Hot Springs, Virginia. Mann then clearly told Rowen what no Administration official had dared admit up to that point: the Nixon game plan had slowed down the economy without stopping inflation, and "an additional step"—that is, a moderate incomes policy—would be helpful.

To the outside world, all this sound and fury surely was a preliminary barrage preparing everyone for a radical shift, to be revealed in the mid-June speech. But the outside world little knew how the Nixon Administration functioned. In fact, most of the agitation for an incomes policy came from second-echelon officials at the Treasury and Budget Bureau operating without the sanction of their bosses. Walker endorsed the Javits bill without telling Kennedy; Mann did not have Mayo's backing when he publicly endorsed an incomes policy (in fact, his knuckles were later rapped in a telephone call from White House aide Peter Flanigan).

Among officials with direct access to the President, only Burns favored an incomes policy, and he made no progress in early May when he again proposed voluntary controls to the President. Kennedy and Mayo were passive and seemingly uninterested in the entire debate. Paul McCracken publicly denounced Burns's initiative. He admitted privately it might have merit but protested vigorously that the Council was not equipped to oversee wage-price decisions as envisioned in the Javits bill. If Nixon needed any further justification for opposing Burns, it came from Secretary of Labor George Shultz. By the spring of 1970, Shultz's unsmiling, slightly intimidating manner had made him a force to reckon with. Now the Secretary turned his new influence with the President against an incomes policy. It would not work, he argued, and besides that, it would lead to shameful abandonment of the game plan by tending to justify a reckless binge of deficit spending. Indeed, Shultz told Nixon, the Hot Springs speech by Burns advocating an incomes policy was inflationary in itself. It would impel businessmen to raise prices quickly *before* an incomes policy was instituted.

With that lineup, the final draft of the speech handed Nixon for his final editing and rewriting did not contain anything that even went so far in the direction of an incomes policy as the very mild Javits bill. A baby step was the announcement of periodic Inflation Alerts to be issued by the Council of Economic Advisers "to call attention to outstanding cases of price or wage increase"—in other words, jawboning *after* the fact. It was a slight departure from total laissez-faire on wages and prices but a bitter disappointment for many who had hoped for a major departure. In his speech to the nation over radio and television at noon on June 17, the President once again indulged his deeply felt bias against Government interference in wage-price decisions in prose unmistakably his own.

Now, I realize that there are some people who get satisfaction out of seeing an individual businessman or labor leader called on the carpet and browbeaten by Government officials. But we cannot protect the value of the dollar by passing the buck. That sort of grandstanding distracts attention from the real cause of inflation and it can be a dangerous misuse of the power of Government.

It was as if the past eighteen months of deepening failure had not occurred, as if Arthur Burns had not made serious proposals that had nothing to do with "browbeating" anybody or "grandstanding," as if serious economists in his own Administration were not turning toward an incomes policy. Never did the failure of communication between the President and the experts in his own Administration come through more clearly.

A few days before that speech, the President took a step that further militated against an incomes policy in the foreseeable future.

In December 1969, Nixon had briefed Robert Mayo on the details of a major reorganization of the Executive Office of the President, not to be publicly disclosed until the next spring, that would transform the Bureau of the Budget into a new Office of Management and Budget (OMB), with greatly enhanced authority for managing the entire Federal Government. In one of those countless misunderstandings, derived from Nixon's often oblique manner of conversation, Mayo got the idea that the job would be his. In fact, however, the President had no intention of giving a post of such vast and pervasive power to a man with whom he had little rapport and in whom he had no great confidence. But he said nothing of this to Mayo. Mayo did not learn the President's real frame of mind until he received a telephone call from a White House aide on June 8, 1970. The aide bluntly informed Mayo that the President on June 10 would name George Shultz as director of OMB, with Mayo shunted off with the title of Counsellor (retaining Cabinet rank), obviously a way station while he found other employment. There was no telephone call from Nixon himself.

The humiliation of Robert Mayo was transcended by the elevation of George Shultz. Having managed to impress the President and shape his policies while operating from the bureaucratic backwater of the Labor department, he now had unlimited possibilities functioning from the White House as general manager for the entire Federal Government. Replacing Mayo on the Quadriad, he would become the dominant force whose influence would far eclipse that of McCracken, Kennedy, and Burns. Behind his back, some of the Government's top economists belittled Shultz, describing him as an academic proficient in the study of wage structuring but not in macroeconomics. They questioned his competence to be the President's most influential adviser on what had become his most serious domestic problem. But that Shultz *was* his most influential economic adviser could be denied by nobody. In terms of mid-1970, that meant an end to any immediate hopes for a meaningful incomes policy, because Shultz's doctrinaire opposition to it would only reinforce Nixon's emotional bias against it. Maurice Mann, one of the most forceful advocates of an incomes policy, quickly perceived the incompatibility of his own economic views and Shultz's, and quietly left the Budget Bureau and the Government. Walker and other Treasury officials pushing for an incomes policy went underground. At the Federal Reserve, Arthur Burns bided his time.

Through the summer and autumn of 1970, inflation and recession worsened together to stunt hopes for significant Republican gains in November. By summer, nothing could be done in time for that year's elections about either inflation or recession. In all fairness to Nixon and his economic advisers, they had inherited from Lyndon Johnson a raging inflation that might have persisted against any proposed remedy, including an incomes policy. Nor was the intensity of the recession wholly attributable to the Nixon game plan: the United Auto Workers struck the General Motors Corporation on September 14, closing plants for the rest of the year and deepening economic distress.

Yet, pervading all the bad luck was a certain thoughtless separation between dream and reality.

In November 5, 1970, two days after the congressional elections, signals began pouring out of the President's Council of Economic Advisers that a change in the economic game plan was in order. "Economic policy like other [policies] has to be responsive to the national will," said Paul McCracken, chairman of the Council. Two days later, another member of the Council, Herbert Stein, flatly predicted a return to full employment by mid-1972. What the Council members were proposing was clear enough: a switch to an expansionary economic policy to fight the recession and give up the struggle against inflation. That would be an attack on one of the two serpent heads of Nixonomics—the one that had caused by far the most damage in the just completed election. Republican politicians who had suffered badly in 1970 and feared even worse for 1972 were pleading for an all-out attack on the recession.

At the Treasury, Secretary Kennedy and Under Secretary Walker were appalled. They argued privately that victory over inflation was in sight if only the Government did not panic by throwing more fuel on the fire. After all, the Treasury men reasoned, the recession that had been induced in a so far unsuccessful effort to slow down inflation had already done its damage to the President and the party. Why make the switch now *after* the election losses? There would be enough time to step up the economy, if need be, before the 1972 election. That line only showed how out of touch with the White House David Kennedy had become. For in fact, McCracken and Stein were reflecting Richard Nixon's views. These had hardened long before the election, but the President had kept silent about them.

In part, the change was due to the growing influence of George Shultz, who had taken over as director of the newly reorganized Office of Management and Budget on July 1. A clue to the revised standings in relative power at the White House came in late summer during a visit to Nixon by Senator Robert Dole [Republican] of Kansas. Dole expressed chagrin at his inability to contact presidential Counsellor John Ehrlichman and told Nixon he would like to meet him some day. *"Ehrlichman?"* retorted the President. "Don't worry about him." Then, picking up his telephone, he said: "I'll put you in touch with somebody who *really* counts: George Shultz."

As one who really counted, Shultz was able to implant his economic views on Nixon as nobody else had in the first two years of the Nixon Administration. By November 1970, Shultz had convinced Nixon of the worth of these economic views:

Full-Employment Budget: An old proposal by liberal economists for the past generation, it envisioned the budget being balanced when expenditures were no higher than revenue would be *if* there were full employment (that is, unemployment no higher than about 4 percent). Thus, with unemployment well over 6 percent, the President could claim a budget balanced on the full-employment theory, even though, in fact, there would be a substantial budget deficit—sheer heresy for a conservative Republican.

Money-Supply Expansion: As a doctrinaire exponent of Professor Milton Friedman's theories, Shultz wanted the money supply expanded at a steady rate and at a faster rate than the Federal Reserve Board under Arthur Burns's leadership was approving.

Incomes Policy: In a slight break with Nixon's iron opposition to any incomes policy of significance, Shultz was advocating an attempt to hold down prices and wages by withdrawing artificial Government supports—such as import quotas and labor union privileges—but in no other way. That meant continued opposition to Burns's proposal for a return to wage-price guideposts.

Long before election day, Nixon was committed to an expansionary policy that would run a considerable deficit, saying nothing about it only because of his adamant political position that conceding that anything at all was wrong with the economy would be playing into Democratic hands. The Treasury's postelection opposition crumpled quickly.

But the Nixon-Shultz plans for money-supply expansion and incomes policy ran into trouble from Arthur Burns, who had recommended George Shultz as Secretary of Labor but felt him inadequate as an economist to be grand designer of the nation's economic policy. On the morning of November 20 in a meeting at the White House, Nixon, reflecting Shultz's viewpoint, urged Burns to expand the money supply at a faster rate. In response, Burns reiterated his old position that some incomes policy, some Government restraint on wages and prices, was necessary. As a specific example, he urged presidential suspension of the Davis-Bacon Act, ensuring that construction workers on Federal projects get the high prevailing union wage rates. That suspension would be a big stick to pressure the building trades unions to hold down their inflationary wage settlements.

In the early months of 1971, Nixon edged ever so cautiously closer to a working incomes policy. He forced a partial rollback of a Bethlehem Steel price increase by threatening to end the import quota on foreign steel, a withdrawal of artificial Government aid that would have fallen within the boundaries of Shultz's doctrinal approval. Nixon finally did suspend Davis-Bacon after first weighing a flat freeze on construction-industry wages and prices proposed by James Hodgson—Shultz's hand-picked successor as Secretary of Labor—but opposed by Shultz. This ended Nixon's adamant opposition through his first two years as President to intervention in wage-price decisions but was nowhere near a full-scale policy to hold down wages and prices on a systematic basis.

The question posed nearly two years earlier, whether Richard Nixon would rather fight inflation than be elected to a second term, was now being answered. While defending the battered old game plan and declaring that "the worst of inflation is over," the President was really abandoning the game plan and saying that inflation was far the lesser evil when compared with recession. The way in which the fight against inflation was being placed in a secondary position became clear when the budget for the year ending July 1, 1972, was submitted to Congress on January 29, 1971. The deficit was calculated at $11.6 billion (under the full-employment budget concept, it would have brought a surplus of $100 million had the country been at full employment, said the President). But this was based on revenue generated by an economy at the level of a $1065 billion Gross National Product—a ludicrously high figure, in the opinion of most economists. In truth, everybody was sure that the deficit would be around $20 billion, producing some $40 billion in red-ink spending for two years, with the budget running wild, out of control, for the years ahead. That was the true extent of the game plan's abandonment.

Equally important as this switch to an expansionary policy in its implications for the future was a change of vast importance in Nixon's economic team made just after the election. The President determined that David Kennedy's disappointing tenure at the Treasury had to come to an end. Kennedy, scarcely a Hickel or a Romney in his self-effacing manner, was happy enough to leave a post that had become increasingly unpleasant. To replace him, Nixon wanted somebody who could dynamically and actively sell his new, expansive economic program (along with his new legislative proposals) to the press, the Congress, the business community, and the nation. Dr. Charles Walker, who in two years had performed most of Kennedy's duties in dealing with Congress and the press, fit that description perfectly and was eager for the advancement. But the tax reform fight had left bad blood between Walker and White House aides John Ehrlichman and Peter Flanigan, who successfully convinced Nixon that Walker would be a mistake. They wanted a prominent bank president from Wall Street or the West Coast. But after the David Kennedy experience, the President was wary of bankers. Besides, with his love for novelty, and frustrated by the premature detonation of the bombshell he had hoped to set off by making Patrick Moynihan ambassador to the United Nations, Nixon wanted a surprise that would stun Washington and, perhaps, energize his drowsy Administration for the two years ahead.

John B. Connally's performance on the Ash Council on Government Reorganization impressed the President. [The President's Advisory Council on Executive Organization, headed by Roy L. Ash of Litton Industries planned the bills for a sweeping overhaul of the domestic agencies of the Federal Government.—Ed.] Like John Mitchell, Connally has the imperious air of authority, self-possession, and masterfulness that Nixon lacks, and therefore so admires in others. Soon after the 1970 election, the President began commenting to close aides about Connally and asking their opinion of him. But nobody faintly guessed that the President was thinking about the Treasury. After ten days and three meetings, Connally, who first refused the job, finally said yes. On December 14, Nixon had his stunning surprise.

From Nixon's standpoint it made sense. He finally had a Democrat in the Cabinet, albeit a very conservative Democrat who for the past decade had led the Tory wing of the Texas Democratic party. Texas Republicans gasped at the betrayal by Nixon in bestowing this honor on their great enemy, but Connally's presence in the Nixon Administration could only help the President's chances to carry Texas in 1972, which might be vital to his reelection. He added strength to a Cabinet that was weak and would become weaker when Mitchell resigned to become campaign manager for 1972. And here was a Stetson-wearing supersalesman who could make Nixon's economic-progress game plan plausible to the nation. The only drawback was John Connally's lack of qualification to be Secretary of the Treasury. An able lawyer, businessman, and politician, he had no familiarity with fiscal and monetary affairs. But that was scarcely relevant; there had not for a long time been a Secretary better qualified than David Kennedy, and look what happened to him.

In the spring of 1971, nobody could be sure whether the mistakes of 1969 and 1970 would cost Richard Nixon a second term. Despite all the heavy deficit spending, unemployment remained over 6 percent in early May and the business recovery was sluggish. Not even optimists felt that unemployment would fall below 5 percent before election day, 1972. The best news was the economic consensus that 1972 would be a pretty good year, though how good was a matter of sharp debate. The Davis-Bacon suspension was called off in return for construction labor's agreement to negotiate limits on wage increases, perhaps the thin end of a wedge on the incomes policy that Nixon had resisted for so long. The rate of inflation had slowed, but not noticeably so in the opinion of the consumer (the 1957-1959 dollar now having dropped in value to 71.8 cents compared with 81.1 cents when Nixon took office). At the Federal Reserve, Arthur Burns was being forced to slow down the rate of money expansion with the attendant danger of boosting interest rates and slowing down the recovery. It was a mixed picture, better than the previous dreary autumn but not as good as it could be.

Nor were the personal power relationships clear. Connally was now the only noneconomist, the only businessman, and the only politician on a Quadriad of strong men, joining economists Shultz, Burns, and McCracken. Unlike them, his mind was open on almost all economic questions. (Arthur Burns confided to friends that he thought Connally was "educable.") How he would act in crisis was anybody's guess. He sided with Burns and against McCracken and

Shultz in being willing to propose personal tax reductions and a reinstatement of the business investment tax credit if necessary to stimulate the economy. In late April, Connally sharply criticized a prime-interest-rate increase by the nation's banks while it was being defended by McCracken. But he was so concerned with emergency assignments (such as the controversial plan to bail out the beleaguered Lockheed Corporation) that his overall power position was uncertain. His strength against Shultz had not really been tested. Nevertheless, with his direct access to the President assured, the certainty was that he would act and act unfettered by doctrine. That would be something new in President Nixon's management of the economy.

RICHARD NIXON SEES THE LIGHT [4]

Late last September [1971], Herbert Stein, then a member and now Chairman of the Council of Economic Advisers, clambered aboard a White House jet to hand-carry a rough outline of Phase II's wage and price controls to Richard Nixon, who was in Anchorage, Alaska, to greet the Emperor of Japan. As Stein had been given only a day's notice of his trip, he was hard pressed to get the outline completed in time. But despite the rush, the memorandum pleased Nixon, and it was on the flight back from Anchorage aboard the Spirit of '76 that Phase II would be said to have been born. That day was also just about the last on which it was free from controversy.

The control machinery did considerable violence to classic theories of management structure. With its two independent boards of citizens, plus a Government council, it seemed an almost circular approach to decision making, whereby the buck could be endlessly passed. In at least one other important respect, it was an oddity among Government pro-

[4] Article, "How the U.S. Got on the Road to a Controlled Economy," by Juan Cameron, Washington editor. *Fortune*. 85:74-7+. Ja. '72. Reprinted by permission of Fortune magazine; © 1972 Time Inc.

grams: a set of economic controls drafted by a man who does not believe in controls and approved by a President who dislikes them just as fervently.

In Nixon's eyes, however, the Stein program had one overwhelming advantage. Though devised by an eminent economist, it was a predominantly *political* solution to the President's problem. It involved both business and labor in the explosive issue of dividing up the national income and making the program work. As an official who helped draft the program with Stein explains: "It was a way to try to do the job without tearing the institutions apart." From this central concept, subsidiary advantages flowed. For one thing, the proposals did not require any massive Federal bureaucracy like the Office of Price Administration and the War Production Board, in which Nixon and Stein toiled in World War II, and which in the process they learned to abhor. Furthermore, the control machinery was designed to keep the presidency two levels above the inevitable wrangling about individual cases. It was, in fact, the kind of program that has become a hallmark of the Nixon Administration: something that could be announced with a bold sweep on television, after which it would be expected to tend to itself. Sometime in 1972, amid economic stability and prosperity—or so the hope went—the President could scrap it.

If that were to come to pass, Phase II would serve as a happy ending to a turbulent and trying period, one that in many ways is without precedent in US economic history. The story of that testing time for the Nixon Administration, beginning roughly a year ago, has never been fully told. It is a story of bitter disputes, tightly disciplined secrecy maintained by deception, and surprising events that even today are known to only a handful of Administration officials.

Nobody in Charge

If the virtues of the Stein plan were immediately apparent to Nixon, the dangers also surfaced quite quickly, once Phase II began. In return for gaining some distance from the daily workings of the controls he so dislikes, the President had also ceded most of his power over the course of enforcement—the most dramatic single instance being his famous memorandum to George Meany. Right from the start, the Price Commission, under the brisk leadership of C. Jackson Grayson, Jr., took a firmer line than did the Pay Board under Judge George H. Boldt. Phase II's most glaring fault was the absence of a clear, single voice at the top. For a program depending upon a large measure of voluntary compliance must be perceived by the public, business, and labor to be working equitably, or in the long run it will not work at all. Within a month after Phase II started, some editorial and business voices were already dismissing it as a failure. [See "Phase II" in Section I, above.—Ed.]

All this pessimism may prove to be premature. Despite the flaws in its structure, Phase II may still work moderately well, at least for a while; it is not supposed to end inflation, after all, but merely ease it. Public attention has focused, naturally enough, not on prices that are holding steady but on cases where the boards have violated their own guidelines. But the whole point of moving from the freeze to Phase II was to gain a measure of flexibility—"a lid with a spout to let some of the inflationary pressures out," says Arnold R. Weber, a public member of the Pay Board. Herbert Stein explains that the program bears about the same relation to the freeze as a military occupation does to war. "It is less glamorous and dramatic, more irritating, political, and controversial than the earlier phase." Unfortunately, in the absence of effective leadership from the White House the program will be even messier than it need be, and it will seem a lot messier than it is.

Beyond its own shortcomings, one of the intrinsic difficulties of the New Economic Policy is that it has been and will be caught up in the politics of an election year. The fight to discredit the economic program, and to pin the blame for its failure on Nixon, has already been joined by organized labor and in congressional politicking over the wide array of legislation necessary to implement it. This constant battling will tend to cloud the working of the program, and could cripple it.

Another difficulty—and perhaps the basic one—is that the entire Nixon economic policy was the product of a divided government acting hastily and yet with great reluctance under the irresistible pressure of events. Even today the President and his closest economic advisers have a deep philosophical aversion to much of the program. George P. Shultz, the powerful director of the Office of Management and Budget, makes no bones about his feelings: "I haven't changed my mind one iota about the wage-price business. It's undesirable. But I agreed completely that we had to do something, something that would work."

In the White House, Treasury, CEA [Council of Economic Advisers], and Federal Reserve there are other equally strong reservations about the surtax on imports, closing the gold window, and the fiscal-monetary mix decided upon last summer. John B. Connally, the Secretary of the Treasury, upon whom Nixon conferred the title of "chief economic spokesman and quarterback," is the lightning rod for some of this unrest. Before he switched to a softer negotiating stance on monetary matters in late November, Connally was under attack from Henry Kissinger and other Nixon advisers, who felt that he was persevering stubbornly in a high-risk strategy that was endangering not only world trade but vital US alliances. At one point these criticisms led Connally's press spokesman, Calvin Brumley, to complain that the "White House staff is trying to stab Connally in the back."

"Pressure, Pressure, Pressure"

Major policy decisions of Government often seem from the outside to have been improvised hurriedly—slapped together by a small group of men meeting secretly in a big room amid an air of crisis. And in the wake of a major turning point in policy, a government tries to dispel this image by means of an imaginative reconstruction in which decisions are made harmoniously and the groundwork is laid weeks and months beforehand.

The New Economic Policy is generally understood to have been the result of eleventh-hour decisions taken by a small group of men meeting with the President on the weekend of August 15 [1971]. The history of the program is quite different from this widely held belief, just as were the various roles played by the President's advisers in shaping it. Through this story run the threads of both careful planning and hasty improvisation. In the end it was the President, buffeted by conflicting advice, who decided to cut with the past and embark on an uncharted economic path leading into the unknown.

Richard Nixon made this fateful decision on the night of August 2, two weeks before the Camp David summit. The decision, says George Shultz, was prompted by the "lackluster economic picture in July and pressure, pressure, pressure on the dollar." But implementation of the program, far sooner than had been planned, was dictated to the President by the largest money run in history, which culminated in a panicked request from the Bank of England for a guarantee against devaluation of its dollar holdings totaling some $3 billion. The British request, viewed as tantamount to a demand for gold, was relayed to the White House on the morning of August 13.

The Salesman Cometh

But if that was the final moment of decision, the first stirrings of change in the Nixon "game plan" can be traced as far back as last winter and the arrival of two new Nixon recruits in Washington: Connally at the Treasury, and Peter G. Peterson at the White House as Assistant for International Economic Affairs. Neither contributed original scholarship to solving the problems of the economy—and, indeed, Connally was slow to accept the seriousness of the monetary crisis that had already begun to build. Both men, however, were receptive to the ideas of others, and each had a talent for advocacy that is in short supply within the Administration. When they saw a problem, both shared the activist's tendency to want to do something about it.

Assistant to the President John D. Ehrlichman believes the appointment last January of Peterson and the studies he subsequently initiated mark the true genesis of the new policy. A former chairman of Bell & Howell Company, Peterson came to Washington with the reputation of a supersalesman and ardent free trader. In his new role, however, he had to cope with the growing protectionist sentiment in Congress and organized labor. His studies reflected the gist of briefings that Paul A. Volcker, Under Secretary of the Treasury for Monetary Affairs, gave Connally after he became Secretary in February. Volcker's message was that the rapidly growing balance-of-payments deficit was caused by a basic disequilibrium of the dollar and that no solution would be found unless new strong steps were taken by the Government. Peterson leaped on this analysis, as he did on the controversial thesis of an obscure Department of Commerce economist, Michael Boretsky, that the United States was gradually losing its superiority in industry and technology to other countries. Skilled in presenting ideas, Peterson wrapped up these strands into what was to become an exceptionally influential report, "The United States in the Changing World Economy," and made a flip-chart presentation to Nixon last April. Soon many of the report's ideas began to crop up in the President's speeches.

The action steps recommended by Peterson in this same report, never publicized, show how he was moving to accommodate protectionist forces. The United States had been neglectful of its vital economic interests, Peterson wrote, and had to adopt a get-tough policy, including imposition of an import surtax, setting temporary limits in certain cases on the rate and level of foreign penetration, and readjusting the exchange rate of the dollar. Specifically, he urged moving in "an orchestrated fashion" with "carrot and stick" to force Japan to revalue the yen, open its markets to US goods and investment, and accept restrictions on the US market for its exports. In Europe, the overriding policy issue was to "minimize the risk and maximize the advantage inherent in Europe's integration process" by negotiating in GATT [General Agreement on Tariffs and Trade] a trade-off of lower US tariffs in return for adjustments in currency values and eased restrictions on US farm exports.

The Figures That Triggered the Plan

Unveiled against a backdrop of the enormous speculative money flows that occurred in the spring, Peterson's chart show had considerable impact. By May, both Nixon and Connally were increasingly alarmed at the deteriorating position of the trade accounts and the dollar. During evening trips down the Potomac aboard his yacht, Sequoia, Nixon began in late June to discuss, with Connally and other aides, taking substantive steps for dealing with these growing pressures. The proposals he had in mind could be traced to Peterson's April paper.

In response to this high-level concern, staff work had been proceeding in the Treasury under Volcker, but not within any time frame for action. On Saturday, July 10, after receiving the report of the third consecutive monthly trade deficit, Volcker called William B. Dale, US executive director of the International Monetary Fund, at his home to ask what sort of June deficit he felt would have a serious impact on the skittish money markets. Dale, after a pause, answered: "$300 million to $400 million." The laconic Volcker replied: "Well we've got it, so we'd better get started on contingency plans." From that weekend until August 15, a small Treasury group under Volcker worked steadily on the ingredients of the monetary package that was ultimately announced.

During this same period, Federal Reserve Chairman Arthur F. Burns was trying to get a message on the domestic economy across to Nixon. But, unlike Peterson's, this was a message the President didn't want to hear.

By the late summer of 1970, Burns, who first made his reputation as an authority on business cycles, was deeply disturbed that huge wage increases were still being won, even though unemployment was high and the economy was in recession. He concluded there were structural difficulties that conventional monetary and fiscal tools were powerless to solve. By the fall of that year he was telling visitors: "We're coming to an incomes policy, not because I want it or some presidential advisers [i.e., Shultz] don't, but because we have to." When William L. Safire, a Nixon speechwriter, pointed out that, like the President, Burns himself had historically been opposed to such a policy, Burns replied: "At my age, you realize that everything you've written has not been chiseled in granite." Although deeply loyal to Nixon, Burns is a man of firm conviction who did not want to see his friend in the White House overtaken by events. He began to speak out publicly for adoption of an incomes policy, and finally this past summer—in a highly unusual step for a Federal Reserve Chairman—began to help a group of Republican senators who were drafting legislation to this end. Although Burns did not know it then, his was an idea whose time had come.

The Famous Four No's

John Connally is known to his colleagues as a "quick study," but also as a man slow to commit himself on important questions. Initially unfamiliar with the Treasury's work, he had listened for months to warnings from his economic adviser, then Assistant Secretary of Treasury Murray L. Weidenbaum, that the President's economic plan, concocted by Shultz, was misguided and a failure. But it was not until early summer, when Representative Wilbur D. Mills underlined this warning, that he began moving toward a position of his own. What finally cut it for Connally was a meeting at Camp David in late June, at which Paul W. McCracken, then Chairman of the CEA, pointed out that unless the economy was stimulated, the Administration would still be facing a 6 percent unemployment rate at the end of the year. Convinced that time was running out politically for the President, Connally argued forcefully that the old game plan was dead, and that the economy needed to be spurred by tax cuts or higher spending. "We knew a change had to be made if the final second-quarter figures looked as bad as the preliminary ones," one participant at that Camp David meeting recalls. "From that point on, it was simply a matter of when we would move." As Nixon's economic spokesman, Connally got the job of declaring publicly after the meeting that no change in policy was planned. But Connally's famous "Four No's"—no wage and price controls, no review board, no tax cuts, and no spending increases —were nothing but a cover.

A few days later, in a meeting with the President in early July, Connally and Burns had a spirited discussion on the need for wage and price controls, and Burns was turned down by both men. But as staff work went on in the CEA and the Treasury, it became clear that the measures needed to stimulate the economy would also add new inflationary pressures and further imperil the already threatened dollar. In late July, Connally swung his powerful influence behind the advice that there was no alternative to putting a lid on wages and prices. When the dismal July figures came in, events had overtaken ideology, and policy was ready to shift.

The Week That Was

At eight o'clock on the muggy night of August 2, the President closeted himself with Connally and Shultz in his suite in the Executive Office Building. At the end of two hours, Nixon said, "This is what we're going to do" and then ticked off the major points: stimulate the economy with tax cuts offset by some budget cuts; seek a readjustment of the dollar's exchange rate through a surtax; and put a temporary freeze on wages and prices. Before the three men parted company that evening, the President swore his two aides to absolute secrecy. He had not made up his mind on when to implement the new policy, although he was thinking at that moment of moving in the fall, when Congress reconvened. Burns was possibly the first person other than Connally and Shultz to know what was afoot. Two days later, after a press conference, the President called his old counsellor at the Fed and said that he might surprise him. Returning home that evening, Burns told his wife, Helen, "You know, I think the President is going to impose a freeze. He didn't say so. But I just think he will." Burns shared his hunch with no one else.

None of these men knew, however, that they would not be given time to complete their planning. An unbroken string of bad economic news on many fronts was followed on August 6 by a report of the Joint Economic Committee of Congress calling for revaluation of the dollar and, if necessary, closing the gold window. Viewed mistakenly abroad as a trial balloon inspired by the Administration, the report started money moving out of the United States in enormous quantities—nearly $4 billion left within a week—and the central banks of Europe were flooded with unwanted dollars.

As this monetary crisis intensified, Paul McCracken dropped his customary reticence about urging bold action and pressed the President to put his August 2 decisions into effect immediately, a move that would be as dramatic in economic policy as the overture to China had been in foreign policy. He began to sense the President was psychologically prepared to move—and he was right. On August 10, Nixon checked with Connally by phone—curiously the Treasury Secretary had been away over the weekend at Alcoa's [Aluminum Company of America's] guest lodge in Tennessee and then had begun a vacation at his own ranch in Texas— and ordered Shultz to get the staff work finished by that weekend. At this point, despite the run on the dollar, there was still no decision to cut loose from gold. But on the morning of Friday the thirteenth, just as Nixon and all of his top economics advisers were preparing to leave for a final conference at Camp David, the British demand was relayed to the White House. It was considered a distinctly foul blow; after all, the United States had helped rescue sterling at least three times during the 1960s. An outraged United States Treasury abruptly turned down the British request.

The Gold Decision

Arthur Burns arrived at Camp David still opposed to closing the gold window. He felt, first, that the shock therapy of the freeze and import surcharge would suffice to check the flight from the dollar. And like any central banker, he recognized it as a fateful step to cast off the world's monetary system from its mooring to gold. But Britain's action had forced the decision. Finally Burns went along—and in retrospect feels the decision was the right one.

There was what one participant has called a "final round of prose" on the major elements of what has become the New Economic Program. Some had considered the 10 percent import surcharge too small to have much economic effect (15 percent was preferred); and others, including Volcker, thought the surcharge unwise. But with Connally and Peterson pushing strongly for it, it was adopted as a temporary measure to convince the world the United States meant business. The rest of the weekend was spent on fitting together the various parts of the program. Small changes were made in the investment tax credit and other fiscal measures. There was a decision not to scrap the ineffectual controls on investment abroad by US companies, and not to impose a restriction on textile imports.

Speechwriter Safire fashioned the smooth TV announcement, which was couched in calm tones that gave no inkling of the deep troubles facing the President. At the strong urging of Burns, it was decided that Nixon should make his announcement Sunday night, so that he would not be speaking against the backdrop of a flight from the dollar that was certain to resume on Monday.

On Sunday afternoon notices went out to Government officials to watch the President's speech. (Private economists like Paul A. Samuelson were called as well.) And finally Pierre-Paul Schweitzer, Managing Director of the IMF [International Monetary Fund], was invited to come over to the Treasury to view the telecast. After he arrived that evening, Volcker handed him a formal ten-line letter written by Connally that afternoon to comply with US treaty obligations. It came right to the point: "This is to notify you that the United States no longer, for the settlement of international transactions, in fact, freely buys or sells gold." The astonished Schweitzer then sat down in Connally's office to listen to Nixon explain the rest of his program on TV.

A Question Left Hanging

When the President stopped talking on that Sunday evening, the most conspicuous question left hanging in the air was what would come after the ninety-day freeze. Burns, McCracken, and Weber had hastily prepared a two-page memorandum on various policies available. But Nixon did not wish to commit himself to Phase II specifics at that time. One of the advantages of the freeze, indeed, was that it provided time for a consensus to develop on the boundaries of the follow-up program and how it would be operated.

Two days later, on August 17, Stein, who had volunteered to draft a Phase II plan, became the head of a task force set up as a working group for the Cabinet-level Cost of Living Council. The Council itself, which Connally headed, became so bogged down in detail that it never functioned efficiently, and the job of designing the follow-on control mechanism fell mainly to the Stein group.

During his stint on the War Production Board during World War II, Stein had concluded that controls work imperfectly at best, and tend to cause distortions that eventually bring about their collapse. As an associate research director for the Committee for Economic Development, Stein played a major role in drafting the CED's 1951 policy paper, "Price and Wage Controls," one of whose major themes was that if controls were necessary they should be flexible, allowing prices and wages to be adjusted continually to reflect changes in relevant costs. This report, which was on Stein's desk as he began work last summer, is reflected in the philosophy of Phase II. Indeed, beyond its chairman's personal views, the Stein task force had precious little to chew on.

Planning Under Wraps

Due to the secrecy imposed by Nixon prior to Camp David, only minimal planning had been done. It was not until August 4—nine days before the Camp David meeting began—that Shultz instructed Arnold Weber, then associate director of OMB [Office of Management and Budget], to get together a study of wage-price controls, telling him it was for use in congressional hearings coming up in the fall. This being the case, Weber was somewhat surprised when on Tuesday, August 10, Shultz asked him to produce a summary of his findings by the next day. His surprise turned to astonishment when Shultz, after hearing his report, said, "Okay, go and deal with the operational problems by Friday morning." Weber and his aide, William H. Kolberg, had been working on a general review of various control mechanisms. They had not focused on a freeze, except to recommend it as a desirable prelude.

To help him in his crash project, Weber had started a search for someone in the Government who might have been doing some planning, and finally turned up Leonard Skubal in the Office of Emergency Preparedness. (Ironically, having worked for twenty years on controls, Skubal left the Government two weeks after the freeze took effect.) Weber conducted a hurried search through library materials and was able to finish an eight-page plan titled "Economic Stabilization Program" on the morning the Camp David meeting was to begin. The Council of Economic Advisers had concluded a similar study that same week, but the final draft was still in a secretary's typewriter when Nixon and his aides helicoptered off to his mountain retreat.

The President's Parameters

If such hurried staff work did not provide much of a base from which to design Phase II, the President's own strong feelings on the subject did. On the one hand he wanted nothing resembling the elaborate OPA [Office of Price Administration] machinery of World War II. On the other hand, as he told Stein in early September, he did want an "executive program," something firmer than what the Administration likes to call the "soft, hortatory approach" of the Kennedy-Johnson jawboning years. This preference for the middle ground dictated a system backed by the force of law but run by a small bureaucracy: the Price Commission was to have a staff of around 400, the Pay Board just over 125. And since such a small bureaucracy would perforce have to limit its monitoring to the doings of the largest corporations and labor unions, the President's wishes also meant an essentially voluntary approach to controls. While this gave promise of creating confusion at least initially, says one White House aide, "It also promised more chance of success in the longer term than us telling the nation what we wanted and how we were going to achieve it."

During late August and September talks were held with a wide assortment of people on how to gain such voluntary cooperation and how to avoid the pitfalls that France, Britain, and Canada had encountered with their incomes policies. Foreign visitors like John H. Young, chairman of the Prices and Incomes Commission in Canada, and Aubrey Jones, chairman of the similar British board, were eagerly interviewed when they happened into Washington during this interval. But the talks were not particularly illuminating. Both the Canadian and the British programs, after all, had worked for a while and then collapsed.

Meanwhile, the President was chafing to announce that he would end the freeze on schedule and move on to Phase II. After the first rough draft was brought to him in Anchorage, Nixon met twice more with Stein and Shultz and then, on October 5, gave his final approval to the Phase II machinery. The setup was awkward, to be sure, but as Stein has said, it at least "reflected the balance of power and responsibility that exists in the country." Business leaders, operating through Secretary of Commerce Maurice H. Stans, had achieved one key objective opposed by both Connally and organized labor: a firm target of reducing inflation to less than 3 percent. George Meany—whose demands were conveyed through Labor Under Secretary Silberman and Meany's friend in the White House, George Shultz—achieved that nearly autonomous Pay Board cumbrously manned by fifteen labor, business, and public members. (Meany, of course, demanded much more that he did not get, including abolition of the CLC [Cost of Living Council].) [See "Phase II," in Section I, above.—Ed.]

Ninety-Day Wonder

When Nixon announced Phase II on October 7, he was able to do so against the backdrop of a freeze that was working with remarkable success and with wide public support. This ninety-day wonder had proved to be a simple if brutal administrative device that accomplished its major purpose of dramatically altering the inflationary expectations of the economy. Under the day-to-day guidance of Weber, the executive director of the CLC, the freeze was run, he says, "by a pickup volley-ball team of fifty people who came from every agency of Government and had never seen each other before. It worked because we weren't smart enough and there wasn't time enough to develop the procedures that would inhibit us." From August to October, the consumer price index rose by only 0.3 percent; wholesale prices eased slightly in the same period. Furthermore, compliance was good. Of some 47,000 complaints of alleged violations, 62 percent were, on investigation, discovered to be unfounded. Where violations were real, the Internal Revenue Service secured voluntary compliance in all but 195 cases.

But the freeze had also built up a veritable mountain of problems that the Pay Board and Price Commission had to try to solve. To no one's surprise, these brand-new institutions spent their first two months hopping from one crisis to the next while the backlog, if anything, grew larger. Considering some of their early difficulties, it is a wonder that the two boards got their frail machinery flying at all.

C. Jackson Grayson, Jr., is a decisive executive who likes and expects a modicum of orderliness. But when, at the urging of his old friend George Shultz, he left his post as dean of the Southern Methodist University School of Business and flew to Washington to become chairman of the Price Commission, he found nothing but a bare suite of offices. There was no staff preassembled, nor any clue on how and where to look for help. Grayson, whose motto is "somebody has to make it happen," picked up the phone and called the Civil Service for advice. The other six members of the commission were just as green as Grayson. "Imagine," he says, "getting seven people in a room without previous experience and expecting them to come up with guidelines in two weeks."

"Pipsqueaks" and "Hatchet Men"

Judge George Boldt faced not only the same staffing and housekeeping problems, but attacks on his personal qualifications as well. By the time the Pay Board had taken one of its first major decisions, not to grant retroactive pay increases—since reversed by congressional legislation—the labor members on the board were in full cry. George Meany regaled an AFL-CIO convention in Miami with a tale of how Labor Secretary James D. Hodgson first telephoned to broach Boldt's appointment and then called to say Boldt was out because he was "totally and completely unfit for this job. He just couldn't handle it."

Then, the way Meany tells it, there came a third call from Hodgson, saying Boldt was in. "I said, 'What the hell are you talking about? He's going to be chairman after your description?' He said, 'Well, there are some people around here who don't agree with my estimate of his abilities, and besides, we couldn't get anybody else.'" (Hodgson insists that he merely expressed "apprehension" about appointing Boldt, who has a top reputation as a jurist but little experience in labor matters.) Meany also denounced Virgil B. Day, a board member and vice president of General Electric, as a "pipsqueak," and Weber, a public member, as Nixon's "hatchet man." This vituperation was followed by leaks from other labor members of the Pay Board designed to show that its proceedings were nothing but chaotic and confused attempts by people who didn't know much about what they were doing. Boldt, when he was a tough, no-nonsense Federal judge, would have responded to such talk with a contempt citation. But in commendable show of restraint, he has limited himself to pointing out that if the board cannot function "with built-in provisions for fairness and equity," the only alternative will be rigid Government controls.

The size of the job ahead for Boldt and Grayson can be clearly seen on the top three floors of a new office building at Twentieth and M streets, where the Pay and Price boards eventually found quarters. Groups of harried business executives and their lawyers mill along the bare, narrow corridors, staring at crude, hand-lettered signs outside office doors and waiting to see they are not sure whom. The confusion is greatest on the sixth floor, where price increases are granted. Many requests have been rejected peremptorily because they have not been signed, as required, by the companies' chief executives. Members of the commission staff complain that all these supplicants are merely fouling up the works with their requests for instant action—which they are not likely to get.

Nearly 400,000 inquiries, complaints of violation, requests for approval of pay and price increases, and appeals for exception poured onto the Phase II mechanism during its first three weeks alone. One major problem was that the boards, neither guided nor restrained by precedent, were obliged to make up the rules as they went along. And the regulations that have so far been drafted are both voluminous and ambiguous.

Happy Times for Lawyers

The first price policy decisions, which essentially were statements of general principle, filled fifty typewritten pages. Many had the mark of having been hammered out by committees of nonlawyers, as indeed they were. For instance, a Pay Board interpretation and policy decision on merit and salary plans was so obscure that a press release was issued ten days later to clarify it, only to have some board members complain that the press release itself was inaccurate. The confusion resulting from these ambiguous directives has complicated the efforts of the more than three hundred field offices of the IRS [Internal Revenue Service] to handle the flood of inquiries and complaints from the public. Because corporations feel an imperative need to know where they stand, Washington law firms have found the coming of controls something of a bonanza, as have business advisory services that purport to be up-to-date on Phase II rulings. But the contradictory vagueness has left a poor first impression on just about everybody else.

At the Price Commission, where more than 1,200 applications for price increases landed within the first month—covering everything from ketchup to steel wool—Grayson is nevertheless optimistic about working off his backlog soon. He has begun handling some requests in batches by approving a single, across-the-board average figure for large corporations, which can spread the approved increase across their product lines however they please. If the commission had not taken this decision, says Peter Carpenter, its deputy executive director, it would have been faced with a million or more individual price decisions a year.

Grayson says he is surprised and gratified by the restraint that many companies have shown, asking for less of an increase than they could have justified under the commission's rules. He also cites a December poll, taken by his commission, indicating that half of the one thousand largest corporations did not intend in the near future to ask for price increases at all. This intention may be due, in part, to the unwillingness of corporations to disclose their books to the commission's controllers, or go through the red tape required to obtain approval. But at any rate it will work to restrain inflation over the short run.

The Pay Board has a harder job in that its decisions are more contentious and involve even more difficult issues of equity. They range from how to deal with a request for a pay increase from baseball star Vida Blue, who earned only $14,000 last year although he was voted the American League's most valuable player, to how to handle deferred or retroactive pay increases contained in contracts negotiated by the coal miners, the auto workers, and the machinists. A stronger hand than the Pay Board has shown so far is obviously needed if labor is to take on its share of the sacrifice.

But if and when the board cracks down, it faces the threat of a walkout by its five labor members and strikes by the unions concerned.

The Carrot Is Phase Three

The carrot for achieving success in Phase II is the prospect of arriving at Phase III and the end of controls. White House aides speak of wanting to end the wage-price program before "muscle and cartilage solidify around it." Connally has held out the promise that many of the controls can come off within a year—just which ones he has not said.

But such promises may be premature. Grayson personally thinks it is too early to tell when and if Nixon's target of 2 to 3 percent inflation will be achieved. He points out that because of the lags involved, and the slowness of economic reporting, there won't be any valid statistical measure of how well the program is working until spring. And he feels that the control mechanisms must be disassembled gradually rather than abruptly terminated. Other economists, like Walter Heller, go much further. They say that the country will never be able to return permanently to the kind of free-market system that operated before August 15.

At the start of 1972 the Nixon Administration had been able to get a handle on some of the economic disorders that led to the abrupt policy shift last August. In a whirlwind of year-end negotiations, the dollar was devalued as part of a broad realignment of currencies, and the surtax on imports was ended. And, at home, the rate of inflation has been slowed. Some of the underlying problems in the US economy, however, still remain to be dealt with. Arthur Burns has urged that the Government use the coming months to find out why the economy has become so prone to inflation. Is it, he asks, because of structural changes in the economy—because business and labor are abusing their economic power to a larger degree than before? Or did the normal growth in US productivity halt at the end of the 1960s for some reason or reasons unknown? "These are a few of the questions that we need to ask and try to resolve," Burns says, "in order to help assure that the controls of Phase II, once dismantled, will not be needed again in our lifetime."

V. IMPACT AND OUTLOOK

EDITOR'S INTRODUCTION

A detailed account of what happened once the President made his decision to administer controls was described in the first section of this book. But how did the nation react? And how did the economy respond? Those are different matters. This section takes a look at both questions.

The first article in the section deals with the immediate response to the President's announcement of Phase I. The second selection gives examples of what happened to individual people and describes some situations brought on by the freeze. The third relates how people in a New England community reacted to the freeze.

Phase II, with its wage and price review boards, created still another situation. In the fourth article, two reporters for the *Wall Street Journal*, visiting an Illinois town to see how people are responding to the new set of ground rules, find that while people are not discouraged they cannot say that they are much encouraged either. In the piece that follows Tom Wicker of the New York *Times*, also sampling the sentiment of Americans, finds the mood to be even less favorable toward the effects of controls. He concludes that this reaction could spell trouble for incumbent Republicans in the 1972 elections.

Indeed, as the next selection (from *Newsweek*) points out, there are many reasons for this. The article makes it clear that Phase II mechanisms have not worked as well as they might have. Some people have fared well under them, but many more have not.

Still, the outlook for the economy itself does seem brighter than it has been in recent years. In the section's last excerpt, Thomas Mullaney sums up the prevailing view that the economy—for all the discontent of some citizens—is definitely on the move again.

THE FIRST REPORT [1]

An outpouring of prepared statements and extemporaneous remarks from business executives, economists and politicians throughout the world followed almost immediately in the wake of President Nixon's announcement of sweeping changes in the American economy.

With the exception of that from labor leaders, domestic reaction to the various points of the Nixon program was almost uniformly favorable—particularly regarding the ninety-day freeze on wages, prices and rents. Reaction from abroad to those points in the President's program affecting foreign trade—the devaluation of the dollar by letting it "float" in exchange markets and the 10 percent surcharge on imports—was largely cautious, with vehemently negative statements emanating from business groups in West Germany and Japan.

Also discernible in the aftermath of the President's announcement was a maximum of confusion and uncertainty concerning implementation of certain aspects of the program. While the broad outline of the President's intentions was clearly understood, the details seemed unclear to many business officials throughout the country.

A lack of clarity, however, in no way alloyed the enthusiasm of most of the nation's top corporate executives for the economic changes. Indeed, most large companies pledged their cooperation for the duration of the wage-and-price freeze, and many officials predicted the results of the program in its entirety would be to stimulate capital expenditures and consumer spending and to lower unemployment— exactly those beneficial effects predicted by the President.

[1] Article, "Nixon's Economics," a *Wall Street Journal* Roundup. *Wall Street Journal.* p 1+. Ag. 17, '71. Reprinted with permission of the *Wall Street Journal.*

Back From a Binge

One such optimist is John T. Hackett, vice president, finance, for Cummins Engine Company. "Industry feels like the fellow who's been on a binge—now he has to tighten his belt and get back in shape," Mr. Hackett says. "It's strenuous, but he'll feel better for it."

Mr. Hackett says the wage-price freeze will force Cummins to rescind a previously announced 3.7 percent price increase on engines, which had been scheduled to take effect September 1 [1971]. He adds, however, "We assume our suppliers of foundry products will roll back their announced increases, too."

"Capital spending will show a good increase (in the fourth quarter)—perhaps 5 percent to 10 percent," Mr. Hackett predicts. "This will be reflected in increased employent in the machine tool, auto and construction industries, which will help the unemployment rate."

Executives throughout the country searched their lexicons for laudatory adjectives to describe the President's new economics:

—"A very good and forceful move at a critical time"—Richard S. Reynolds, Jr., chairman and president of Reynolds Metals Company

—"Excellent"—E. B. Barnes, president of Dow Chemical U.S.A.

—"Bold and timely"—Allison R. Maxwell Jr., chairman of Wheeling-Pittsburgh Steel Corporation

—"Bold, aggressive, decisive"—Raymond C. Firestone, chairman of Firestone Tire & Rubber Company

Galbraith's View

Despite such extravagant praise from the business community, the nation's economists seem somewhat more muted in their appreciation of the program. "The key problem . . . is that it's an emergency program," says Edwin H. Yeo III, vice president and economist for Pittsburgh National Bank. "The boat has sprung a leak, and we're stuffing some rags in the hole. But we have to come up with a credible long-range program" to deal with American economic and monetary difficulties.

Professor John Kenneth Galbraith of Harvard, while conceding that wage and price controls may help slow the nation's inflation, declares that "the President's program isn't as expansive as I think it should be. It would have been much better if the President increased grants to the cities to reduce unemployment. There are so many things the cities need. They could put on more police, help with housing programs, even clean the streets."

On the worldwide spectrum of criticism, however, Professor Galbraith's remarks are exceedingly temperate. The West German Chamber of Commerce and Industry, for example, called the 10 percent surcharge on imports a "heavy blow" to world trade. The French Auto Industry Federation expressed "hostility" to the same measure. And an official of the Japan External Trade Organization, a semiofficial trade promotion body, termed the surtax "one step short of a total suspension of imports on the part of the United States."

Between the extremes of accolades and barbs for the President's plan as a whole, a number of business officials and economists here and abroad have expressed praise for some points of the program, while at the same time voicing reservations about other facets. A point-by-point capsulation of this reaction:

Wage, Price and Rent Freeze: The response of most companies and economists is favorable, and many top corporate executives have pledged their immediate cooperation. However, the fact the freeze is only for ninety days has caused some executives to have misgivings concerning its ultimate effect. James F. Bere, president of Borg-Warner Corporation, for example, says the freeze won't be of any benefit if it "just delays or stores up the inevitable increases. The President's advisers will need all of that time to work out a satisfactory next step."

The freeze also has created considerable confusion in some quarters of the business community. Are previously announced price increases to be rescinded in every case? (Yes, if not in effect.) Should previously promised wage hikes not yet in effect be uniformly suspended for the duration of the freeze? (Yes.) Many executives say they just don't know.

The uncertainty is particularly acute in those industries that are currently being struck or have recently emerged from strikes. "We just don't know where we are. . . . We don't even know if we're going to be permitted to settle," says an official at Cleveland's Addressograph-Multigraph Corporation, where about 1,600 workers have been on strike since early June [1971].

Confusion also seems rampant in some railroad and copper companies with recently ratified labor contracts calling for price boosts.

Floating the Dollar: Floating the dollar, coupled with the 10 percent surcharge drew the most reaction from abroad. Comments were mixed. While cries of "protectionism" resounded in many capitals, a number of businessmen expressed cautious optimism. "In the longer term it is a healthy sign that [Britain's] largest customer is taking steps to set his house in order financially," says Alexander Stone, chairman of the British Bank of Commerce, Glasgow, Scotland.

In Israel, David Horowitz, governor of the Bank of Israel, Tel Aviv, says President Nixon's economic measures were "essential and (will) have a positive effect on world finance." In Sweden, Volvo, which has projected exports of 50,000 cars to the United States this year, says it isn't "seriously worried" by the surcharge.

But many are worried. The British National Association of Scottish Wool Manufacturers calls the surcharge a "bad blow" to the Scottish tweed trade. In a similar vein, a spokesman for Germany's Volkswagenwerk AG dubs the measure "a hard blow," adding that the giant auto maker is "terribly dependent" on US markets. And J. C. Whitelaw, executive vice president of the Canadian Manufacturers Association, says the Nixon economic package raises the specter of American isolationism, and creates the danger of a worldwide chain reaction.

NIP—OR TINGLE? [2]

"This was all thrown together overnight," admitted one White House aide of the President's surprise program on the economy. Then the aide added what turned out to be the understatement of the week: "There are bound to be some inequities and anomalies." A sampling of the first week's crop:

John Gluck, a twenty-seven-year-old junior-high-school teacher in Toms River, New Jersey, was one of thousands of teachers across the country who had been counting on a raise this fall. In his case, the money was earmarked to help pay for a new car—an American make, by the way—and to meet mortgage payments on his home. "Being a teacher," he said glumly last week, "I felt I could rely on an annual salary increase." With one child and another coming, Gluck may opt for an additional way to boost his income: reenlisting in the Army Reserve. A first lieutenant, Gluck would have been released next month, but now he's relying on a promotion to the rank of captain for some extra money.

With most football, basketball and hockey players' contracts becoming effective in the fall, professional athletes felt a special nip from the freeze. New York Jet defensive back Mike Battle, who hadn't signed his contract when the freeze was announced, chose to play out his option at 90 percent of last year's contract and added: "If this thing doesn't break soon, I'll be a free agent." Chicago Bear star receiver Dick Gordon, a contract holdout, was told by coach Jim

[2] From "The Freeze Can Nip—or Tingle." *Newsweek*. 78:14-15. Ag. 30, '71. Copyright Newsweek, Inc. August 30, 1971. Reprinted by permission.

Dooley: "Well, you don't have to worry anymore, Dick. The President settled your contract." Even the athletes who signed contracts before August 14 [1971] may have to accept last year's salaries. New rates normally take effect at the start of the sport's season; during the training period, pro football players are paid $13 a day expense money. "Maybe we'll have to play the whole season for thirteen bucks a game," yelled one Bear during a workout. "Even for George Halas, that would be low," one of the other players standing on the sidelines replied, referring to the notoriously tight-fisted Bears' owner.

The frantic activity at the stock exchanges that followed the President's announcement meant more commissions for the traders. It meant, too, that a seat on the New York Stock Exchange would cost more; a membership sold last Thursday went for $205,000, up $5,000 from the last sale on August 9. A seat on the Exchange, apparently, is exempt from the Administration's freeze. According to an exchange spokesman, "A membership isn't a commodity or a service. It's a privilege, really."

Stuart Long, who runs Long News Service out of the Texas capitol building in Austin, has a policy of paying his reporters $5 weekly above Newspaper Guild standards. After the President's announcement, he discovered that two of his staffers were up for $10 a week raises on September 1. Long told the two men: "I'll go ahead with the raises, of course, on the condition that one of you will pay the $5,000 fine [for violating the wage-price order] and the other will agree to go to Leavenworth."

One of the first reported violators of the President's price freeze was Edward Sullivan, the seventy-year-old owner of the Jolly Washer, Inc., a coin-operated laundromat in Fairmount, New York, just outside Syracuse. It seems Sullivan had announced price hikes—from 30 to 35 cents on some washers, from 35 to 50 cents on others—last month, to be effective August 9. But his new coin equipment didn't arrive until last week; he then ignored the freeze and raised his prices, whereupon he was promptly reported by a customer to the Office of Emergency Preparedness in New York City. Replied Sullivan to the charge: "It's either this or welfare."

One of the few food categories exempted from the freeze, because of its major seasonal fluctuations, was raw farm produce such as fresh vegetables and fruits, eggs and honey. Processed food is subject to the freeze—which led the Cost of Living Council into some involved discussions on what food was processed and what was raw. Finally, the council ruled, cucumbers are exempt but not pickled cucumbers. Pasteurized milk is also considered processed. Oranges, even though packaged, are exempt, but frozen orange juice is, indeed, frozen. Some stores apparently chose not to wait for clarification of the freeze announcement. A registered nurse, whose $50-a-month raise had been put on ice, was shopping in a Houston supermarket the morning after the President's speech. "It looks," she said, "like everything in the store has gone up 5 or 6 cents since I was here last week." The checker nodded: "They were busy last night marking them up."

Most manufacturers and retailers of seasonal clothing had already determined the prices for their winter items. Among those who had not was Ski-Craft Manufacturing Company, maker of children's winter slacks, which was caught with 20 percent of its goods unticketed. "I was planning a 7 percent increase but I won't raise prices now," pledged owner Bernard Horowitz. Retailers of snowmobiles and other winter hardware claim that this year's models will be modified, so prices can be modified too. High-fashion houses make the same claim about winter and spring apparel. But for some of the big retailers that use mail-order catalogs, there's an added problem. In November, Sears, Roebuck and Company, for instance, must begin printing the thirteen million copies of its spring-summer catalog for 1972. With the possibility that the freeze may be extended, Sears won't know for sure whether it can raise any prices in the new catalog, or whether it will have to hold the line on all of the thousands of items it offers.

At the giant Western Electric Company plant in suburban Cicero, Illinois, the first checks containing a 78-cent-an-hour increase for 18,000 workers had been printed and were ready for distribution last Tuesday. But after the President's speech, the company confiscated the checks and printed new ones at the old wage rate. Adding to the confusion: the plant did pay the higher rate, plus retroactive pay, to those employees who drew their advance vacation pay the Friday before the freeze.

ONE TOWN'S VIEWS [3]

David Carlo, a sixteen-year-old junior at Taconic High School in Pittsfield, Massachusetts, isn't sure how he feels about the freeze on wages and prices.

On the one hand he's glad prices have stopped zooming upward, and even sees the pause as an opportunity. "Last week I spent $33 in ten minutes on two pairs of pants and a shirt," says David. "I'm buying now before the price goes up," he explains.

On the other hand, David doesn't like the way the freeze has affected his family's income. "My Dad fixed up the bathroom in an apartment the family rents out. But now he can't jump the rent."

David's mixed feelings about the freeze are echoed by many other people—not only in this New England town of 60,000, but in towns, cities, and farms across this nation. Almost everyone likes the freeze on prices of things they buy. But few people care for the freeze on the price of things they sell. Some, like teachers who had been promised higher salaries and now can't have them (at least during the freeze) are deeply disappointed or even angry. At the same time a

    [3] Article, "One Town's Hot & Cold Views of the Freeze," by George A. Nikolaieff. *Senior Scholastic.* 99:11-13. O. 11, '71. From *Senior Scholastic*, October 11, 1971. Copyright © 1971 by Scholastic Magazines, Inc. Used by permission of the publisher.

great many businessmen feel the controls are long overdue and should be extended past their present ninety-day limit. But many labor leaders feel the terms of the freeze are unfair to labor.

Nearly everyone's waiting anxiously to see what happens and what new rules are made for the time after November 13 [1971] when the freeze ends.

"The working man is held down by the freeze," says John Foley, Chief Steward of IUE Local 255, which represents most of the 10,000 people working for the General Electric Company in Pittsfield. Members of the IUE (International Union of Electrical Radio and Machine Workers) won't get the 8-cent-an-hour cost of living increase that they'd been expecting this month.

The only thing nearly everyone agrees on is that the freeze is the most sudden, widespread jolt within recent memory to the way Americans earn a living. Until mid-August the Nixon Administration had seemed content to follow a hands-off policy toward the nation's economy. Then, in a quick reversal, it announced a series of measures all aimed at halting inflation while pepping up the pace of business activity.

Some parts of the new program—including such incentives as lower sales taxes on automobiles—need congressional approval. Their impact has yet to be felt. The effect of others, like a 10 percent levy on imports, will also take a while to evaluate simply because of the time and distances involved in international trade.

But the ninety-day freeze on wages and prices has had an immediate impact on almost everyone. It is especially apparent in a community such as Pittsfield, whose economy includes a large industrial plant as well as other businesses.

Take Everet Murch, a community relations specialist at General Electric. "I was due for a raise on August 15," he says, the very day the freeze took effect. "The timing couldn't have been worse."

He's not the only one feeling blue. A standard business practice is to give management and professional employees an annual salary review. With the freeze on, all salary reviews are canceled. "The only thing I know is that my husband won't be getting a raise this year," snaps a well-dressed woman hurrying along North Street.

Some of the most disgruntled are the 750 teachers in the Pittsfield school system. "They got trapped by the freeze," explains assistant school superintendent Leon Siegal. All of them had been expecting an increase of about 6 percent, or $300, for this school year. But because their contracts didn't begin until September 1, they can't have the extra money. (Ironically, the total funds come to about $150,000, according to Siegal. The town has already collected this money from taxpayers, and town officials will now have to figure out what to do with it.)

"I'm a little disappointed," says Mrs. John Arienti, an attractive grandmother who works as a teacher's aide. She had been expecting a 15-cent-an-hour increase. Her disappointment, though, is mild compared with her son-in-law's. A full-time teacher and the father of two, he had been counting heavily on the boost and now "is very bitter" that he won't be getting it, Mrs. Arienti says.

In Washington, D.C., George Meany, president of the AFL-CIO, has said that the wage-freeze portion of the President's program is unfair to labor. The working man whose wages are frozen, he argues, suffers more than the businessman or business enterprise that has no limits on the profits it can make.

IUE's local leadership agrees. "On October 25 we were to start the cost of living increase," says Chief Steward Foley. "The cost of that increase to us has already been calculated in GE prices. Since the employees aren't getting this money, all this does is increase the company's profits."

In many other ways, though, the very same wage freeze benefits workers. "We've got one (housing) development right now whose existence depends entirely on not just this freeze but the chance that controls will be extended after mid-November," says Edward Carman, the youthful president of Berkshire Housing Development Corporation.

Carman is talking about a $1.8 million renovation of a large building into 90 inexpensive apartments for elderly people. Berkshire is a nonprofit company, and the way it raises money and finances its projects is very complicated. If it is able to make the renovation it will provide a good number of jobs. Furthermore, the longer wages and prices hold steady for the builder, the less he will be charging the Berkshire Corporation. The less Berkshire pays out, to contractors, the lower the rent they can charge the elderly people who will live there.

"It goes all the way back to the tenant," says Carman of the freeze's effect. "The ninety days is just a start. We have a great interest in longer term controls."

Even Mrs. Arienti, who is disappointed about her wage increase, is not unmindful of the effects of inflation. She realizes that the price of her groceries—which had been rising at a furious clip—has also been frozen. (Some food prices can still go up, however—nonprocessed foods, such as fresh fruit, for example, can go up in price.) "It really irritated me the way prices kept rising," she says.

"I suppose," she says, weighing the frozen prices against her frozen wages, "it probably balances out for me."

Curiously, a great many merchants—precisely the people whose prices have been frozen—are in favor of the freeze. "I'm all for this thing," says Emanuel Cohen, owner of Michael's shoe store near the town's common. "It will help me keep some of my customers. After all, a lot of them are straining to pay the prices right now."

Cohen goes on to explain that over the past several years prices have risen so fast that some of his customers have had to downgrade—buy cheaper shoes. And, while he doesn't say

so, the ultimate effect of downgrading is that people stop
patronizing a quality shop like his and seek out a place
where cheaper shoes are sold.

Adams Supermarkets, a local grocery chain, even tried
to get price rollbacks for its customers. When suppliers refused to withdraw a price increase on certain products—
which would in turn have meant an increase at the retail
store level—the supermarket simply refused to carry their
merchandise any longer.

Not all merchants, however, have been all that scrupu-
lous. Some are hard at work on gimmicks that will let them
get around the freeze and increase their prices. A few winter
ski resorts, for instance, are planning to stretch the amount
of time they will operate their tows. Technically, since this
is an increase in service, they're entitled to make an additional charge for it. Such actions violate the spirit of what the
freeze is all about—a nationwide effort to halt inflation.

But not all ski resort operators play that game. "For me,"
says Paul Bousquet, operator of a nearby ski area, "It's difficult to pass on an increase by extending hours. That's
immoral."

PHASE II IN DECATUR [4]

As a consumer, Ray Livasy is happy with President
Nixon's wage and price controls. "They've slowed down inflation, no doubt about that, and it's sure welcome," he says.

But as president of Milliken National Bank, the largest
bank in this central Illinois city of 90,000, Mr. Livasy takes
a somewhat different view. "Businessmen here have been
holding off to see how things turn out before making the
sort of moves that might get our economy going again," he
says. "As of now, I can't say I'm encouraged about our prospects for '72. 'Not discouraged' would be a better way to
put it."

[4] Article, "Citizens of an Illinois Town, After Four Months of Economic
Controls, Increasingly Doubt Gains," by Frederick C. Klein and Terry P.
Brown, staff correspondents. Wall Street Journal. p 20. Ja. 3, '72. Reprinted
with permission of the Wall Street Journal.

Mr. Livasy isn't alone. In fact, his dual appraisal of the President's new economic policies is widely shared in Decatur, even by persons who view the business scene from a less advantageous perspective.

... The President's wage-price freeze was greeted here by a wave of gratitude. Approbation all but drowned out the disappointment of those whose pay raises were delayed by the move and the uncertainty of some about where it all might lead. Now that the freeze has been replaced by an increasingly complex set of wage and price rules, a return visit reveals continued general approval of the President's plan. At the same time, however, there seems to be increasing doubt over whether controls will help turn back the high unemployment and lack of business expansion that has plagued this community—and others—for many months.

What's Next?

"With things the way they are today—the layoffs and all —I can't see buying anything big," says Mrs. Dorothy Brown, a tester at a local General Electric Company plant and the wife of a truck driver. "You don't know what's going to happen next."

Others express considerable concern about how the new controls will be administered. Some merchants are decidedly uneasy about organized labor's plan to monitor their prices through a so-called watchdog committee; it smacks of "vigilantism," the merchants say. Among workers, including union members, there is concern that large, powerful unions will be able to push big pay raises through the Government wage board while others will have to settle for less.

Decatur was picked as a place to examine reactions to controls because of its central location and economic diversity. The city is best known as a corn and soybean processing center; A. E. Staley Manufacturing Company and Archer-Daniels-Midland Company, two large producers of agricultural products, are based here. But Decatur also has a large manufacturing work force making everything from heavy construction equipment to phonographs, and it's the shopping center for a region of 450,000 persons.

In a number of important ways, the Nixon economic program seems to be serving Decatur well. Except for some widely noted jumps in the price of a few uncontrolled food items (heads of lettuce lately have been selling for as much as 59 cents in local groceries, up from 29 cents last summer), it's agreed that retail prices generally haven't risen much from freeze levels. This stability, retailers say, helped contribute to brisk Christmas business hereabouts; and while merchants say their overall sales gain from 1970 might not match the 8 percent to 10 percent retail advance forecast for the nation as a whole, the final figure probably won't fall much short.

Decatur sales of new homes and American-made automobiles have also been helped by the Nixon program. Home builders, aided by a lowering of mortgage interest rates and a greater availability of mortgage funds, say they are enjoying their best year since 1965. Sales of new US cars were stimulated by the mid-August to mid-November price freeze, and dealers are hoping that the recent repeal of the 7 percent Federal excise tax will offset price increases of 2.5 percent to 3 percent just put through by American auto makers.

But the other side of the picture is quite gloomy. Decatur-area unemployment in November stood at 3,075 persons, or 5.1 percent of the work force. This was down only slightly from the prefreeze July rate of 5.3 percent and it's expected that figures for December will show another jump in local unemployment.

Caterpillar Tractor, the city's largest employer, laid off 325 workers at its construction equipment plant here in November on top of some 300 layoffs in June, reducing its local work force to less than 4,000. The layoffs were the company's biggest here in more than a decade, and a plant official says no quick recall of workers is planned.

The outlook is much the same with other employers. General Electric's peak employment at its hi-fi plant here this year was 1,400, down from 2,000 in 1970, and prospects for 1972 are "flat," an official says.

Trimming Costs

A. E. Staley's work force here on September 30 numbered 2,721, down from 3,072 on the same date in 1970. The drop stemmed from transfers and attrition, and no upturn is in sight. "If anything, the probability that controls will make price increases more difficult to come by should intensify our need to trim costs in all areas," says a spokesman.

Other observers say the President's declared intention to hold price boosts nationally to an average of 2.5 percent has inhibited local firms from embarking on the kind of capital spending programs that might spur employment.

This spending caution on the part of businessmen is being matched by many Decatur consumers. According to the Federal Home Loan Bank of Chicago, money is flowing into area savings institutions at more than three times the rate of 1970.

An explanation for the seeming paradox of savings deposits rising along with retail sales is provided by Sam Loeb, proprietor of a downtown men's clothing store. Directing a reporter to a rack of suits priced from $200 to $345, Mr. Loeb declares that sales are "great." He adds: "There are a lot of people in this town who are making good money, and they're spending it. They are executives and professional people. They aren't bothered by layoffs and such." This reasoning is shared by other local merchants. Some people in Decatur are bothered by layoffs and make no bones about the fact that they are currently trying to hold on to as much money as they can. "There are rumors of more layoffs at the plant, and I don't want to be caught short," says Dennis Ray, a twenty-six-year-old Vietnam veteran who works at Caterpillar.

A Sure Thing

One thing that's sure to happen soon here, as elsewhere, is that prices are going to start rising again in earnest. Cars bearing the auto companies' new, increased tags have begun to arrive on dealers' lots. The local electric utility has a request pending for a 15.3 percent rate increase. And local property taxes are expected to climb by 3 percent to 5 percent in 1972 as a result of the passage of library and transit bond issues.

"Nobody wants to be the first" retail store to raise prices, "but we have to start looking for increases around the first of the year," says Earl Ownbey, manager of Carson's seven-story department store in downtown Decatur.

Price controls have thus far rested easily on this community. The local office of the Internal Revenue Service, which is charged with overseeing the new regulations, reports it has had only a handful of price or rent complaints since the freeze took effect in August. IRS men say all were based on misunderstandings by the merchant, landlord or the person placing the claim and were easily disposed of.

But price matters are expected to become more complicated after January 1, the date all retailers must post lists of freeze ceiling prices. And the increasing complexity of the rules governing what businessmen can and can't do could well complicate matters further. The IRS has only two full-time employees assigned here to watch prices, rents and wages in a four-county area, and the unit admits it will need help from private citizens to root out violations.

Organized labor, however, is moving to take a hand in policing prices. Decatur's ninety local unions, following the direction of AFL-CIO chief George Meany, have formed what they call the Watchdog Committee for Price Control. Its chairman is Raymond Maulden, former president of a rubber workers' union local.

Mr. Maulden says his unit is distributing copies of Government price regulations to "more than one hundred" wives of union members throughout the region. The women will be assigned to periodically check certain retailers for possible violations. "If a complaint is made, we'll send a committee around to talk to the store owner," says Mr. Maulden. "If we can't settle it ourselves, we'll call in the IRS."

Businessmen here don't relish the prospect of being forced to justify their price moves to an ad hoc union group. Retailers aren't anxious to make statements on the matter, but James Patrick, executive vice president of the local chamber of commerce, says, "The whole thing smacks of a vigilante operation. Our inclination now is to watch and see what happens, but if things get out of hand we might have to take steps."

Problems are also looming here in the area of wages. Despite the Administration's 5.5 percent guideline on pay boosts, the largest labor contract negotiated in this area since the freeze began resulted in pay increases, effective November 14, of 8.7 percent for some 1,700 workers at A. E. Staley. Another big increase (about 10 percent) is scheduled to take effect February 1 at an Archer-Daniels-Midland plant under a pact negotiated last year.

Keeping Up With the Mine Workers

Union leaders here make it clear they'll try to get all they can in coming talks with employers. "Look at the mine workers' union—they got 15.5 percent," says Dwight Patrick, an AFL-CIO staff representative and a member of the executive board of the Decatur Trades & Labor Assembly, a multiunion group. "If they can get it, why shouldn't we?" he asks.

On the other hand, companies whose employees don't belong to unions say they intend to regard 5.5 percent as a wage-boost ceiling. "That's what the President wants, and that's what we will pay," says an officer of one Decatur bank.

The sales manager of another local firm says he sees the pay guideline as "a chance to put my men back on a merit pay schedule." He explains: "We'll use 5.5 percent as an average. Men who produce will get 8 percent or 10 percent. Men who don't will get a little or nothing. I never did buy the idea that people should get raises automatically, just because they show up for work."

Such discrepancies aren't lost on Decatur wage earners. "The big men—labor management—will get what they want and the rest of us will be out in the cold," says a butcher who adds he was supposed to get a pay raise during the freeze but still hasn't received it. "With the job situation being as tight as it is, I just have to sit and take it."

Other Losers

Others here also rate as losers because of the new economic policies. Sellers of foreign cars, for example, have been hurt. Harold Lipe, owner of Lipe Motors, a Datsun dealer, says he sold thirty of the Japanese-made cars in the fifteen days after the President announced the freeze as buyers hurried to beat price increases caused by higher import duties; but since then his business has been off about 50 percent from year-ago levels. Volkswagen and Toyota dealers report similar slides.

Farmers are critical of the way controls have affected them. The prices they receive for their produce aren't controlled and have dropped in recent months; but the prices they pay for equipment are on their way up again with the lifting of the freeze. "I had to increase my yield to stay even this year, and there's a limit to how often I can do that," says Marion Alsup, who runs a farm near town. "The President hasn't done us farmers any favors."

But Mr. Alsup and many others in and around Decatur are glad that the freeze and the new controls have been holding down the price of many things they buy. "Without the controls, things probably would be a lot worse than they are now. At least he (President Nixon) seems to be trying," says Mrs. Charles Harris, of nearby Taylorville.

"If the controls work the way they are supposed to, it will be good for everyone," says John Blasingame, a sales supervisor for Illinois Power Company. "I just hope the people in charge of carrying them out don't let things get out of hand."

DOUBTS REMAIN [5]

The economists and the big businessmen may be predicting a great year for business and wage-earners but on the assembly line and in the shopping centers, the American people aren't so sure.

Economic projections mean less to them than the price of groceries. Estimates of the Gross National Product can sound like one more empty political promise. Wage and price controls may look like a mess, and an unfair mess at that. Devaluing the dollar is of little interest to a worker without a job. Small tax cuts, like those due this year, are not particularly impressive to a man trying to put his kids through college.

Talking to a reporter, A. J. Joyce, Jr., of Pine Bluff, Arkansas, put in perspective the prospect of getting back a few tax dollars next April. "That's customarily the way I catch up on my pledge at church," he said.

None of this will be news to Richard M. Nixon, whose chances for reelection . . . may be substantially influenced by whether the man and the woman in the street think wage-price controls are working and the economy is on the move.

Conventional American political wisdom holds that an improving economic situation will help Mr. Nixon at the polls next November, and vice versa. The President himself

[5] New York *Times* National Economic Survey entitled "But Doubt Nags American People," by Tom Wicker, associate editor. New York *Times*. p 1-2. Ja. 9, '72. © 1972 by The New York Times Company. Reprinted by permission.

is said to be a profound believer in that idea, which was clearly one of the reasons for his plunge into wage and price controls and the other measures of his New Economic Policy.

But the conventional wisdom tends to get out of date, and in recent years some analysts have seen other issues becoming as important as the pocketbook issue—or more so. In the general spread of affluence since World War II, they have argued, and in the greatly changed social conditions of the nation, some voters now worry more about the "quality of life"—a range of issues that runs all the way from law-and-order through school busing to ecological questions.

A spot survey taken in late December in various parts of the country for the New York *Times* gave some support to both theories, without refuting either. Above all, however, it suggested that Americans, a skeptical breed when it comes to political promises, are taking a wait-and-see attitude toward Mr. Nixon's new economic program.

Of ten persons checked in the Milwaukee area, for instance, nine thought they were personally worse off this Christmas than last and none could see how the Nixon economic program was helping much. Yet, none of the ten was planning on that basis to change his presidential voting plans.

Paul Dippolito, a Pittsburgh steel worker who has been in and out of a job last fall and this winter, said an "undeclared war" caused inflation, which was "not Nixon's fault." On the other hand, he said, "Nixon flopped miserably on law and order. When I think about who to vote for in 1972, I'll see what Nixon does on law and order."

Similarly, a Pittsburgh telephone worker, Jay O. Elker, shrugged off what he called "fluctuations" in the economy as only to be expected. He said he was "more concerned about politicians who want the vote of people who don't work."

The more conventional view was well stated by another Pittsburgher, Allegheny County Commissioner Thomas Foerster, a Democrat:

> If the economy gets worse and unemployment continues to rise, they'll take it out on Nixon. This is the one issue that can defeat the President. I don't think the Vietnam war will do it. It will revolve around jobs, if people are working. If they have no confidence in what the President is doing about getting people back to work, they'll vote against him.

Union men in many areas seemed to maintain traditional emphasis on the economic issues. And in Miami, where unemployment is now over 6 percent, Ed Stephenson, an AFL-CIO official, asserted a wide-spread view—that wage-price controls are unfair to the "little guy."

Another American political tradition is distrust of politicians, and there seems to be plenty of that when it comes to the Nixon economic program. Mrs. Hubert Garrison, a housewife in San Diego, said the President "appears to me to be playing a game, playing off business against labor." Conservative southern California is one area where Mr. Nixon appears to be in trouble with those who once supported him most strongly—in trouble not merely because of the economy, but because of his overtures to Communist China, the ouster of Taiwan from the United Nations, and the President's income program for welfare recipients.

This right-wing reaction against Mr. Nixon is reported to center on a conservative group called United Republicans of California, which has its greatest strength in the President's legal residence, Orange County. An effort apparently is being made to get an uncommitted California delegation to pressure Mr. Nixon at the San Diego convention.

Moreover, in the same general area of southern California, unemployment is still high and anti-Nixon sentiment among workers is reported rising.

Officials of the Hod Carriers and Laborers said their unemployment rolls were the worst in seventeen and a half years, and a Ladies Garment Worker spokesman argued that "freezing wages was not a fair shake to the working man when food prices continue to rise."

If right-wing reaction should combine with wage-earner discontent in southern California—where Mr. Nixon must roll up a big vote if he is to carry the nation's most populous state—that could be a problem of serious dimensions for the President.

On the other hand, in Texas—another state crucial to the President's reelection plans—a spot survey found him in good shape. This was partially due to the fact that former Governor John B. Connally is now, in effect, Mr. Nixon's economic manager as Secretary of the Treasury.

A surprising number of people did not blame Mr. Nixon for the economy and its difficulties—including some who do not plan to vote for him, like Donald J. Hayward, an optician in Quincy, Massachusetts. "Somebody else would have had the same problems," he said. "I believe Nixon deserves recognition because he tried to do something to fight inflation. This is the first concerted attempt to stop it."

Others put the blame elsewhere. Mrs. Harvey F. Moore of Chicago, a housewife whose husband is a photoengraver, said she didn't think the economy would improve "until the welfare and tax situations are taken care of. The whole burden rests on the middle-class people, who are being taxed to death to support others. Something has to be done about the tax structure."

Illinois Republicans, particularly Governor Richard G. Ogilvie, are considered in political trouble because of the new state income tax they helped institute in 1969.

But wherever voters were checked, the old pocketbook attitude was never hard to find. A working woman in Dorchester, Massachusetts, put it bluntly to the *Times's* interviewer: "I voted for Nixon in 1968, but I'm damn sorry I did. My son graduated from college this year and can't get a job."

Thus, Mr. Nixon would be counting his votes long before they can be hatched if he came to the risky conclusion that the economic moves he has made so far mean that the economy necessarily will be working for his reelection. . . . Assuming that the pocketbook still is the "gut issue" of American politics, there appear to be more things that might go wrong than right by November.

The mere existence of wage-price controls is not a lasting asset. If Mr. Nixon is to derive votes from the Phase II apparatus, it has to be seen to work—specifically to reduce prices without undue penalties in lost wages and unemployment. To what extent such gains will be a reality by next fall is the big question.

Moreover, wage-price controls could prove to be a liability in at least two ways. One would be if they became a visible bureaucratic nightmare, tangled in their own problems and inadequacies—as the Pay Board already seems in danger of becoming—or if they were so administered as to be riddled with infuriating loopholes and inequities.

The other danger in wage-price controls lies in expansive voter expectations. The Field Poll of California reported in November, for instance, that the new Nixon economic program had strengthened the President's standing with the voters, with 66 percent favoring his moves. But it also reported that 42 percent of the respondents expected personally to be financially better off in November 1972.

That 42 percent might not think so much of Mr. Nixon if, in fact, they know themselves to be no better off, or worse off, when he solicits their votes next fall.

BENDING CONTROLS [6]

When the Nixon Administration unveiled Phase II of its New Economic Policy . . . , the public was given the impression—for strong political reasons, if not for valid eco-

[6] From, "Controls: Bruised, Bent, Broken." *Newsweek*. 74:69+. Ja. 31, '72. Copyright Newsweek, Inc. January 31, 1972. Reprinted by permission.

nomic ones—that the Big Brothers on the Pay Board and the Price Commission would be zealously watching every nook and cranny of the nation's economy. The word was that a corner grocer could no more get away with price gouging on a can of peas than Big Steel could boost the price of a ton of rolled steel—and woe betide organized labor if it squeezed from management a wage increase worth more than 5.5 percent!

All this, of course, has proved to be pure fantasy—an amiable deception. But even so it could boomerang badly come election time. For in the past, whether they were administered well or poorly, price and wage controls have tended to lose popularity after the first burst of enthusiasm. And this process has already begun for Mr. Nixon. "I think most people are coming to believe it's all a farce," says consumer advocate Steven Schwab in Chicago. "And if that's true, then the President is in trouble."

There's no dispute that, in the weeks since Phase II took its tenuous hold on the economy, the Administration's wage and price guidelines have been thoroughly bruised, bent or broken. In some instances, it was the fault of the regulatory groups themselves, with the Pay Board the worst offender. The board's first major action was its blithe approval of a 16.8 percent first-year wage increase for soft-coal miners. And though the board recently sliced back an aerospace industry wage boost to 8 percent, even that was well over the supposedly absolute ceiling of 7 percent adopted as policy in late December [1971]. In its operation, Washington observers agree, the Pay Board has been hobbled by the inexperience of chairman George Boldt, a former Federal-court judge, and by personality conflicts. When labor representatives aren't feuding with the businessmen on the board, both are apt to be tangling with Arnold Weber, a bright but abrasive former professor at the University of Chicago.

A Tale of Two Bottles

While the Price Commission has been far more effective than the Pay Board—at least, at its Washington headquarters —its enforcement machinery at the grass-roots level has been either hit-or-miss or nonexistent. In northern Illinois, Internal Revenue Service agents found that fully 70 percent of 20,000 retailers checked did not have posted lists of pre-freeze prices. In Chicago, an irate woman stormed into the offices of the National Consumers Union with two identical bottles of Vitamin C—one bought during the early days of Phase II for $1.39, and the other purchased . . . [in January 1972] for $3.57. And New Yorkers, many of them with frozen paychecks, have already forked out or will soon absorb hefty increases in the cost of electricity, gas, telephone service, taxes, rents and transportation.

The list goes on and on, and with it goes public confidence in the effectiveness and fairness of the controls program. "I remember back in World War II," recalls a supermarket manager in San Francisco, "the Government did the job right. They had people watching prices everywhere. This time, no one is watching." Adds Father Robert McEwen, a Boston College professor who surveyed price-posting violations: "The role of consumers has never been clear. At one time, consumers are encouraged to report suspected violations. But in the next breath, consumers are warned that it is virtually impossible for them to judge whether a price increase is legally justified or not."

The Power and the Gravy

Nor are consumers the only ones with a gripe. Non-unionized workers don't have even token representation on the tripartite Pay Board, and they are finding that their wages are the most effectively controlled part of the economy. Among unions, the Pay Board spreads the gravy less on considerations of equity than in deference to sheer economic power. "Big unions with a lot of muscle can get pretty much what they want," says AFL-CIO economist Nat Goldfinger, "and the little unions are left out in the cold." And as the coal industry learned to its consternation, the mere fact that the Pay Board approves an outsize wage boost doesn't mean that the Price Commission will let an employer add the extra cost to his prices.

Mr. Nixon's controllers insist that most of the confusion is due to the necessarily hasty improvisation of the whole program. "We wound up with obviously a far less tidy mechanism than you could have had with total controls," Donald Rumsfeld, executive director of the Cost of Living Council, conceded to *Newsweek*'s Rich Thomas. But at least as much of the trouble could be traced to a highly political decision. Many economic theorists argue, and the Administration's experts agree, that it would have been enough to clamp controls only on the biggest industries and unions whose wage and price decisions could be made almost regardless of economic conditions. But for window dressing, the controls were applied to nearly everyone and then allowed to go unenforced.

With public disillusion rising last week, the COLC announced a new set of "refinements" of the rules—in effect dialing back to legalize the most widespread kinds of noncompliance. The council eased rent controls to free about 42 percent of the nation's rented housing units from supervision, and decontrolled all retail-sales establishments with gross sales of less than $100,000 a year—some 75 percent of the stores in the country.

How effective has the whole exercise been? So far, the returns are as confused as the controls program itself. First-year increases in union contracts, for instance, actually rose a bit to an average of 15 percent in the third quarter of 1971, which included most of the freeze. The wholesale price index dropped slightly during the three-month wage-price freeze, but shot up by eight tenths of 1 percent in December. The Administration said that was "expected," as was a rise of four tenths of a point in . . . [the] consumer price index—the first signs of the "big bulge" in prices that had been predicted to follow the freeze.

If the Administration's predictions continue to come true, the bulge will flatten again in two months or so, inflationary psychology will wane and both prices and wage settlements will subside comfortably below their officially permitted ceilings. The figures to prove this won't be on the books until May or June, at the very earliest. But already there is rising speculation, both in and out of official circles in Washington, as to how soon the controls apparatus can be dismantled. Some observers, such as Columbia University economist Jacob Mincer, expect an end before the election; others, like labor official Frank White of the San Francisco Bay Area AFL-CIO, predict: "Now that Nixon has his hands on controls, I don't believe he'll ever let go."

In truth, he may not. Controls were imposed in the first place because the Administration was convinced, to its alarm, that conventional economic remedies were failing and new, unknown forces were at work: despite a recession that had raised unemployment to the 6 percent level, inflation was spinning unabated. If the new conditions prove permanent, some form of controls may be needed indefinitely—and some of Mr. Nixon's top advisers are at least half convinced that this is the case. Others, however—notably budget director George Shultz and Herbert Stein, chairman of the Council of Economic Advisers—are adamantly opposed. . . .

This internal debate has surfaced in the form of contradictory signals and speculation by top officials as to when controls may be lifted. Finally, Treasury Secretary John Connally intervened to lay down a firm line banning further speculation. Controls, he told a group of businessmen . . . [in late January 1972] are "the only game in town," and they will last as long as they are needed.

Nonetheless, the question remains quivering in the economic air. It seems clear enough that the President himself would be delighted to lift controls before November. But to do so without clear evidence that inflation was quiescent would pose still greater hazards for a second term. At the same time, rising public resentment over the inequities of the program could push Mr. Nixon to the opposite tack: clamping down even tougher controls to prove his fairness.

"We Mean Business"

The best bet now is for a combination of the two—an end to the pretense of controls in areas where they don't really matter and enforcement is impossible, and at least the semblance of tough enforcement of the controls that are left. . . . [At the end of January 1972] for instance, the Cost of Living Council announced that it had filed lawsuits against seventy retail firms, including auto dealers, liquor stores and pet shops, for failing to post base-price lists. The sudden surge of law-enforcement activity produced more than thirteen times as many cases as have been filed since Phase II began. . . . "We're at the point where we're going to enforce," Rumsfeld vowed. "You're going to see more and more suits filed. People are going to get the message that this thing is serious and that we mean business."

Maybe so, and that would certainly help to defuse the potential time bomb in Mr. Nixon's closet. But it seems likely that no matter how evenhanded the enforcement from now on, the only convincing sign of success will be an easing of the pinch on the wage earner's wallet. Without clear evidence that inflation is really under control, Mr. Nixon would suffer heavily in . . . [the 1972] election. But if the controls do their work—and barring catastrophe on some other front —that alone could well be enough to insure his reelection.

ECONOMY ON AN EXPRESS TRACK [7]

Unless some unforeseen political or economic obstacle derails it, the American economy should be speeding on an express track in 1972, even picking up momentum as the year progresses.

All of the reliable gauges of business activity and prospects were giving positive readings as 1971 ended.

They pointed toward a substantial gain of 9 or 10 percent in total economic activity in . . . [1972]—which would be a record jump of some $100 billion. If realized, it would put the United States back on the remarkable growth path that prevailed for nine years in the 1960s.

The economic indicators showed, too, that, despite a full catalog of challenges, complexities and uncertainties, the year just past provided a recovery from the moderate recession of 1969-1970. It closely followed the predictions made for it twelve months ago.

Even so, there was a large quotient of discontent in the business and investment worlds over the economy's performance in 1971, and a big sigh of relief when the year expired.

What was widely overlooked was that the economy had succeeded in emerging—firmly although not spectacularly—from its fifth recession of the last three decades and had proceeded to new heights.

Little acclaim was accorded such accomplishments as the first trillion-dollar economy; a continued rise in the number of people at work to a total of more than eighty million; new records in personal income and consumer spending; broadened Federal programs to combat hunger, expand job opportunities and increase medical care, and a slight moderation in the rate of inflation for the first time in five years.

[7] From New York *Times* Economic Review entitled "Economy on an Express Track," by Thomas E. Mullaney, financial and business news editor. New York *Times.* p 1-2. Ja. 9, '72. © 1972 by The New York Times Company. Reprinted by permission.

Instead, business and investment sentiment became severely depressed over the negative aspects of the economy—the high level of unemployment, the cost squeeze suffered by business and the public, the recurrent crises in the monetary area and various tensions in society.

To be sure, these problems still cry out for solution, but the atmosphere seems to be improving, even though the nation continues to be enmeshed in a web of caution over the political and economic outlook.

The prospective enlargement of an already gigantic American economy this year should be extremely satisfying to a nation hungering for mammoth progress to better the lot of its 209-million population. But the glow is dimmed by the realization that 1972 could be contentious in many ways.

On the domestic side, there may well be considerable periods of strife as the nation seeks an equitable allocation of resources to care for the jobless, those with substandard incomes and other disadvantaged elements of society and to improve the quality of life in decaying urban areas.

The year ahead may be marred as well by such divisive issues as the economic controls program, labor policy and the debate that develops in every national election year. And, in the international area, there are the overwhelming problems relating to wars, political differences and trade practices.

Those who expect better things to happen in 1972 are counting chiefly on a continuance of the rising economic activity that has prevailed in the last few months.

They are also encouraged because 1972 is a presidential election year and an Administration in power will be bent on playing every card it holds to assure its return to office.

Early . . . [in the summer of 1971], when the nation was suffering from a severe breakdown in confidence over inflation, unemployment, the deteriorating trade balance, international pressures on the dollar and the disarray in the securities markets, a prominent businessman with close ties to the

Administration said that President Nixon would "turn heaven and earth" to get the economy moving strongly again before the 1972 election. . . .

On August 15, in the year's most dramatic action, at least part of the promise was fulfilled when President Nixon announced a historic offensive to get the economy moving more strongly, arrest inflation and restore the nation's competitiveness in world markets.

He called for a big tax-reduction program, instituted a freeze on wages and prices and imposed a 10 percent surcharge on imports. The new economic package represented a significant turnabout in Administration policy.

The fruits of this bold shift in Washington's domestic and international game plan soon became evident. It created a climate of euphoria in the financial markets, a higher level of confidence in the business world and a recognition in foreign capitals that the United States was indeed serious about trying to get its economic house in order.

The new program, however, was not universally applauded—it did create some uncertainties, criticism and resentment. Still, it achieved a large measure of success and the promise of greater accomplishment in 1972.

Phase II of the program followed on November 14, when the Administration set up stabilization panels to hold wage and price increases to moderate levels following the three-month standstill.

A little later, other facets of the program were put into place. Congress enacted a wide-ranging bill to put more spending power in the hands of business and the public with tax reductions totaling more than $26 billion. And the leading Western nations acquiesced to the United States by adopting a broad package of currency realignments that provided an effective 12 percent devaluation of the American dollar.

The basic objectives were less inflation and more jobs for the American economy as well as a major swing in the payments deficit, which . . . [in 1971] was ranging between $12 billion and $23 billion by the various calculations.

Will the Nixon Administration obtain the payments swing that it wants, the reduction in inflation to an annual rate of 2 to 3 percent and the addition of some 500,000 or more jobs? Its hopes remain high that it will, but many private analysts are less sanguine. Most are confident that some significant measure of success will be realized, but they caution that it may well take some months before the scope of the achievement can be discerned.

While the Administration is relying heavily on its control program to gain economic stability, many in the private sector are skeptical of its efficacy. And so is labor, which has criticized the Administration program as inequitable.

Leif H. Olsen, chief economist for the First National City Bank of New York, recently voiced an assessment of the control program that is frequently echoed in business and economic circles. He remarked:

> A program which achieves some arbitrary standard of equity in allocating labor income, corporate income and investment income is not necessarily a program that enhances the growth and performance of the economy, nor one that assures the maximum reduction in the rate of inflation.
>
> If monetary and fiscal policies are kept on a noninflationary path, the controls will appear to work and probably will get the credit—and hopefully [be] retired early. The widespread opinion that controls represent an efficient means of forcing prices to behave runs contrary to theory and also to a long and unhappy chain of experience.

Even though Congress late . . . [in 1971] voted to extend the President's economic-control authority until the end of April 1973, few commentators expect them to last that long.

Despite the business world's traditional abhorrence of governmental interference in the free market, there was wide endorsement of the Administration's control program when it was suddenly adopted late in the summer.

Businessmen and others had become convinced that some drastic action was needed to stem the inflationary tide of wage settlements and the erosion of confidence in the financial markets.

If it did nothing else, the control program did dampen the spirit of inflationary expectations that reigned so widely among the public, investors and businessmen.

The ebbing of that tide and the wave of confidence that flowed in after it constitute the main source of optimism that now prevails over prospects for . . . [1972].

It became evident early . . . [in 1971] that the recession of 1969-1970 had definitely ended and had been replaced by a new, although halting, recovery movement. The sluggishness of the upturn was disappointing to some, but it was hardly surprising in light of the mildness of the contraction that had preceded it.

If the recession had not ended, the economic numbers for 1971 would have been much less satisfactory than they were. Unemployment might have been as high as 8 percent; industrial production would still be declining; corporate profits would not be showing an upward tendency, and the Gross National Product would not have negotiated the gain it did in real terms.

As it turned out, 1971 saw unemployment remaining high (although it halted at the 6 percent level); corporate profits rising about 15 percent; industrial production starting up again, and the Gross National Product gaining some $80 billion, an overall increase of about 7.3 percent. Real growth devoid of inflation represented a little less than 3 percent of the gain.

The upturn in the GNP [Gross National Product] last year pushed it above the one-trillion-dollar mark for the first time and to the area of $1,052 billion. That was virtually right on the target predicted a year ago by most forecasters, although it did fall considerably short of the overly optimistic $1,065 billion predicted by Government officials in last year's economic messages.

With Government spending reduced and business investment for capital equipment and inventories curtailed significantly, the impetus for the 1971 growth in the economy came from revived consumer spending for autos, housing and an array of durable goods and services.

Predictions for . . . [1972] are all quite glowing on the assumption that consumer outlays will show a further rise, on the order of 8 percent, while business capital spending, buttressed by restoration of the 7 percent investment tax credit and liberalized depreciation rules, will increase by perhaps 10 percent. Added to this would be heavier spending commitments by business for inventories as sales continued upward.

A recent survey by *Business Week* magazine among twenty-six leading economists, plus the forecasts of seven computerized econometric models, developed a consensus prediction of a $1,148 billion GNP in 1972—up about $96 billion, or 9.1 percent, from this year's estimated figure. The real growth would be a healthy and impressive 5.7 percent.

If this turns out to be an accurate forecast of the economy's performance, the unemployment rate should be reduced—gradually—from the recent level around 6 percent to perhaps 5 percent, or slightly lower, by the end of 1972.

That would still be high, leaving some 4.5 million people without jobs, but at least it would be a move downward. Ordinarily the reduction in unemployment might be expected to be greater in view of the sharp upturn in the economy. However, business will probably proceed slowly in rehiring workers, as it seeks to increase productivity and to offset rising costs in a tightly controlled pricing environment.

Greater productivity, or output per man-hour, is sorely needed to improve the profit picture. Productivity increased . . . [in 1971] by about 3.6 percent, but that was well below the average 5.5 percent gain realized in the first year after previous recessions.

The great hopes for 1972 are pinned largely on another boom year for automobiles after record sales of 10.3 million units in the year just past; another strong performance by general retail sales following their 10 percent rise in 1971; a vigorous rebound in steel production and shipments; a second consecutive year of 2 million new housing starts; a big improvement in business capital spending and inventory accumulation, and modest gains in Government spending and US exports.

To assure these results, business and consumer confidence must be maintained at high levels; inflation must be kept under tight rein; the nation will have to make progress in solving its social problems, and the world will have to be peaceful and prosperous.

It will be Washington's job, in a tumultuous election year, to exercise initiative and leadership to assure the climate the economy needs to attain its projected growth and to permit the implementation of programs improving all Americans' health, education, welfare, prosperity and mode of living.

VI. UNANSWERED QUESTIONS

EDITOR'S INTRODUCTION

If all the intricate steps that the Nixon Administration has taken work—or even if they do not—what does the action portend for the future of the economy—or, for that matter, for the nation as a whole since the political process is as much involved as the economic?

Articles in this concluding section of the book examine these questions and prospects. The first article asks whether the economic theories that became so popular during the 1960s are still viable. The author takes a look at fiscal and monetary policy and concludes that it may be too early to tell. He does suggest that, on the other hand, the Nixon Administration may itself be at fault for certain imbalances because of its spending policies. The second article, from *The Christian Science Monitor,* deals with those massive spending policies. The Administration's willingness to overspend—in order to get the economy moving and thus reduce unemployment—is also going to leave the Government short of cash at some point. To raise such vast amounts Government economists are looking with increasing favor on a new kind of tax—the value-added tax. The article explains just what that tax is.

The third selection focuses on the gradual strategy that the United States will probably pursue in international trade now that it has taken the bitter pill of devaluation. For all the effort that went into devaluation, there is clear evidence that much more negotiating lies ahead.

The fourth selection is a *Wall Street Journal* editorial which argues, with great earnestness, for a return to a more classic economy with few man-made restrictions. Government interference in the economy, now usually taken for granted, is opposed in this editorial, which argues instead for movement away from controls, away from restrictive trade barriers. Without such movement, it warns, we risk a worldwide depression.

The article that follows, from *Time*, pours some oil on those troubled waters. First it asks whether the new Nixon Economic Policy means that we have abandoned the free enterprise system. Then it concludes that our free enterprise system was not as free as we have tended to assume.

The final article touches on a new but increasingly popular dimension in economic thinking. The Nixonites—and most of those who oppose them—have one common ground. They agree that the economy must continue to grow. The article, however, reports on a special study which suggests that we stop making our economy grow, pointing out that we are exhausting too many resources as it is. What we must do, according to this view, is to stabilize our economy at a level where it supplies our needs but does not constantly expand.

ARE THE THEORIES DEAD? [1]

"I see by the papers," Herbert Stein, President Nixon's rotund chief economist, told the National Press Club the other day, "that the economy is going to be a big issue in the 1972 campaign."

While Mr. Stein, who is widely known for his acerbic wit, despaired that his Democratic opponents would ever get beyond assailing Herbert Hoover, there is indeed a great (and substantially nonpartisan) debate raging among economists over how the Government should manage the economy.

The irony has not been lost that Mr. Nixon—in many ways the archetype of an economic conservative who came to office with a gradualist, hands-off strategy designed to re-

[1] From "Nixonomics—Do the Old Economic Theories Still Hold?" by H. Erich Heinemann, assistant to the financial editor. New York *Times*. p F 1+. Mr. 5, '72. © 1972 by The New York Times Company. Reprinted by permission.

store a "steadier and more even-handed management of our economic policies"—should be defending a system of direct, if limited, wage and price controls in his reelection campaign.

The President's good intentions to the contrary notwithstanding, both the Administration's fiscal (that is tax and spending) policy and the Federal Reserve System's monetary policy, which controls (or some say should control) the rate at which money is created, have gyrated widely between economic restraint and stimulus in the last three years.

On the political stump, the major economic issues of 1972 are likely to be the apparently sluggish recovery from the 1970 recession and the persistence of higher-than-acceptable rates of both unemployment and inflation.

The economic professionals are mindful of those shortfalls—if, in fact, they be such—in the management of the nation's productive system, but the major questions with which they are wrestling are far more fundamental:

What are the causes of economic instability, and how can these be minimized? To what extent does the Government, in seeking to be an economic stabilizer, actually achieve a perverse result? Has the structure of the economy—indeed of the society—so changed in recent years that the "old" economic rules no longer hold?

The presidential campaign may be lending a certain shrillness to the debate, but in the meantime, several other, quite independent events have served to bring some of the issues into sharp focus. These were:

In late December [1971] at the annual meeting of the American Economic Association, Andrew F. Brimmer, a member of the Federal Reserve Board, presented a biting attack on the monetarist school of economics led by Professor Milton Friedman of the University of Chicago, and concluded that it would be "misleading," "extremely risky" and possibly "disastrous" for the central bank to follow the policy of fairly steady growth in the money supply advocated by the Friedmanites.

In February, Darryl R. Francis, president of the Federal Reserve Bank of St. Louis—which has long been known for its "Brand X," that is, monetarist, approach to central-bank policy—gave an equally testy rebuttal. The burden of his argument was that it was at least premature to inter monetarism as a failure inasmuch as its central recommendation, a relatively steady rate of expansion in money over a period of time, had never been adopted.

More or less concurrent with this exchange of intellectual brickbats, two of the leading monetarists—Beryl W. Sprinkel of the Harris Trust and Savings Bank in Chicago and A. James Meigs of the Argus Research Corporation in New York—published books designed to explain their doctrines to the layman.

Neither of these volumes—*Money and Markets,* by Mr. Sprinkel, published by Richard D. Irwin, Inc., and *Money Matters,* by Mr. Meigs, from Harper & Row—makes any pretense at overall objectivity.

Both seek to advance the monetarist view; yet, both also have the outstanding virtue of presenting the rival fiscalist (or Keynesian, after the late John Maynard Keynes) case in simple, straightforward, and accurate terms.

Greatly abbreviated from the original, this is how Mr. Meigs sets forth the issues:

The Monetarists, he says, believe that changes in the rate of growth of the supply of money in the economy (which is generally, but not necessarily, defined as the total of most checking accounts at the banks and currency in the hands of the public) will, following an average lag of six to nine months, produce corresponding changes in the growth rate of money incomes.

Should an accelerated growth in the money supply lead to an expansion of money balances to a greater level than people desire to hold, Mr. Meigs explains as a case in point, this would lead to adjustments—either debts would be reduced or new assets acquired.

Thus, the immediate, or first-round impact of monetary expansion shows up in increased demand for goods and services and hence higher real output (that is, production measured in dollars of constant purchasing power). Naturally, the converse—a monetary deceleration—can be expected to lead to economic contraction.

The change in the rate of growth of nominal income [measured at current prices, Mr. Meigs asserts] usually shows up first in real output and hardly at all in prices. The effect of a change in money-supply growth on prices comes about six to nine months after the effects on income and output. Therefore, the average delay between a change in monetary growth and a change in the rate of inflation is about twelve to eighteen months.

Two points to remember are (1) that only changes in the growth trend of the money supply—not the erratic week-to-week and monthly shifts—are likely to be important in influencing overall business activity; and (2) that the timing of those influences is both long and highly variable.

Thus, precisely for the reason that the authorities cannot know when or just how a given change in policy will affect the economy, Mr. Meigs goes on to say, "the proper role for monetary policy, in the monetarist view, is to provide a stable framework in which markets can function, not to direct the markets."

In Mr. Sprinkel's words,

Excessive monetary growth, in the view of the monetarist has accounted for all known sizable inflations, domestic and foreign, modern and ancient. A rising trend of money per unit of real output has inevitably brought inflation, whereas stabilization of money growth in line with output growth has brought price stability.

In contrast to the monetarist view of the private economy as responding primarily to changes in money growth, the Keynesian analysis stresses business investment—which is considered to be highly unstable—and Government spending as the principal elements that induce economic change.

The propensity of individuals to consume is thought to be relatively stable, or as Lord Keynes put it, "men are disposed, as a rule and on the average, to increase their consumption as their income increases, but not by as much as their income increases."

On the other hand, investment depends on a variety of unpredictable elements both within and without the system.

Since in the Keynesian scheme, changes in income are largely the function of erratic changes in investment, it falls to Government—as a powerful "exogenous" force, outside of, but heavily influencing, the private sector—to use its spending power to stabilize investment activity and through that, incomes.

In the real world of Government economic policy makers, of course, there is never a sharp and clear distinction between opposing camps of theorists. The "new economists" of the Kennedy and Johnson Administrations, for example, included some of the nation's leading Keynesian scholars, and there is no question but that their advocacy of a tax cut in 1964, represented a grand laboratory experiment in fiscal economics.

But the new economists did not ignore monetary policy any more than President Nixon's advisers—who are often described as being sympathetic to the monetarist approach—have ignored fiscal policy. Indeed, in the Economic Report that Mr. Nixon sent to Congress in January [1972], monetary expansion seems distinctly to get a second billing in the Administration's program to stimulate the economy.

According to the Council of Economic Advisers, which is headed by Mr. Stein,

the role of monetary policy in the expansion ahead will be to provide for the increase of liquidity required to support increases in activity and income. This outcome will involve a resumption of the growth of the stock of currency and demand deposits, after five months in which there has been relatively little growth. The expectation of an increase of GNP around $100 billion is based on the assumption that the required monetary growth will be forthcoming.

The implication, it would appear, was that the forward thrust to the economy would come from the Administration's decision to run a deficit of close to $65 billion in the two years ending in June 1973, with money growth following afterwards in a supportive role. This is hardly a monetarist description.

The decision that the Federal budget (as measured on the high, or "full employment" basis) should swing from an annual rate of surplus (which means restraint) of almost $15 billion late in 1969 to a deficit (or stimulus) of more than $20 billion in the second quarter of 1972 reflects President Nixon's political judgment about the needs of the economy.

What is less clear is why the Federal Reserve System has encouraged such wide swings in the rate of money expansion in the last two years—5.7 percent annual rate in 1970, 11.6 percent in the first half of 1971 and then 1.5 percent in the second half of last year.

The purpose of the ninety-four-page paper that Mr. Brimmer of the Federal Reserve presented to the American Economic Association was to trace the development of Federal Reserve policy-making techniques through the 1960s to what he described as "the high-water mark of monetarism" in March 1970, when the Federal Open Market Committee, which directs Federal Reserve policy, began specifically to mention rates of growth in the "monetary aggregates" (the money supply, as one example) as among its targets.

Mr. Brimmer left no doubt of his personal opinion that it is just as well that 1970 represents a high-water mark. The monetarists, he asserted, "have not demonstrated convincingly that the relationship between the money supply and economic activity is especially close."

To this charge, Mr. Francis, the president of the St. Louis Reserve Bank, answered in effect—How do you know, since you have never followed our approach? "One has only to look," he said, "at the growth rates of the money stock over the past four years to see that monetarist recommendations were not implemented."

No one can say for sure whether American society has so changed in recent years that the old economic rules are no longer working. But failing an answer to that question, Government itself might well examine its own house to see whether [through its own massive spending—Ed.] it is at the root of some of the inflation and unemployment with which it is now struggling to deal.

TO PAY THE PIPER—A NEW SOURCE OF FUNDS [2]

No reporter can hope to explain intricate things—let alone the value-added tax—without Mr. Smith and Mr. Jones.

"Smith, Jones—will you please step forward?"

"With families?"

"Oh, yes, with families, of course."

Two bright-faced families of four—the standard family for economists and sociologists—appeared.

"Very well, Mr. Jones, for today's exercise you represent the affluent family with income of more than $20,000; Mr. Smith, you and Mrs. Smith are the under-the-poverty-line family, with income around $3,500."

Mr. Jones at once looked as though he had just stepped out of a Buick, while Mr. Smith took on a chastened and hungry look.

[2] From "Explaining Value-Added Tax, With Help of Smith and Jones," by Richard L. Strout, staff correspondent. *Christian Science Monitor.* p 1+. F. 4, '72. Reprinted by permission from *The Christian Science Monitor.* © 1972 The Christian Science Publishing Society. All rights reserved.

Mass National Sales Tax

"As you are aware, the value-added tax, in effect, is a mass national sales tax. President Nixon appears to be moving closer and closer to it. He hinted a comprehensive tax change in his State of the Union message. The White House says specifically that Mr. Nixon has a 'positive' approach to the value-added tax. America's great annual ritual of making out its income tax is hardly known abroad—"

"Sir," interrupted Mary Smith, age four. "Can I sit down while you talk?"

"Certainly, but don't make a nuisance of yourself. Where was I? Now Smith—you're the poor one, remember—how much of your meager income goes to consumer items?"

"Practically all of it, sir. It's terrible; we spend it as fast as we get it. We can't save a thing."

"Stick to facts, Smith, my good man. Virtually all of it, eh? And now Mr. Jones, I admire that $20,000 of yours; how much goes to consumer expenses?"

"Food, clothes—that sort of thing?"

"Yes, and all the rest; heat, rent, cost of living generally?"

"Oh, about 62 percent, that's according to latest figures."

"Exactly, so if we have a national sales tax on consumer goods it will apply 100 percent to your expenses, Smith, and only 62 percent to Mr. Jones here."

"That's the way it always is," complained Mrs. Smith wistfully.

[The Nixon Administration indicates that the regressive effects might be alleviated by rebates to taxpayers at or below certain income levels.]

Income-Tax Difference

"If the tax were raised by the graduated income tax, which is progressive—adjusted upward with income—how much tax would you pay, Smith?"

"None, sir," said Mr. Smith cheerfully, "I'm under the tax."

"Mr. Jones?"

"It's a despicable tax!" he replied. "Still I pay it from duty. I'm in the 25 percent bracket even after those tax-exempt bonds, and the deductions my lawyer showed me. Thank goodness Mr. Nixon is reducing the tax! In his economic message he said he'd cut it $22 billion in three years."

"Stick to the facts, please. You know a lot of economists are sorry to see the income tax cut; they say it helps narrow the gap between rich and poor. Now we will go on to the matter of dividends, dividends from common stock. Smith, what part of your paltry income comes from dividends?"

"Oh, none at all, sir."

"So you aren't taxed on what you don't get. . . . Mr. Jones?"

"Income from dividends in the over-$15,000 income rate averages around 6.7 percent," said Mr. Jones complacently. "I've done very well with my Xerox stock."

"Very good. So far as we've come, VAT [Value-Added Tax], or the national sales tax, probably would hit you a lot harder, Smith, than a rich man."

"Oh, yes sir," interrupted Mrs. Smith. "You should see the city sales tax we pay!"

"You're a jump ahead of me. The White House says a Federal value-added tax to raise $16 billion is contemplated, probably to be called a 'school tax,' to pay about one third of the cost of public and elementary schools. It would pay some of the property taxes. A 1 percent rate on a national sales tax would raise $5 billion—it's a gusher—so presumably a VAT of 2 or 3 percent is contemplated. Probably food and clothing would be exempt. That's in deference to all you low-income people, Smith.

"You say you have a city sales tax?"

"Three percent for the state and 4 percent for the city!" said Mr. Smith.

"Exactly. Right now forty-four states have retail sales taxes, over 97 percent of our population lives in those states, with 97 percent of all retail establishments. The usual rate is 5 percent, but some run to 8 percent. They are regressive, and if you include concealed costs of property taxes, and taxes on Social Security—which are regressive, too—they are quite a burden. Smith, what is your tax rate—as a ratio of total income?"

In a sing-song voice Mr. Smith recited: "Families in the under-$2,000-a-year bracket paid 50 percent of their total income in taxes. Those between $2,000 and $4,000 paid 34..6 percent, of which 18.7 percent was Federal—income tax 3.5; corporate profit tax, 4.3; and Social Security, 6.5—and 15.7 [percent] was state and local—property 7.5 percent and sales tax 4.9 percent."

"Very good; and that was for 1968?" Mr. Smith nodded. "Now, Mr. Jones?"

"I'm a self-made man," he said, swelling a little. "My income is $20,000. I pay about 30 percent in taxes."

"Why—that's less than Smith."

TRADE STRATEGY [3]

President Nixon sees a major shift in the world's balance of economic power reflected in the latest international monetary agreement.

And the Administration has a multiphase policy in mind to cope with the new situation. After the exchange rate realignment . . . [in December 1971], President Nixon defined that situation as a "new world" in which "instead of just one strong economic nation, the nations of Europe, Japan and Asia, Canada and North America, all of these nations are strong economically, strong competitors. . . ."

[3] From "How the U.S. Plans to Ride World Economy," by David R. Francis, business and financial correspondent. *Christian Science Monitor*. p 1+. D. 21, '71. Reprinted by permission from *The Christian Science Monitor*. © 1971 The Christian Science Publishing Society. All rights reserved.

Japanese to Backtrack?

The monetary side of the first phase is now completed. First-phase trade issues—modest unilateral trade concessions which the United States seeks from its trading partners—should be resolved over the next few weeks.

Canadian negotiators met with United States officials . . . [in December 1971] to discuss these short-term issues. President Nixon's top trade negotiator, William Eberle, talked with his Japanese counterparts . . . Saturday, December 18, while the monetary talks were going on. Because the Japanese agreed to such a substantial upward revaluation of the yen, there is a suspicion . . . the Japanese may now want to backtrack a little on the trade side.

Resolution of the Japanese-American trade questions may await the January meeting of Japanese Prime Minister Eisaku Sato with Mr. Nixon in Washington.

Mr. Eberle meets with European Community officials Tuesday, December 21 in Brussels. The United States is expected to insist that the Common Market give its negotiators more leeway to make concessions. . . . Treasury Secretary John B. Connally, Jr., described the negotiating "mandate" given by the Common Market to its negotiators last week as "barely positive."

The second phase of the Administration's program calls for some trading issues of mutual concern in the trade area, to be tackled by the United States and its allies in 1972.

These items will be dealt with on the basis of reciprocal concessions. One aim will be just to show that such efforts to trim trade barriers can be successful.

Phase 3 on the trade side calls for broad-ranging talks between the United States and its trading partners on the whole range of trade issues—the system, nontariff barriers, tariffs, international rules of trade, and other items. . . .

These talks may not be concluded with one major balanced package of trade concessions. Rather, they may result

in a string of agreements put together as the negotiators work
through the many issues over several years. . . .

French President Pompidou agreed to participate in such
long-term trade talks at the little summit with Mr. Nixon
in the Azores.

Up to then, European Common Market [European Economic Community] officials had not expected to engage in
serious talks on the broad-range trade issues until late in the
decade, when the expansion of the Community was complete.
By then, it was thought, Europe would be stronger and in a
better bargaining position. Further, the trade discrimination
against outsiders inherent in a customs union would have
helped unite Europe.

Now the Pompidou commitment means the broad-range
talks . . . could be outlined next year and get under way in
1973. . . . A communiqué of the Group of Ten indicated that
the other members of the Six have agreed to such talks.

What Other Reserve Asset?

Phase 2 of the monetary side (no Phase 3 is planned)
involves long-term international monetary reform.

Several topics were spelled out in the communiqué.

For instance, one issue will be when and how to make
the dollar convertible into another reserve asset. During the
negotiations over the weekend the Europeans wanted a
United States pledge of convertibility for some time in the
future to ensure that the dollar would be subject to "balance-
of-payments discipline."

In other words, the Europeans wanted to obtain through
convertibility some influence on the management of the US
economy.

The United States apparently refused to agree to this demand, considering it part of Phase 2.

Negotiators in the forthcoming talks will be fully aware of their bargaining strengths and weaknesses. Mr. Connally often spoke of this fall's monetary dispute in terms of a card game.

Cards held by the United States would include these:

1. The United States has by all standards the biggest domestic market in the world. Thus it is not quite so reliant on exports and imports for its welfare as most of its trading partners.

2. The United States has huge material resources and a wealth of personal talent.

3. The dollar is the predominant international monetary vehicle.

4. The United States is the biggest trading nation.

5. The United States gold reserves of around $10 billion before devaluation—about $11 billion after devaluation—still represent the largest bullion kitty in the world.

6. The United States has the foremost money and capital markets in existence. The stock and bond markets can absorb more investments than all their counterparts across the globe put together.

7. The United States is the biggest debtor of all times—from a bargaining standpoint, a strength.

8. The United States remains the biggest military power and generally the leader in technology and science.

Cards for "Other" Side

Cards held by the "other" side include:

1. The rest of the world taken together is a far bigger sales territory than is the United States for the leading industrial nations (except in the case of Canada).

2. The prestige of the dollar has been weakened by its troubles in recent years.

3. Official bullion holdings of the ten nations that are to be in the European Common Market stand at more than $16 billion.

4. The enlarged European Community surpasses the United States in trade, with combined exports of $88.7 billion last year, compared with $43.2 billion for the United States.

5. Other nations know that as an ultimate weapon they hold national sway over some $80 billion of direct US foreign investment—money sunk into plants, stores, mines, etc., in Europe, Canada, Japan, and dozens of other countries.

A WORLDWIDE DEPRESSION [4]

That's a scare headline, of course, one that does not apply to the conditions of the moment. Unless nations begin pursuing wiser economic policies, however, before long the words may be only too appropriate.

Economic nationalism has become the order of the day. Underdeveloped countries, desperately in need of foreign capital and technology, frighten it away by seizing foreign assets with little or no compensation. "Chile for the Chileans" makes a ringing slogan, but it's a poor way to build up a poor country.

The problems of the poorer lands are aggravated by a similar chauvinism in the industrial nations, countries that ought to know better. In a revival of old mercantilist notions, exports are eagerly sought but imports are something to hold down as much as possible.

If the underdeveloped nations are ever to develop—and thus to provide expanding markets for the industrial countries—they have to begin somewhere, and a logical way to start is with labor-intensive industries such as textiles. But these industries need markets, too, and increasingly they find the markets of richer countries more or less closed to them.

Nearly all countries, rich and poor alike, appear to think they can purchase lasting prosperity with expansive monetary and fiscal policies. In the backward lands the result has

[4] From editorial, "A World-Wide Depression." *Wall Street Journal.* p 20. O. 28, 1971. Reprinted with permission of the *Wall Street Journal.*

often been nearly ruinous inflation. The sophisticated industrial nations think they can control the price pressures with "incomes" policies, but the results in the past have differed only in degree from those in underdeveloped nations.

Inflation helps to lead organized labor everywhere to press for ever-higher wages, even though in the process the unions are often pricing their members' products out of the market. The upshot of all of this is the present period of economic weakness and uncertainty, conditions that are by no means unique to the United States. . . .

Unemployment is creeping upward almost everywhere in Europe. On a seasonally adjusted basis, joblessness in Britain is the highest in thirty years. Swedish unemployment, on a similar basis, is the highest since the nation began keeping such statistics in 1955.

In few countries does anyone seem to see that a prime cause of present problems is excessive governmental meddling in the economy. Most countries, in fact, appear to think that the way out is for the government to meddle quite a lot more.

The United States for its part, is trying to check inflation by freezing prices and wages; . . . [in November 1971] the freeze will begin to thaw in a manner that is anything but settled. With a 10 percent import surcharge, America is also trying to coerce other countries into opening their markets wider to US goods; so far, the more noteworthy results have been Japanese agreement to "voluntary" quotas on textile sales to the United States—and threats by other countries of retaliation against American goods.

United States officials firmly deny that they're trying to build a sort of "fortress America," but actually nearly every nation seems to be trying to build a little fortress of its own. Many countries evidently accept the idea that, in the future, there will be fewer economic gains to share and they want to make sure of theirs while they can.

"The world economy is entering a stage of lessened growth in which, within a few months, problems of activity and unemployment will raise universal concern," Valéry Giscard d'Estaing, the French minister of economy and finance, said recently. In some areas the concern is already here.

There is no easy solution. It should be apparent, though, that the post—World War II world prospered through growing cooperation, not through growing chauvinism. It should be obvious too that inflationary finance buys only inflation, not perpetual prosperity. Sound growth must be based on relatively stable prices and the freest possible markets, in labor as well as in business.

If every nation insists on trying to enrich itself at the expense of its neighbors, the result will be that worldwide depression. In the interdependent world we inhabit now, that's even truer than it was in Adam Smith's day.

HAS "1984" ARRIVED? [5]

The United States is universally recognized as the capital of capitalism, the land of free markets and the home of resourceful entrepreneurs. More than any other country, it has been known for leaving an entrepreneur free to decide prices for his products and set wages for his workers, free to grow and prosper—and free to go bankrupt if he failed. Historically, the United States Government has often done much to strengthen those twin pillars of free enterprise, private ownership and unfettered competition. Americans have grown so accustomed to living under free enterprise that they rarely even think in terms of class struggles, expropriation, the proletariat or other concepts that mark national debate elsewhere.

[5] Time Essay entiled "The Future of Free Enterprise," by Donald M. Morrison. *Time*. 99:50-1. F. 14, '72. Reprinted by permission from *Time*, the weekly newsmagazine; © Time Inc. 1972.

Only in the United States are airlines, radio and television networks, telephone systems, power companies and all other major industries owned primarily by private individuals. By contrast, Japan is a corporate state in which government and industry are so closely interrelated that it is difficult to tell which segment is in control. Half of France's auto industry is owned by the state; 35 percent of Italy's industrial production is state controlled.

Recently, however, free enterprise in the United States has been under heavy pressure—not so much from the New Left or consumerist critics as from some of the system's primary defenders, namely the Republican party and private businessmen. By ordering the first controls in the nation's history (outside of a military emergency) clamped on wages, prices and rents, President Nixon made one of the boldest encroachments so far on the free-enterprise system. Nixon's New Economic Policy is, in fact, only the latest and most dramatic in a series of events that seem to challenge the principle of free enterprise. In business, the role of Government is fast growing larger—as savior, subsidizer, owner, regulator, decision maker.

It is business leaders themselves who often urge the Government to step in. When the aerospace industry tumbled into trouble last year, its generally conservative captains importuned Washington for subsidies to bail out Lockheed (successful) and save the SST (unsuccessful). When the housing industry slumped in the late 1960s, home builders pressured the Government to increase subsidies greatly; under the present Administration, the number of federally assisted housing starts has jumped 150 percent, to almost 400,000. After passenger rail service had become a hopeless drain on profit, Congress last year relieved the railroads of that burden by creating Amtrak, the Government-sponsored rail corporation.

The Government's recent actions raise troubling questions. Does free enterprise have much of a future? If so, what should be done to preserve and strengthen the system? If not, what will replace it?

Actually, the system has never been as free as its folklore suggests. Business and Government have often been partners in a common-law marriage. What is happening now is largely an intensification of a long process of Government involvement.

Many early American capitalists built their fortunes by prying favors and subsidies out of the Government including publicly financed roads and canals that were tailored to their needs, direct land grants and protective tariffs. The first steps toward Government regulation of industry were prompted not primarily by bureaucrats or muckrakers but by businessmen themselves. Around the turn of the century they persuaded the Government to referee ruinous competition, stabilize markets and guarantee a steady line of credit by creating the Interstate Commerce Commission, the Federal Trade Commission, the Federal Reserve System and other agencies of the Progressive era. Some businessmen urged the Government to go even further. As Judge Elbert Gary, first chairman of United States Steel Corporation, told a somewhat startled congressional committee in 1911: "I believe we must come to enforced publicity and Government control, even as to prices."

As conservatives have never ceased grumbling, Franklin Roosevelt's New Deal pushed the Government even deeper into free-market restraints by creating the Securities and Exchange Commission (which regulates the securities business), expanding the Reconstruction Finance Corporation (which started the Government rescuing companies from bankruptcy), and introducing the minimum wage law (which set a precedent for some wage controls). During World War II and the Korean War, the Government imposed temporary wage and price controls.

The most important incursion of all came when Congress passed the Employment Act of 1946, which once and for all committed the Government to take all necessary steps "to promote maximum employment, production and purchasing power." Using that broad political charter and the economic principles of John Maynard Keynes, every President since 1946 has wielded the powers of Government in attempts to keep the level of jobs high and prices low. Richard Nixon's controls are by far the most drastic moves toward that goal in the past quarter-century. Yet in the Government's arsenal, controls are merely one form of economic weaponry, along with fiscal and monetary policy.

The Government's influence on the private economy will become even greater in the future. But the nation is not creeping toward a corporate state or outright socialism. Aside from the special case of railroads, for example, there is little popular support for having Washington take control of basic industries. Still, the Government will increasingly exert its great power in three ways:

First: Washington will involve itself more and more as a goal setter and rules maker for business—largely because many business leaders want it to do so. Banker David Rockefeller, General Motors' ex-Chairman James Roche and American Telephone & Telegraph Chairman H. I. Romnes are among the prominent nonrevolutionaries who have endorsed the National Urban Coalition's proposed "counterbudget," which calls for the Government by the mid-1970s to establish a guaranteed annual income, start a national health-insurance program, and double Federal outlays for education. Only the Federal Government is in a position to direct an attack on a wide array of national problems—environmental pollution, urban deterioration, auto and job safety. The business community is too fragmented, and individual managers are too preoccupied with their own companies' affairs, to undertake the task alone.

At the same time, the Federal role will be restricted by the fact that not even the Government is rich or powerful enough to solve all the nation's needs and problems without help from business and the public. A prime example is pollution control. Businessmen are urging the Government to set clear, firm national standards. Only in that way can entrepreneurs compete on equal terms; no one will be able to use plain self-interest or lax local laws to cut his antipollution costs. But if the Government were to attempt to spend all the billions necessary to clean up the nation's air and waters, it would break the already deficit-ridden Federal budget. The cost of cleanup is so enormous that it can be met only by adding to the prices of the major products of pollution—gasoline, electric energy, steel, fertilizers and others—and thus ultimately making consumers pay the bill. Thus the Government may set the goals and standards, but the problem can be solved in the private market.

Second: The Government will become a sterner policeman of private enterprise. Responding to a surge of rising public expectations about corporate performance, Washington is stepping up its regulatory efforts. Nixon-appointed heads of Federal agencies are already outdoing their Democratic predecessors in bedeviling businessmen with tougher rules on auto safety, toy safety, food and drug quality, truth in advertising, disclosure of financial information and other securities practices, as new regulations proposed . . . [in February 1972] by the SEC [Securities and Exchange Commission] indicate. In 1970 Congress passed environmental protection and industrial safety acts that empower the Government to seek court orders banning certain methods of production, and even closing down some plants in basic industries—notably autos, steel, oil, electric power and coal mining—when they violate Federal pollution or job-hazard standards. By 1975, Federal officials will be responsible for almost as many basic decisions in auto design as the auto companies' engineers. Stiffer regulation, however, is not a constraint on free enterprise. In an increasingly large and complex economy, regulation is what prevents the pursuit of profit from leading to harmful products, destructive diseconomies like pollution, the exploitation of customers and other threats to the stability of the business system.

Third: The Government will likely continue some form of surveillance over wages and prices. In his economic report to Congress two weeks ago, President Nixon implied that controls will remain at least until the end of . . . [1972] and perhaps longer. Beyond that, the United States will probably have some looser form of Government wage-and-price supervision more or less indefinitely. At his farewell press conference in December [1971], Paul McCracken, the President's outgoing Chief Economic Adviser, said that the Government may have to take steps to moderate prices "for a long time to come, even after Phase II has done its thing."

Many economists and businessmen favor a system of voluntary wage-price guidelines, such as existed with varying success during the Kennedy-Johnson years. Companies and unions would probably be reluctant to transgress these guidelines, if for no other reason than the Government, having set a precedent for peacetime controls, could always go back to them. Says Walter Heller, a member of *Time*'s Board of Economists: "Things will never be the same again. Even after controls are lifted, there will be the threat of their reimposition. As Al Capone put it: 'You can get so much farther with a kind word and a gun than with a kind word alone.' "

If the Government, whether under Republican or Democratic auspices, can curtail inflation and revive the economy by using such tools as controls and guidelines, free enterprise will be greatly strengthened. When the economy is growing, entrepreneurs have a much greater opportunity to start and enlarge businesses. When costs are stable, established businessmen find it much easier to lower the prices of their own products in pursuit of competitiveness.

Free enterprise should be valued, preserved and strengthened. It is not fundamentally endangered by Government attempts to set rules or goals for business to solve social problems or by efforts to straighten out the economy by setting wage-and-price controls. The real threat comes from quite another source: the steady increase of economic power concentrated in large corporations and large unions. Today the 100 biggest industrial corporations control about half the nation's corporate manufacturing assets, an even greater percentage than the 200 largest companies controlled twenty years ago. These corporations may be beneficent and efficient, though smaller firms are often better in both categories. The sheer size of the giants, however, hampers new entrepreneurs from entering some industries and expanding in others. A handful of companies dominate auto, aerospace, steel, aluminum and computer manufacturing so thoroughly that new companies find it nearly impossible to break in. If the United States wants to expand free enterprise in these and other basic areas, the Government will have to become more vigorous in pursuing antitrust policies.

Free enterprise is also restrained by giant national unions. Because they are often more powerful than their generally small employers, the building-trades unions can demand—and get—exorbitant wage increases, make-work practices, and restrictions on the use of new methods and materials. Similar abuses are committed by the Teamsters, the maritime unions and the civil service workers. Sooner or later, some US President will have to challenge union power and put an end to such enterprise-sapping practices as the union hiring hall and featherbedding. That man may as well be Richard Nixon, since the great majority of union leaders already vehemently oppose him and he has little to lose.

The United States should make free enterprise even more competitive and more responsive to the nation's needs. That may require some more effective form of Government planning to coordinate the resources of businesses with the spending and taxation policies of Federal, state and local governments. The capitalist economy may thus eventually take on some features of socialism, just as socialism over the years has adopted some practices of capitalism. Yet a nation that accounts annually for nearly half of the non-Communist world's gross national product, and has more individual business enterprises than many countries have people, is surely strong and diverse enough to accommodate the best features of both systems.

MAYBE WE'RE ALL WRONG [6]

High-ranking figures in government, diplomacy, business, the military and the academic world gathered . . . [in Washington, March 2, 1972] to ponder the implications of a controversial computer study that says the world must put a quick end to economic and population growth or face total collapse of human society.

The 250 or so senators, representatives, ambassadors, agency heads, industrialists, scientists and generals reached no consensus on whether the warning was valid or on how to cope with it, but their comments suggested that it was provoking wide international debate.

Among the participants in the symposium, held under the soaring Romanesque columns of the great hall at the Smithsonian Institution, was Elliot L. Richardson, Secretary of Health, Education, and Welfare. He said that the study was "too thoughtful and significant" to ignore, but he reflected the underlying concerns of many in saying that he hopes the regulation needed to halt growth would not result in "the destruction of our liberties and freedom."

He added that "the mind boggles" at the problems involved in trying to distribute goods and services equally throughout the world, if that is required to achieve a global economy based on no growth.

[6] From "Warning on Growth Perils Is Examined at Symposium," by Robert Reinhold, science reporter. New York *Times.* p 41+. Mr. 5, '72. © 1972 by The New York Times Company. Reprinted by permission.

"Global Equilibrium" Needed

The burden of the study, performed at the Massachusetts Institute of Technology under the aegis of an international group called the Club of Rome, is that the planet is finite and is rapidly reaching its capacity to support human life and unrestricted industrial growth. If governments do not achieve a state of "global equilibrium," it says, then uncontrollable collapse, through disease and starvation, is likely within one hundred years.

This conclusion emerged from an eighteen-month project in which the MIT group built a mathematical approximation, or model, of the world system. The preliminary results are to be published . . . under the title "The Limits to Growth."

The conclusions have been disputed by many, particularly by some economists, who have argued that the computer model bears little relationship to reality and the numbers fed into it are not scientific. Nevertheless, it was apparent the work had made a deep impression on the group gathered today.

The purpose of the session, according to the head of the Club of Rome, Aurelio Peccei, the Italian industrialist, was to alert decision makers of all ideologies to the urgency of the situation. "We dearly hope that the debate which starts here today will have wide repercussions, opening a new phase of awareness, inquiry, and finally political action," he said.

With the help of large charts covered with soaring and dropping curves in blue, red, yellow and brown, Dennis L. Meadows, the soft-spoken twenty-nine-year-old director of the project, described what his group had done. Then open discussion was invited.

The debate focused on two main questions: Was the model valid; and, if so, How was the transition to no growth to be achieved in a world in which the goal of growth and improvement seems to underlie so much of human behavior?

As Senator Claiborne Pell, Democrat of Rhode Island, put it: "You presume man is rational, but man is an emotional creature. How do you convert this into an action program?"

Dr. Meadows replied that legislators such as the senator were better equipped to answer that question, and that the role of science was to provide the "rational input" to help them act.

Great International Cooperation Required

It was clear to many that action would require great international cooperation. "It is not likely to happen without global decision making," remarked Philippe de Saynes, Under Secretary-General for Economic and Social Affairs at the United Nations. "There is none now. The UN has power to influence attitudes, but it has very little world power."

Ambassador L. K. Jha of India was concerned that a state of equilibrium, if not accompanied by equalization of income, might mean that "the poorer nations would slide down to starvation." In an interview, he said, "No growth would have to reflect a much more equal state of affairs," which he hoped would come about "not by authoritarian means but by adoption of techniques that will carry a good deal of world support."

A man who identified himself as representing the World Bank said that he was not optimistic that the industrialized countries would reduce their consumption. Dr. Meadows agreed that this study said little about this, but added, "The fundamental question is whether the distribution problem is more likely to be solved by current practice than by moving into equilibrium." He indicated he did not think so.

Mr. Peccei told . . . the symposium that what was required was not just technical information on sociopolitical change, but "a thorough revision of our whole cultural basis."

According to Donella H. Meadows, Dr. Meadows' wife and a collaborator in the study, this is not impossible. She said that she took heart because young people today were discovering that "alternative life styles" that do not require great material consumption "are not sacrifices—they are fulfilling."

Professor Jay W. Forrester, an MIT engineer who has pioneered in computer analysis of large systems, said that equilibrium did not require complete equality world wide. Each area of the world, he said, would have the freedom to make certain "trade-offs" between population and standard of living.

As to the validity of the model, there was some question about whether the MIT study had taken adequate account of the possibility of new energy sources that would push back the limits to growth. Dr. Meadows insisted that the computer curves showed that even the most optimistic assumptions about energy availability did not ward off collapse.

In an effort to refine and extend the conclusions, the Club of Rome is embarking on a "Phase II" that it hopes will help solve some of the questions of distribution and provide decision makers with some guidelines for action.

The Club of Rome was founded in that city in 1968 and is a worldwide group of scientists, economists, educators, businessmen and specialists in systems analysis. The group sought to work together to avert a breakdown in society it felt was intrinsic in uncontrolled growth of technology and population.

BIBLIOGRAPHY

An asterisk (*) preceding a reference indicates that the article or a part of it has been reprinted in this book.

Books, Pamphlets, and Documents

Egle, W. P. Economic stabilization. Princeton University Press. '52.

*Evans, Rowland, Jr. and Novak, R. D. Nixon in the White House: the frustration of power. Random House. '71.
  Excerpts. Atlantic. 228:66-76+. Jl. '71. Nixonomics: how the game plan went wrong.

Gross, B. M. Action under planning; the guidance of economic development. McGraw. '67.

Hansen, A. H. Business cycles and national income. Norton. '51.

Johnson, H. G. Money, trade and economic growth. Harvard University Press. '62.

Keynes, J. M. Essays in persuasion. Norton. '63.

Keynes, J. M. General theory of employment, interest, and money. Harcourt. [originally published in 1936] '65.

Lekachman, Robert. The age of Keynes. Random House. '66.

Meigs, A. J. Money matters: reflections of a practicing monetarist. Harper & Row. '72.

Metzler, L. A. and others. Income, employment, and public policy: essays in honor of Alvin H. Hansen. Norton. '48.

Mishan, E. J. The costs of economic growth. Praeger. '67.

Okun, A. M. The political economy of prosperity. Brookings Institution. '70.

Phelps, E. S. Fiscal neutrality toward economic growth. McGraw. '65.

Robinson, Joan. Economics: an awkward corner. Pantheon Books. '67.

Roll, Sir Erich. The world after Keynes. Praeger. '68.

Rostow, W. W. Stages of economic growth; a non-Communist manifesto. Cambridge University Press. '60.

Silk, Leonard. Nixonomics. Praeger. '72.

Sprinkel, B. W. Money and markets: a monetarist view. Dow Jones-Irwin. '71.

Stewart, M. S. Can we avoid economic crises? (Pamphlet no 471) Public Affairs Committee. 381 Park Ave. S. New York 10016. '71.

Ulman, Lloyd and Flanagan, R. J. Wage restraint: a study of incomes policies in western Europe. University of California Press. '71.
        Review. New York Times. p F 12. Ag. 1, '71. Incomes policy clarified. E. M. Fowler.

PERIODICALS

America. 120:296. Mr. 15, '69. Disinflation, not deflation.

America. 124:223. Mr. 6, '71. What Mr. Burns really said: testimony before Joint Congressional Economic Committee.

America. 124:398. Ap. 17, '71. Inflation, incomes policy and all that. B. L. Masse.

America. 125:109-10. S. 4, '71. Mr. Nixon's New Economic Policy.

America. 125:448-50. N. 27, '71. Nixon's NEP [New Economic Policy] and the developing world. P. J. Henriot.

America. 125:475. D. 4, '71. Moral rules and economic quarterbacks. B. L. Masse.

Annals of the American Academy of Political and Social Science. 379:78-82. S. '68. Fiscal and monetary policy. C. C. Balderston.

Annals of the American Academy of Political and Social Science. 396:90-104. Jl. '71. Control of inflation and recession; address, April 1971. F. W. Schiff.

Annals of the American Academy of Political and Social Science. 397:40-7. S. '71. Need for increased public investment. M. J. Shapp.

Business Week. p 39-40. D. 7, '63. Slow growth is no. 1 problem: survey by campus economists.

*Business Week. p 35-6. N. 20, '65. Will the guideposts hold?

Business Week. p 42-3. F. 22, '69. Nixon team maps out its economic strategy.

Business Week. p 31-2+. D. 13, '69. Farther than ever from a fiscal policy [with editorial comment].

*Business Week. p 16-17+. My. 8, '71. Hot dollars spark a global crisis [with editorial comment].

Business Week. p 24-5. Je. 12, '71. Unemployment as a way of life.

*Business Week. p 64-7+. Jl. 3, '71. The U.S. searches for a realistic trade policy.

Business Week. p 18-19+. Jl. 31, '71. Administration takes on the Fed.

Business Week. p 24-5. Ag. 14, '71. World downgrades the dollar.

Business Week. p 21-30+. Ag. 21, '71. Administration blockbuster: 90-day freeze.

Business Week. p 18. Ag. 28, '71. CLC [Cost of Living Council] warms up to its job.

Business Week. p 14-15. S. 4, '71. Congress bones up on Nixon economics.

Business Week. p 37. S. 25, '71. Newest Nixon looks Galbraithian.

Business Week. p 32. N. 20, '71. Zigs and zags of setting prices.

Business Week. p 31. N. 27, '71. Price rulings gather speed.

Business Week. p 31. N. 27, '71. Wobbly line on nonunion pay.

Business Week. p 18. F. 12, '72. Pay board looks beyond union wages.

Changing Times. 25:35-9. Ag. '71. Coping with inflation: what readers report.

Christian Century. 88:992. Ag. 25, '71. Nixon's N. E. P. [New Economic Policy].

*Christian Science Monitor. p 1+. D. 21, '71. How the U.S. plans to ride world economy. D. R. Francis.

*Christian Science Monitor. p 1+. Ja. 25, '72. Nixon primes economy with deficit tide. C. R. Sheldon.

*Christian Science Monitor. p 1+. F. 4, '72. Explaining value-added tax, with help of Smith and Jones. R. L. Strout.

Commonweal. 93:539-40. Mr. 5, '71. Balancing the books; national myth of progress.

Commonweal. 94:443-4. S. 3, '71. Out in the freeze.

Current History. 60:171-4. Mr. '71. State of the Union message, January 22, 1971; excerpts. R. M. Nixon

Department of State Bulletin. 50:864-7. Je. 1, '64. Perspective on the tasks of the 1960's; address, May 11, 1964. W. W. Rostow.

Department of State Bulletin. 64:105-10. Ja. 25, '71. Conversation with the President, January 1971.

Department of State Bulletin. 64:212-18. F. 15, '71. World inflation and the international payments system; address, January 14, 1971. P. A. Volcker.

Department of State Bulletin. 65:42-6. Jl. 12, '71. Mutual responsibility for maintaining a stable monetary system; address, May 28, 1971. J. B. Connally, Jr.

Department of State Bulletin. 65:253-6. S. 6, '71. Challenge of peace.

Department of State Bulletin. 65:450-2. O. 25, '71. President affirms U.S. cooperation in world economic affairs; remarks, September 29, 1971. R. M. Nixon.

Department of State Bulletin. 65:458. O. 25, '71. Group of Ten
    ministerial meeting held at Washington; text of communiqué,
    September 26, 1971.
Dun's (Dun's Review and Modern Industry). 92:96. D. '68. Presi-
    dent Nixon and the economy.
Dun's (Dun's Review). 97:9. F. '71. Nixon-Burns battle? Robert
    Lekachman.
Dun's (Dun's Review). 98:13. Ag. '71. Waning game plan. Robert
    Lekachman.
Dun's (Dun's Review). 99:11. F. '72. Those economic forecasts.
    Gardner Ackley.
Editorial Research Reports. v 1, no 13:249-66. Ap. 7, '71. State
    capitalism. R. C. Deans.
Forbes. 107:52. Je. 1, '71. Game is over.
Fortune. 67:72-5+. Ja. '63. Real case for a tax cut. Max Ways.
Fortune. 70:27-8. D. '64. Boom ad hoc.
Fortune. 70:104-7+. D. '64. Next turn in taxes. E. K. Faltermayer.
Fortune. 74:113-14. O. '66. Case for doing almost nothing.
Fortune. 75:110-15+. Mr. '67. U.S. economy enters a new era.
    William Bowen.
Fortune. 79:23-4. Mr. '69. Gradualism.
Fortune. 79:15-16. My. 1, '69. Pattern of moderation.
Fortune. 80:85-6. O. '69. Choices that will shape the future.
Fortune. 83:72-7+. Ja; 80-5+. F; 92-5+. Mr. '71. U.S. economy
    in an age of uncertainty.
Fortune. 83:22. F. '71. Puzzling aspects of unemployment.
Fortune. 83:17. Ap. '71. After the disappointing rebound.
Fortune. 83:33. My. '71. Stirrings of spring in the economy.
Fortune. 83:272. My. '71. Fall-off in jobs.
*Fortune. 84:70-3+. S. '71. A strategy for winding down inflation.
    R. V. Roosa.
Fortune. 84:17. N. '71. Bottom line in a controlled economy.
*Fortune. 85:74-7+. Ja. '72. How the U.S. got on the road to a
    controlled economy. Juan Cameron.
Harper's Magazine. 241:29-34. Ag; 16. O. '70. Money in America.
    Robert Lekachman.
Harvard Business Review. 42:49-61. Jl. '64. Inflation danger ahead?
    G. L. Bach.
Harvard Business Review. 49:68-78. S. '71. Price stability and full
    employment too? G. L. Bach.
*Life. 60:4. Ja. 7, '66. 1966: booming but look out [editorial].
Life. 67:46. O. 17, '69. When bad news is good news.

Life. 71:30. Ag. 13, '71. Kicking the inflation habit.

Life. 71:32. S. 10, '71. From the freeze to Phase II.

Monthly Labor Review. 86:51. Ja. '63. Presidential committee report on fiscal and monetary policy, November 19, 1962.

Monthly Labor Review. 94:68-71. F. '71. Inflation versus unemployment: the worsening trade-off. G. L. Perry.
    Adapted from "Changing labor markets and inflation," Brookings Papers on Economic Activity no 3.

Monthly Labor Review. 94:51-4. My. '71. Manpower approach to the unemployment-inflation dilemma. C. C. Holt and others.

Monthly Labor Review. 94:26-36. Jl. '71. Labor market twist, 1964-69. D. F. Johnston.

Nation. 212:677-8. My. 31, '71. Soviet gold.

Nation. 213:99. Ag. 16, '71. Matter of models.

Nation. 213:164. S. 6, '71. Thunderclap politics.

Nation. 213:293-6. O. 4, '71. Nixon's N. E. P. [New Economic Policy] & the Constitution. A. S. Miller.

National Review. 23:186-7. F. 23, '71. New warning signs for the dollar.

National Review. 23:994. S. 10, '71. Down the primrose path. F. S. Meyer.

National Review. 23:1043. S. 24, '71. NEP [New Economic Policy] of a different color.

National Review. 24:202. Mr. 3, '72. Who controls the controllers?

Nations Business. 59:40+. Mr. '71. Mixing politics and economics. C. H. Madden.

New Republic. 164:11-12. Ja. 2, '71. Two years of Nixonomics.

New Republic. 164:16-19. F. 13, '71. Better than revenue sharing. M. J. Ulmer.

New Republic. 164:6. Ap. 17, '71. TRB from Washington: views of Arthur Burns.

*New Republic. 164:15-18. Ap. 24, '71. Applied Nixonomics: inflation/unemployment seesaw. M. J. Ulmer.

New Republic. 164:7. My. 22, '71. Saga of the dollar.

New Republic. 165:16-18. Ag. 7, '71. What to do about the economy. E. J. McCarthy.

New Republic. 165:7-8. S. 4, '71. New Nixonomics.

New Republic. 165:15-17. S. 4, '71. Deceptive package. Ralph Nader.

New Republic. 165:12. S. 25, '71. Public employment.

New Republic. 165:11. O. 2, '71. Public service jobs.

New Republic. 165:19-21. D. 11, '71. Non-answer to Nixonomics. M. J. Ulmer.

New Republic. 166:4. F. 19, '72. TRB from Washington: upstaging the economy.

New York Times. p 24. My. 11, '71. Mills doubtful of revenue vote.

New York Times. p 17. Je. 2, '71. G.O.P. hints shift on tax sharing. Eileen Shanahan.

New York Times. p 1+. Je. 3, '71. House panel cool to fund sharing. Eileen Shanahan.

New York Times. p E 2. Je. 6, '71. Revenue sharing: the big brawl over how to cut the cake.

New York Times. p 1+. Je. 11, '71. Mills proposes tax-sharing plan to aid cities only. Eileen Shanahan.

New York Times. p 20. Jl. 4, '71. Mills to present revenue-sharing plan to committee this week. Eileen Shanahan.

New York Times. p 1+. Jl. 22, '71. Tax-sharing plan altered to heed big-city demands. Eileen Shanahan.

New York Times. p F 1. Ag. 1, '71. Gold troubles. C. H. Farnsworth.

New York Times. p 24. Ag. 14, '71. Stuttering in steel [editorial].

New York Times. p 1. Ag. 16, '71. Highlights of Nixon plan.

*New York Times. p 14. Ag. 16, '71. Transcript of President's address on moves to deal with economic problems.

New York Times. p 15. Ag. 16, '71. Truman imposed last wage-price curbs in '51. R. E. Tomasson.

New York Times. p 26. Ag. 16, '71. Call to economic revival [editorial].

New York Times. p 1. Ag. 17, '71. Congress likely to vote Nixon tax cuts; stock market up 32.93 in record trading; most world currency dealing is halted. Marjorie Hunter.

New York Times. p 1+. Ag. 17, '71. Observers say Nixon aim is 12 to 15% devaluation. H. E. Heinemann.

New York Times. p 16. Ag. 17, '71. Excerpts from Connally news conference on Nixon Administration's economic steps.

New York Times. p 17. Ag. 17, '71. Texts of Nixon's orders on freeze and surcharge.

New York Times. p 34. Ag. 17, '71. The New Economic Policy [editorial].

New York Times. p 20. Ag. 18, '71. Government's questions and answers [policy guidance on wage-price freeze].

New York Times. p 37. Ag. 18, '71. At last, devaluation. P. A. Samuelson.

New York Times. p 40. Ag. 20, '71. Japan curtails foreign exchange buying after new surge of dollar sales. Takashi Oka.

New York Times. p 1+. Ag. 21, '71. President to meet Hirohito in Alaska. J. M. Naughton.

New York Times. p 13. Ag. 21, '71. Trading on Japanese markets calmer. Takashi Oka.

New York Times. p 48. Ag. 22, '71. Permanent shift in yen doubted. R. A. Wright.

New York Times. p F 1. Ag. 22, '71. Monetary uncertainty. C. H. Farnsworth.

New York Times. p 42. Ag. 23, '71. Tokyo and Detroit: two views on trade. Takashi Oka; J. M. Flint.

New York Times. p 36. Ag. 29, '71. Polls indicate a majority of labor union members support Nixon economic moves. Damon Stetson.

New York Times. p E 1. Ag. 29, '71. The yen. Tokashi Oka.

New York Times. p 20. S. 10, '71. Transcript of Nixon's address to Congress asking support for his economic plan.

New York Times. p F 1. S. 12, '71. The Common Market is torn by dollar crisis. C. H. Farnsworth.

New York Times. p E 2. S. 19, '71. Post-freeze. A. H. Raskin.

New York Times. p F 1. S. 26, '71. The magnificent fiction. J. M. Lee.

New York Times. p 1. S. 29, '71. Six nations ask end of dollar's role as key currency. E. L. Dale, Jr.

New York Times. p E 1. O. 10, '71. Phase II. A. H. Raskin.

New York Times. p F 1. O. 31, '71. Phase Two buoys bonds, depresses stocks.

New York Times. p F 1. N. 28, '71. Controls bog planning. Gerd Wilcke.

New York Times. p 28. D. 1, '71. Mills offers a fund-sharing plan tied to local needs.

New York Times. p F 2. D. 5, '71. Monetary: Alice's dollar and some other currencies. Leonard Silk.

New York Times. p 32. D. 10, '71. Two views of Lindsay. John Herbers.

New York Times. p 1. D. 19, '71. 10-nation monetary agreement reached; dollar is devalued 8.57%; surcharge off. E. L. Dale, Jr.

New York Times. p F 1. D. 19, '71. Living with devaluation. H. E. Heinemann.

New York Times. p E 1. D. 26, '71. The dollar: why it feels so good to devalue. E. L. Dale, Jr.

New York Times. p 1+. D. 29, '71. Some on Pay board find panel largely ineffective. Philip Shabecoff.

*New York Times. p 1-2. Ja. 9, '72. But doubt nags American people. Tom Wicker.

*New York Times. p 1-2. Ja. 9, '72. Economy on an express track. T. E. Mullaney.

*New York Times. p 41+. Mr. 5, '72. Warning on growth perils is examined at symposium. Robert Reinhold.

*New York Times. p F 1. Mr. 5, '72. Nixonomics—do the old economic theories still hold? H. E. Heinemann.

New York Times. p 1+. Mr. 23, '72. Revenue sharing clears a hurdle; Ways and Means Committee reaches agreement on bill.

New York Times. p 1+. Ap. 2, '72. Most business analysts discern upturn, but economy is still key election issue. H. E. Heinemann.

New York Times. p 35. Ap. 7, '72. Needed now: "jobs now." W. W. Heller.

New York Times. p 49+. My. 1, '72. Curb on profits dispiriting many businessmen; Phase 2 view is different for economists. M. C. Jensen.

New York Times Magazine. p 27+. Mr. 18, '62. We must grow, or we sink. A. H. Hansen.

New York Times Magazine. p 8+. Ag. 4, '63. Economic oracles of the New Frontier. R. E. Mooney.

New York Times Magazine. p 36-7+. Ap. 4, '65. We are depression (but not recession) proof. E. L. Dale, Jr.

New York Times Magazine. p 50-1+. S. 18, '66. Another look at the new economics. E. L. Dale, Jr.

New York Times Magazine. p 32-3+. F. 16, '69. After peace breaks out, what will we do with all the extra money? E. L. Dale, Jr.

New York Times Magazine. p 18-19+. S. 26, '71. A bitchy society will be an inflationary society. E. L. Dale, Jr.

New York Times Magazine. p 70+. O. 3, '71. Nixon of the O.P.A. Milton Viorst.

New Yorker. 47:83-7. F. 5, '72. Letter from Washington [Nixon's new policy]. R. H. Rovere.

Newsweek. 62:20. S. 30, '63. To the people: President Kennedy's television talk.

Newsweek. 65:85. My. 17, '65. Bad guys, good guys: economic expansion v. balanced budget. H. C. Wallich.

Newsweek. 73:63-4. F. 10, '69. To tune or not to tune?

Newsweek. 73:105. My. 26, '69. Money and inflation. Milton Friedman.

Newsweek. 77:81. My. 3, '71. Money explodes. Milton Friedman.

Newsweek. 77:78-9+. My. 10, '71. Europe feels symptoms of "stagflation."

Newsweek. 77:80. Je. 14, '71. That old spiral.

Newsweek. 78:15-16. Ag. 9, '71. U.S. economy off the tracks.

Newsweek. 78:19. Ag. 9, '71. Game plan: will it work?

*Newsweek. 78:59-60. Ag. 16, '71. Inflation scores on the game plan.

Newsweek. 78:69. Ag. 23, '71. Devaluation economics. P. A. Samuelson.

*Newsweek. 78:14-16. Ag. 30, '71. The freeze can nip—or tingle.

Newsweek. 78:22-3. Ag. 30, '71. Verdict of *Newsweek*'s three economists. Milton Friedman, P. A. Samuelson and H. C. Wallich.

Newsweek. 78:83-4. S. 13, '71. Freeze: planning for thin ice.

Newsweek. 78:84. S. 13, '71. Have controls ever worked?

*Newsweek. 79:69+. Ja. 31, '72. Controls: bruised, bent, broken.

Newsweek. 79:71-2. F. 14, '72. Case of the jitters; monetary system unstable.

Newsweek. 79:68. F. 28, '72. Good news, bad news.

Ramparts. 10:46-8. F. '72. Phase Two strategy for the Left; a mass movement for people's control of the economy. Staughton Lynd.

Reader's Digest. 99:77-80. D. '71. Fighting inflation is everybody's business. R. M. Nixon.
    Adapted from speech delivered on October 7, 1971.

Reporter. 28:22-5. F. 14, '63. Economic education of John F. Kennedy. M. J. Rossant.

Saturday Evening Post. 237:92. D. 5, '64. Let's cut taxes again.

Saturday Evening Post. 238:14. S. 25, '65. Where do we go from here? Stewart Alsop.

Saturday Review. 46:13-15+. D. 14, '63. Can anyone explain capitalism? R. J. Monsen, Jr.

Saturday Review. 52:19-21. D. 13, '69. How not to tinker with the economy. J. F. Wharton.

Saturday Review. 54:15-18. Mr. 6, '71. Training a pleasant demon. Robert Lekachman.

Senior Scholastic. 86:12+. Ap. 15, '65. U.S. dollar: can it stand its popularity?

Senior Scholastic. 99:15-16. S. 27, '71. Remember the dollar? the reaction abroad.

*Senior Scholastic. 99:11-13. O. 11, '71. One town's hot & cold views of the freeze. G. A. Nikolaieff.

Time. 86:81. S. 10, '65. Embattled guidelines: Council of economic advisers' guidelines.

*Time. 86:64-7B. D. 31, '65. We are all Keynesians now.

Time. 94:85-6. N. 14, '69. Economy at the turning point.

Time. 97:85-6+. My. 17, '71. Dollar crisis: floating toward reform?

Time. 97:79-80. My. 31, '71. Struggle to stay competitive.

Time. 98:4-14. Ag. 30, '71. Nixon's grand design for recovery.

Time. 98:7. Ag. 30, '71. Putting on the freeze.

Time. 98:34. Ag. 30, '71. Assessing the new Nixonomics; press reactions.

*Time. 98:10-12+. O. 18, '71. The economy: a drive to beat infla-
tion—and Democrats.

Time. 98:29. N. 29, '71. Labor's disturbing challenge; President
Nixon and George Meany as speakers at AFL-CIO convention.

Time. 98:31. N. 29, '71. Learning to live with Phase II.

Time. 98:18-20. D. 13, '71. Forthcoming devaluation of the dollar.

Time. 98:17-18. D. 20, '71. Everything you want to know about
Phase II.

Time. 98:19. D. 20, '71. Take charge price czar: C. Jackson Grayson, Jr.

Time. 98:22-3. p 22. D. 27, '71. The quiet triumph of devaluation.

Time. 98:24+. D. 27, '71. The advantages of the unthinkable; results of currency realignment.

Time. 99:18-20+. Ja. 10, '72. At last, the year of real recovery.

Time. 99:20-1. Ja. 17, '72. Breaks in the wage-price spiral.

*Time. 99:50-1. F. 14, '72. The future of free enterprise. D. M.
Morrison.

Time. 99:23-4. F. 21, '72. Phase II: tackling the sticky ones.

Time. 99:20+. F. 28, '72. The simmering VAT [Value Added Tax].

U.S. News & World Report. 58:48-51. Ap. 19, '65. What is money,
anyway? answers to your questions.

U.S. News & World Report. 60:27-8. Ja. 24, '66. LBJ's decision:
guns and butter; concerning State-of-the-Union message.

*U.S. News & World Report. 64:27-9. F. 12, '68. Guns and butter
—failure of a policy.

U.S. News & World Report. 70:82-4. Ap. 19, '71. Dollar survives
still another crisis.

*U.S. News & World Report. 70:55-7. My. 10, '71. "Economic policy
on course," says top Nixon aide. G. P. Shultz.

*U.S. News & World Report. 71:30-2. Ag. 2, '71. Jobs for all; any
time soon?

U.S. News & World Report. 71:15-24+. Ag. 30, '71. Nixon's New
Economic Policy; with interview with P. W. McCracken.

U.S. News & World Report. 71:18. Ag. 30, '71. Who's in charge of
wage-price curbs?

U.S. News & World Report. 71:26-8. Ag. 30, '71. Can anybody manage a free economy?

U.S. News & World Report. 71:15-16. S. 27, '71. After the freeze: what comes next?

U.S. News & World Report. 71:25-8. O. 4, '71. Spotlight on productivity: why it's a key to U.S. problems.

U.S. News & World Report. 71:88. N. 22, '71. Pay rules: official guidelines; statement by the Board, November 8, 1971.

U.S. News & World Report. 71:40. D. 13, '71. Price controls get tougher.

U.S. News & World Report. 72:70-2. F. 28, '72. Will 1972 wage settlements torpedo the Pay board?

U.S. News & World Report. 72:73. F. 28, '72. Labor council glum on economic outlook.

Vital Speeches of the Day. 35:346-9. Mr. 15, '69. Economic problems: stabilization; address, February 27, 1969. W. M. Martin, Jr.

Vital Speeches of the Day. 37:253-6. F. 1, '71. Squeeze-freeze dilemma; address, January 20, 1971. R. H. Larry.

Vital Speeches of the Day. 37:263-5. F. 15, '71. Inflation's impact on consumer behavior and attitudes: a little inflation tolerable; address, January 14, 1971. George Katona.

Vital Speeches of the Day. 38:73-6. N. 15, '71. Economic game plan, thoughts from labor; address, October 4, 1971. Leonard Woodcock.

Wall Street Journal. p 1+. Ag. 5, '71. The crisis. Ray Vicker and Richard Janssen.

Wall Street Journal. p 6. Ag. 6, '71. The peril of escalator clauses. B. E. Calame.

*Wall Street Journal. p 1+. Ag. 17, '71. Nixon's economics; a *Wall Street Journal* Roundup.

Wall Street Journal. p 1. Ag. 20, '71. Strained relations. Robert Keatley.

Wall Street Journal. p 26. Ag. 23, '71. Contingency planning. R. E. Winter and Jim Hyatt.

Wall Street Journal. p 1+. S. 13, '71. A lesson for U.S. Bowen Northrup.

Wall Street Journal. p 1+. S. 27, '71. Monetary muddle. R. F. Janssen.

Wall Street Journal. p 1+. O. 8, '71. Foggy Phase II. R. F. Janssen and A. R. Hunt.

Wall Street Journal. p 1+. O. 13, '71. Confusion, Inc.

*Wall Street Journal. p 20. O. 28, '71. A world-wide depression.

Wall Street Journal. p 1+. N. 10, '71. Budget blues.

Wall Street Journal. p 1+. N. 11, '71. Reverse twist. R. F. Janssen.

Wall Street Journal. p 1. N. 24, '71. Phantom Phase 2? A. R. Hunt.

Wall Street Journal. p 1+. D. 13, '71. The early results.

Wall Street Journal. p 1+. D. 14, '71. Economics 101. R. E. Winter.

*Wall Street Journal. p 1+. D. 20, '71. The new dollar. R. F. Janssen.

Wall Street Journal. p 6. D. 22, '71. Wage-price controls won't work. W. A. Wallis.

Wall Street Journal. p 1. D. 24, '71. The enforcers. Bill Paul.

Wall Street Journal. p 1+. D. 27, '71. Battle plan. A. R. Hunt.

Wall Street Journal. p 1+. D. 28, '71. Too little, too late. Richard Martin.

Wall Street Journal. p 6. Ja. 3, '72. Controls: could Democrats do better? A. R. Hunt.

*Wall Street Journal. p 20. Ja. 3, '72. Citizens of an Illinois town, after four months of economic controls, increasingly doubt gains. F. C. Klein and T. P. Brown.

Wall Street Journal. p 1. Ja. 10, '72. Continuing crisis? Charles Stabler and Ray Vicker.

Wall Street Journal. p 30. Ja. 21, '72. Full employment remains a Nixon target. R. F. Janssen.

Wall Street Journal. p 32. F. 9, '72. Surprising smell of success. A. R. Hunt.

Wall Street Journal. p 12. Mr. 1, '72. A new try at fine tuning.

*Wall Street Journal. p 1+. Mr. 24, '72. Nixon vs. labor; Pay board's policies are unlikely to change; walkout called political. B. E. Calame.